MW00451369

GOTCH

AN AMERICAN HERO

ALSO BY MIKE CHAPMAN

Two Guys Named Dan
Kings of the Mat
Toughest Men in Sports
Evy and the Hawks: The Glory Years
Gotch to Gable: A History of Iowa Wrestling
Iowans of Impact
Nick and the Cyclones
Gotch: World's Greatest Wrestler
Encyclopedia of American Wrestling
Fighting Back

The New Breed: Living Iowa Wrestling
(with Lou Banach)

GOTCH

An American Hero

by

MIKE CHAPMAN

CULTURE HOUSE BOOKS

GOTCH: An American Hero

A Culture House Book / November 1999

For information address: Culture House
                             P O Box 293
                             Newton IA 50208

Library of Congress Cataloging-in-Publication Data
Chapman, Mike, 1943 -
    Gotch: An American Hero / Mike Chapman
  1. Gotch, Frank. 2. Wrestling. 3. Humboldt, Iowa.
  I. Title.

ISBN 0-9676080-0

PRINTED IN THE UNITED STATES OF AMERICA

First edition

Whoever excels in what we prize
appears a hero in our eyes.

Thomas Carlyle
"On Heroes and Hero Worship"

Thomas Carlyle captured the essence of hero worship with the quote above. This book is dedicated to all the athletes who have taken to the wrestling rings and mats in order to test themselves. No sport receives less publicity than amateur wrestling and that is a shame, for no sport demands more from an athlete. My special thanks go to Bev Chapman and Dale Anderson and to my children Jacquie, Jenny and Jason for their continual support. I also owe a debt of gratitude to Lou Thesz, Verne Gagne and Dan Hodge for their great inspiration. Lou, Verne and Dan have walked in the footsteps of Frank Gotch and knowing them helped me to write this book.

PREFACE

The day was long and hot, as were most of the days that summer, and every summer I can recall, for that matter. Iowa summers are a special breed. The humidity is always high, and you battle both the heat and the wetness. Every movement causes a trickle of sweat. At first, you walk and play delicately, hoping you can enjoy the movement without perspiring. But all it takes is one spontaneous burst of running - like playing tag, or scouts and Indians - and you've lost the battle to stay dry.

But then, children are supposed to play, to feel the excitement of each day in the summer heat while youth still allows. The time will come soon enough when you take to the fields along side your older brother and father, to help earn a living for the family, and some day for yourself. Life was hard in most Iowa towns, where the wild and wooly frontier was fading slowly. After all, this was 1907, and there were still plenty of folks around who could spin yarns about the Indian days. Now and then, we would catch sight of a real Indian - probably of the Sac and Fox tribe, or maybe even a Sioux - in town for one reason or another. We tried to be polite and not stare, but the temptation was just too strong for some of us, myself included. Once, when I stopped and turned to watch the one the men called old Sitting Bull - of course, he wasn't the famous chief who played a role in the destruction of General Custer and his men - my ma grabbed hold of my arm and pulled me along down the boardwalk after her, my shirt half out of my pants and flapping in the breeze.

"You needn't look up to the likes of him," she told me that night, by a warm fire, as she turned to her knitting. "There are plenty of examples for a boy to look up to. We have a fine president in Mr. Roosevelt, and those Wright brothers down in North Carolina are men to be admired. Why, they actually made a machine fly a couple of years ago. I doubt if anything more will come of it, but just those pictures of men sitting in a flying machine, way up off the ground, is something wonderful to ponder. And if you're looking for a sports hero, there's still Jim Jeffries, the old champion of the ring. Why, he'd box the ears off that Jack Johnson fellow, if they was to meet...."

My pa always chuckled when my mother would mention Johnson, the great Negro fighter. Although she would never mention it to me, I had heard he fooled around with white women, and white folks didn't like him for that. Everyone admitted he was a master boxer, maybe the best ever. Still, most white people wanted him to get whipped good.... "Just so's he wouldn't flaunt himself," they'd say....and my ma was one of them. After all, times were hard here in Iowa and no one needed to be reminded that an uppity negro was having the time of his life by beating up white contenders, racing around in his expensive automobiles, traveling the world and sporting his famous grin of gold. No siree, Jack Johnson was no one's hero these days, except for the poor oppressed Negroes around the country who looked to him for a sort of self-pride. And I can't say I blames 'em for that, because most of us young fellows here in Iowa....and particularly here in Humboldt....certainly had our hero.

He was home grown, a product of our times and our town. We didn't see a lot of him in those days, because he was always off somewhere in the United States wrestling someone, and winning. Frank Gotch always won; at least, that's the way it seemed to us. If he ever lost, the older folks must have kept it from us. But, I suspect that he never did lose much at all.

I remember the first time I saw Frank Gotch. I was only twelve years old. It was another of those scorchers and I and a bunch of pals were swimming in the Des Moines River on the outskirts of town. Billy Turner had just caused a bit of excitement by pretending he was drowning, and then almost drowning for real when he swallowed too much water and began coughing and hacking. It was all real funny afterwards, but a few of us were downright scared for a while when old Billy couldn't catch his breath, and turned ghost white.

We were relaxing in the shade of a big oak tree when we saw some movement down the long, dirt road that led up to our spot. We could see a figure coming, but we couldn't make it out. All we knew was someone was running toward us, and that usually meant it was time to scatter. But, we reasoned we hadn't been stealing anything; heck, there wasn't even a watermelon patch within two miles. We were sort of nervous, like maybe this was the last of the Indians on a solitary warpath, and for a minute I had visions of us all being scalped, and I could almost read the headlines in Tab Jones' newspaper the next week. But one of the boys finally spoke up.

"Hey, it's Mr. Gotch," John Marks said, clamoring to his feet. "That's Frank Gotch, the wrestler. My dad says he's going to be world champion some day."

All of us had heard of Frank Gotch, of course. His dad worked the old farm south of town. We would see Mrs. Gotch in town from time to time, but the men folk stayed to the farm. The story was that Frank was real strong and real quick, the finest wrestler ever in these parts, and let me tell you a lot of great wrestlers were born in Iowa, before and after the days of Frank Gotch. But the Gotch boys - Frank had an older brother, Charlie, whom folks said was even stronger than Frank, but was slightly different in the head, I guess, and never was seen by hardly anyone - stayed to themselves. Of course, now that Frank was famous and chasing the world wrestling champion, George Hackenschmidt, the man they called the Russian Lion and who people said was the strongest man in the world, he was gone from Humboldt a lot. But folks sure talked about Frank; they were proud - very proud - that a boy from Humboldt was making good in this old world.

We could see him clearly now, coming up the road. His head was down, watching his footing, more than likely, so that he didn't step into a chuckhole and turn an ankle, or break one. But every so often, he would lift his head up high, sniffing in that clean Iowa air, as if it would help make him stronger. Then, he'd twist his head from side to side real quick, and roll it back and forth on that big, powerful looking neck, never breaking stride. It was while doing this that he caught sight of us, and he broke into a big grin.

He was almost beside us boys - eight in all - and we stood in silence, waiting for him to go streaking past. But he stopped right there on the dusty path and walked over to us. He rested his arms on a fence post, and gazed at us. I can still remember the tremor that raced down my back when his eyes lit on mine. I had been staring at his huge, muscled arms, the biggest I had ever seen on any man. His black hair, parted down the middle, was slapped up a bit on both sides of his head, from running into the slight wind. He had thick brows and gray eyes, and he was a very handsome man, I thought. Sweat was running down his forehead, and he lifted up a hand to flick away the drops before they ran into his eyes, where they would burn like the devil.

He wore a white flannel shirt, with the sleeves whacked off high in the middle of his arms. The shirt was soaked with sweat, as he must have come at least three miles from the farm south of town. The thick pants had spots of sweat showing through, and he wore a heavy pair of black boots.

"What you fellows doing?" he asked with a stern look on his face, as though he was about to bawl us out for swimming in the river. He glanced at each one of us with those gray eyes, and I was frightened. But he must have sensed our discomfort because he broke into a big grin.

"Aw, I'm only fooling with you," he said easily, a slight chuckle in his voice. "Why, anyone half smart would be swimming on a day like this instead of running."

We all laughed nervously, and several of the boys walked up to the fence.

"What are you doing, Mr. Gotch?" asked Billy Turner, who always had more courage than the rest of us. "Why are you running on a day like today? Did your cows get loose, or somethin?"

Frank laughed heartily at that one.

"Naw, son, nothing like that," he replied. He straightened back up then, leaving the post. "But you know, I guess I am chasing something....two things. I'm chasing the Russian Lion, a fellow named George Hackenschmidt, and a dream of my own."

"I know who that Russian Lion is," said Jeffrey Harrison, a towhead who always knew everything, even in school. "My pa says that he's the strongest man in the world, and the best wrestler, and the best fighter. My pa says even if you are a friend, and even if you are from Iowa, that Mr. Hackenschmidt will murder you once he gets you in the ring." A hush fell over us, not knowing what to say or how Mr. Gotch would react. But it didn't last long.

"Well, lots of folks would agree with your pa," said Frank, smiling again. He shifted his gaze, looking up at the sun overhead, and squinted. He ran his hand over his forehead again, tossing the sweat away. "But that's why I'm out here running, son. You know, that Russian Lion is pretty strong all right, but he gets tired easily. He's too strong; those big muscles slow him down. And I'll just tire him out and when he's all tuckered, why I'll slap the old toe hold on him and make him yell uncle."

Several of the boys - including me - let out a gasp when we heard him mention the toe hold. Why, it was the most feared hold in all the world. We'd all heard stories about Mr. Gotch getting some poor fellow on the ground and tuckering him out, and then putting on the toe hold. None of us boys knew how to do it for sure, although we all tried it in the grass on each other on a number of occasions. But, it was one terrible situation, of that much we were certain.

Frank knew he had made an impression on us. "Well, guys, I gotta be movin' on," he said. Then he turned to Jeffrey Harrison. "Your pa may be right," he said, pointing at young Jeff, "but you tell him not to bet against old Frank, okay?" With that, he gave us all a wink and was off down the road, running harder than ever. We stood and watched in silence as he disappeared on the other side of a hill, and we turned to our swimming again.

On the trek home, with the heat hanging despite the fact the sun was setting, we were more quiet than usual. Finally, Jeffrey Harrison spoke up. "I'll bet that Russian Lion guy murders Frank Gotch," he said. And for some reason - one that I wouldn't be able to understand or explain for many years - I got mad, fighting mad. I grabbed him and spun him around.

"You listen here, Jeff Harrison," I said, the words coming out hot and heavy. "Frank Gotch will whip George Hackenschmidtter, or whatever his name is, and everyone else in the world, too." We stood toe to toe, and the others gathered around us, sensing a fight. Several tried to goad us on with rough words, but Jeff didn't seem in the mood. And we all went home quietly.

Later that night, when we were sitting on the porch and just about ready to turn in, I told my pa what had happened. Ma, my sister and two brothers were in the house, making ready for bed. We had a long day ahead, all of us, in our different ways, and bedtime came early, around 8 o'clock. I had to ask pa if I did wrong to stick up for Mr. Gotch.

Pa puffed long on his corn pipe, rocking in his black chair, as if formulating an answer.

"No, you didn't do wrong," he said to me that day, long ago. "You see, we all got to have heroes in life, someone to look up to, someone for us to want to be like. And I couldn't think of no better man for my son to be like than Frank Gotch. I've known him since he was your age, and he's a fine man, always friendly and courteous. He's a big shot now, and travels all around the country, meeting famous people. But Frank Gotch is always the same when you pass him on the street, always friendly and neighborly."

We were quiet for several minutes. Then, just when pa began to shift, like he was getting up to go in, I asked him the question I had to ask: "Pa, he'll beat that Russian Lion, won't he?"

"Well, son," he said, placing a hand on my head. "I doubt they'll ever meet. I doubt George Hackenschmidt will ever come here to America. The Russian Lion is too darn popular in Europe to come over here to wrestle."

"But, if he did, Mr. Gotch would win, wouldn't he?" I was persistent, I had to know. I had to know that I was right, and Jeffrey Harrison was wrong.

I'll never forget what pa said next; I love my pa, now that he's long gone, more than I ever knew back then. But at the moment I could have almost swung at him, though it wouldn't have done any good.

"No, I don't think so," he said. "I don't think any man living, even our Frank, could beat the Russian Lion in or out of the ring."

I stepped back and stared at my pa, and he must have known that he had wounded me. I couldn't find words at first, but then they came in a flurry.

"You'll see," I said, almost crying, "you'll see. Mr. Gotch will beat the Russian Lion and everyone else, too. Everyone will know he's the greatest wrestler ever."

I ran down from the porch, toward the barn. Pa called after me twice, but I ran into the barn and fell into the hay. I was panting, out of breath, even after that short run. I couldn't keep my heart quiet....I listened for steps that would tell me pa was coming after me, to take me to the house. But they never came. I fell asleep, and spent the night in the barn. When I woke, it was broad daylight, and I walked out of the barn up to the house, stiff and sore and with hay buried in dozens of places under my clothes. Ma was at the stove, her back to me, but she heard the screen door bang shut. She turned around, and stared at me.

"Hungry?" she asked. I nodded that I was.

She busied herself making flapjacks, and brought over a bowl of honey to pour over them. She sat down and watched me wolf them down. I could tell she was building up to something.

"So, you've found yourself a hero, have you," she said. I didn't answer, but she continued. "Well, Mr. Gotch is a fine man, but so's your pa. Your father knows a lot about wrestling, was pretty good himself one day. Maybe not as good as Frank Gotch, but pretty good.

Just don't you go forgetting in your new enthusiasm for Mr. Gotch that your pa is deserving of some respect now, too."

Ma's words surprised me that day, but I didn't forget; nor have I after sixty years.

I went to town later on, hoping to see Mr. Gotch somewhere, and I went to town for the next week daily, until I heard some fellows talking at the general store on main street. They said Frank was gone again, out east to wrestle some fellow named Jenkins for the American championship. They said they thought he'd win that one, but then some fellow mentioned Hackenschmidt - they called him Hack, but I knew who they meant - and they all fell sort of quiet, shaking their head. They didn't think our Frank could win, either.

But I knew, I mean really knew, different. There was something about that man, something I saw that day by the river, when he stopped to talk to a bunch of wet and scraggly kids. I knew he would tire out Hack and get the toe hold on him and that the Russian Lion couldn't take it; I knew it all to be true because Mr. Gotch had said it would be.

The rest of the summer passed, and many summers in quick succession. Frank Gotch made a great impression on me, my town, my state, and even the world. I would never forget that first day I saw him, and several meetings in between, and I will always, always remember that cold day in December when I walked to the cemetery with three thousand others to say good-bye to the greatest wrestler the world has ever known. I promised myself years ago that I would write a book about Frank Gotch, so the world would know how great he really was.

The following pages are that promise come to life.

CHAPTER 1

The track meet had just ended. The track itself was only a strip of land drug over a dozen times by several horses pulling a log through the middle of a cornfield, and sprinkled heavily with cinders for good footing; but it served the purpose. Nearly sixty boys and young men, representing the town of Humboldt and nearby Luverne, took part. The Humboldt team came out ahead, thanks largely to the efforts of Frank Gotch, a strapping nineteen-year-old farmer. Frank won firsts in the short dash and the long run, and also won the hammer throw and the demanding wheelbarrow race.

Everyone was so caught up in the camaraderie and spirit of the event that they didn't even notice when a stranger, nattily attired in a white shirt tucked into gray trousers and carrying a small leather case, appeared halfway through the meet. He had seen the activity from a window of a passing train some thirty minutes earlier and got off at the Humboldt train station. He hitched a ride in a buggy to the makeshift athletic field and watched the proceedings with interest. He took note of several of the young men, particularly Gotch. He smiled as he watched some of the clumsier men struggle in vain in the various events, but couldn't hide a trace of respect when Gotch took his turn. He also measured the pride of the young Gotch, making a quick assessment.

Shortly after the competition halted and the teams gathered together for small talk, he approached a group of four young men.

"Say, that was some event," he said, trying to sound country and camouflage his slight Eastern accent. The men looked over at him and nodded quickly, and turned back to their conversation.

The stranger waited a moment or two, glancing around casually, hands in his pockets, then spoke again. "Got some athletes here," he said. "Any wrestlers?"

The question gained the immediate attention of the men. They turned to the stranger with new interest, sizing him up. He appeared polished and slick....like a setup man, but not a wrestler. He smiled at them.

"Well?" he asked with a shrug of impatience, keeping his smile.

"Yeah," said one of the men, a farmer, trying to sound casual too. "We got a wrestler or two around. Why?"

"Well, thought I'd drum up a match, if anyone cared to go a bit."

The stranger felt the cool eyes of appraisal on him. It only took a couple of seconds, and the reply was what he had hoped for.

"Yeah, we could get you a match," said the farmer, wiping perspiration from his brow with a handkerchief.

The stranger smiled even wider. "That's fine, fine," he said. "And who will it be....you?"

"Naw," said the farmer, holding his hands up. "I can wrestle some, but nobody around here can touch Frank. He'll go a bit with you." He turned and grinned at his friends, all of who grinned back, nodding.

"Which one is this....Frank?" asked the stranger, already suspecting the answer. "That sturdy looking character over there?"

The spokesman turned, looked in the direction the stranger indicated, then faced him again.

"Yep, that's Frank, all right," he said, more than a trace of pride in his voice. "That's our Frank."

The stranger was delighted. The situation was perfect, all he could ask for. He stuck out his hand. "Name's Jonas, David Jonas. Pleased to meet you."

The farmer returned the gesture.

"Elmer Smith," he said as the two shook hands. Smith shouted over to his friend, talking idly with several others. "Hey, Frank, got a fellow here who wants to wrestle. Wants to wrestle you, even!"

The buzzing of conversation in the scattered groups ceased abruptly, as all heads turned toward Smith and Jonas. The stranger felt the eyes on him, probing and scrutinizing. He flashed his smile, and nodded in the direction of all the little groups. He gave a short wave, also. He knew the game well, just how to play it. To these people, he was a stranger passing through. To him, this was life....and his livelihood.

Gotch ambled over; his sweat-soaked gray shirt with the sleeves rolled up and baggy trousers presented a striking contrast with Jonas. The two sized one another up, until Jonas broke the silence, offering his hand. "Jonas....David Jonas is the name," he said.

The youngster stuck out a hand and when they clasped, Jonas felt the strength the fellow possessed. The hand was hard as a board, and the grip had no slack. The eyes, gray and probing, stared out from underneath heavy, dark brows.

"I'm Frank Gotch," he said matter of factly.

"You a wrestler, Frank?" the man asked. He heard the snickers and guffaws from the crowd, now circling the two. He glanced about quickly, smiling widely, playing to their affection for Gotch. He shrugged his shoulders, raising his hands up in a gesture of ignorance.

"Just passing through," he said. "I'm not too familiar with Iowa wrestlers. Except, of course, Farmer Burns. Ain't none of you the Farmer, in disguise, are you?"

That brought forth a round of chuckles. Iowans were extremely proud of their wrestling and wrestlers, and Farmer Burns was already a legend, even though under forty years of age. Burns wasn't around to prove the point, but this stranger was about to learn a rough lesson, regardless, they figured.

"I can wrestle some," said Gotch, still eyeing his new rival. "How about you? Where you from?"

"Out East," said Jonas. "Done a little wrestling out East. Nothing serious."

"We take our wrestling pretty serious," said a voice from the back.

"You will too, after you grab hold of old Frank here," shouted another. The crowd broke into a good-natured laughter, but neither Frank nor Jonas joined in. They kept their eyes glued on one another.

"Well, then, shall we proceed?" said the newcomer amicably. He took a step back, holding his case as though he was about to look into it. "But," he added at the last moment, as though it were an after-thought, "would anyone care to make a wager on the outcome?"

"What are the rules?" someone yelled from the back. Jonas turned to Gotch.

"Catch-as-catch-can?" he asked. Gotch merely nodded and walked ten feet away, where he started to limber up, swinging his arms back and forth and doing a few deep bends at the knee.

Jonas busied himself making some wagers, moving easily

through the crowd. He was amused at how eager these hicks were to part with their hard-earned money. When he had about a dozen bets lined up, he began to limber up. The crowd watched intently as he stripped to the waist, revealing a torso which was lean but very well muscled. His abdominal area fairly rippled with muscle, and the arms, long and sinewy, looked as though they contained far greater power than one would have guessed with his shirt on.

Gotch was unruffled by the maneuvering or the physique of his rival, but several in the crowd seemed impressed, and perhaps just a little worried about their wagers. If Jonas was deceiving in appearance, they reasoned, maybe he was deceiving in attitude. Maybe a calm, seasoned professional lurked behind that quick smile and ready handshake. They were soon to discover just how real their suspicions were.

Jonas walked to Smith and handed him a hundred and fifty dollars.

"Here's my money," he said. "Reckon you're an honest man, and can remember who owes me, once we're done." He paused. "You capable of refereeing, too?"

Smith looked over at Gotch. "Well, I can keep the money for you. But as to refereeing....well, Frank and I are friends."

"That's okay by me," said Jonas. "Reckon all of you are his friends. Just soon have you be the ref as anyone else."

Jonas nodded his agreement. The preliminaries over, Jonas motioned to his young foe.

"C'mon over, Frank; we may as well get under way," he said, standing in the thick grass.

Gotch stood rooted in the middle of the track, cinders strewn all about him. "No," he said. "Not there..." He pointed down at his thick boots, in the cinders. "Here."

Jonas was surprised.

"No," he laughed a bit nervously. "Certainly, you're kidding. We should wrestle in the grass."

"Footings too uncertain there," said Gotch simply. "We won't slip here, and you won't be able to run and hide."

Jonas drew himself up straight.

"I don't run and hide from any man, son," he said, and stepped briskly forward. Word of the match had spread to several groups of nearby picnickers, and the gathering had almost doubled in size since Jonas had first appeared. It promised to be a thrilling spectacle, an old-fashioned, Iowa-style wrestling match between a cocky stranger and the local hero.

They nodded briefly at one another, then stepped cautiously forward. They circled for a moment, then grabbed one another's arms and neck in a tie-up position, testing one another's strength, each hoping to build confidence from the exchange. Neither came away fortified with false courage, as they found one another to be hard as rock, and of good balance. They continued to spar until Jonas feinted for a headlock. Gotch lifted his arms high to fend off the attack, and Jonas dove underneath Gotch's arms, grabbing a leg and toppling Gotch to the ground. Thinking he had secured a considerable advantage, Jonas leaped to seize the fallen man in a pinning hold, but was shocked at the quickness Gotch displayed in rolling away. Like two cats, the men were on their feet again, parrying.

The pace quickened as each sought a hold which would result in a pinning of the other's shoulders, or a hold that could end in a submission. As the match wore on, it became apparent the strength and quickness of Gotch was holding its own with the expertise displayed by the stranger. Slowly, the crowd - and Gotch - began to realize Jonas was a man of vast skills, undoubtedly honed and refined in hundreds of such pickup bouts over the years.

Thirty minutes passed, with neither man able to score decisively. Sweat was mingled with dirt and laid thick on their bodies. They rolled through the cinders time and again, gouging small patches of skin from their bodies. Gotch had not stripped to the waist, as had Jonas, but his shirt hung on him in shreds, until at last he cast it away, displaying thick hair growing over a heavily muscled body. The two locked on to one another continuously, pushing and shoving, panting heavily, each working for a hold that would give him the advantage.

Fifty minutes into the bout, Gotch wrapped his arms around Jonas' waist, lifted him off the ground, and slammed him hard to the cinders, dust rising up over them and caking their sweaty bodies. The crowd surged forward, urging their hero on. Gotch gritted his teeth and smashed Jonas back to the earth each time the stranger tried to rise. Dirt filled their nostrils and mouths, and both fell into coughing seizures, with Gotch still clinging precariously to the top position.

Jonas appeared done in; he was gasping and blood was flowing from half a dozen spots on his arms and legs. Then, suddenly, he exploded. Gotch had moved up high on Jonas' back in an attempt to turn his man, and Jonas seized the opportunity. He shifted his weight in a flash, catapulting Gotch over the top of him. Jonas grabbed the young Iowan's head and pulled with all his might, bending Gotch's body over the top of him, Gotch's legs trapped beneath Jonas' body. Gotch was caught in a vice-like grip and fought desperately to free himself. Jonas, sensing victory, grew more determined.

Slowly, with hands locked tightly behind Gotch's neck, Jonas forced the younger, heavier man over the top of him. Gotch was bent nearly in half. His shoulders touched the ground, his body held in a tight arch. The crowd, shouting wildly only moments before, fell into a death-like silence. Their champion, a man they had never seen even close to defeat, was being slowly crushed to the earth before their very eyes. Gotch was struggling frantically, almost in a rage, to free himself, but Jonas persisted in his deadly game.

At last, Smith, who had little to do the first fifty minutes other than stay out of the way, stepped forward. There was no longer movement in the wrestlers save the heavy grunting and gasping. Jonas clearly was the victor. Gotch, with his shoulders planted solidly to the ground and unable to move more than a toe or finger, was pinned.

Dejectedly, Smith slapped the ground hard, then patted both men on the shoulders.

"It's over," he said dourly. "The stranger is the winner." In the excitement he had forgotten Jonas's name.

Jonas relinquished his hold and the two men began to unwind. Gotch rolled free and slowly came to his feet. He shook his head from side to side, rubbing his neck, which might have snapped from Jonas's hold, had it not been so powerful. Jonas was slower in rising; his face was red, his tongue dark. He coughed up phlegm, and seemed on the verge of collapse. His torso, so tuned and magnificent an hour earlier, was covered with dirt and streaks of blood. There were tiny black spots all over, cinders ground deep into the flesh. He looked at Gotch, and extended his hand.

"How old are you?" he asked, respect in his voice and his gaze.

"Nineteen," came the reply.

Jonas whistled, and shook his head. He walked to his bag and picked it up, rifling through it. He pulled out a small bottle, unpacked it and held it up to his nose. He took a deep whiff before withdrawing with a horrible expression, shaking his head wildly.

"Well, Mr. Gotch," he said, picking a towel from his bag, "you are one fine wrestler. I've been around a few parts of this grand country, and I can say I've never met a stronger man, or a more fierce competitor. You're going somewhere."

"Yeah," came a voice from the crowd. "He's gonna go home and get whipped by his mother for wrestling; she don't approve."

The crowd laughed and so did Jonas. Jonas toweled himself off, and began to pick cinders from his body. Several came off easily, but others were deeply imbedded. He grimaced.

"Have you met Farmer Burns yet?" he asked, glancing at his young foe.

"No," said Gotch. He didn't feel like making conversation with this man who had just defeated him in front of his friends. He wanted to wrestle again....now.

Jonas sensed Gotch's mood, and smiled quickly.

"Hold on, young fellow," he said. "Let me recuperate. I've got some twelve years of experience on you in this business, all of which I needed just to survive here today. I'm not going to wrestle you again....today or tomorrow or the next day, for that matter. You're too good too strong, too eager. You just need some coaching, and you'll be the best."

At last, the young farmer was pacified, at least somewhat.

"Where do I get coaching?" Gotch asked. "I already know more about wrestling than anyone else around." He said it not in the manner of bragging, but with disappointment. He was eager to learn more, so that he could beat men like this Jonas.

"I'm headed over to Fort Dodge, and I'll tell the Farmer about you. That's the best thing that could happen to you, meeting the Farmer," said Jonas.

It was a long trek home for Frank. His clothes were torn, his muscles ached, he was humiliated by the loss. But those causes of discomfort hardly ranked with the true source of his misery. His mother, Amelia, was passionately against her son's preoccupation with wrestling. She and her husband, Frederick, were born in Germany and emigrated to the United States in 1860, bringing with them their fierce pride and puritan work ethic, both of which demanded that a man and woman spend their waking hours in honest and gainful pursuit, fashioning a meaningful way to live and a means by which to support a family. Participating in any sporting activity, wrestling most of all, was not condoned by Amelia Gotch, although her husband was less opposed.

Frederick had brought his young wife from Germany to Lewis County in New York State, but soon was caught up in the American civil war - as were thousands of other Americans, both north and south of the Mason-Dixon Line. As a soldier in Company A of the 186th New York Volunteer Infantry, Frederick Gotch took part in the capture of Petersburg, as well as several other major campaigns. He served in the Army of the Potomac under General Ulysses S. Grant, a man destined to become the eighteenth President of the United States.

Though he had survived the great war without major injury, Frederick found misfortune in Iowa. Moving to a spot near Humboldt after his discharge, a tree he was cutting fell on him, crippling his right arm and leg. The injury slowed him considerably in farm work, and he and his wife became even more dependent on the strong arms of their seven children - especially young Frederick, Charles, George and Frank - in running the farm.

Amelia had viewed with grave misgivings the interest Frank had shown at an early age in both boxing and wrestling. He idolized John L. Sullivan, the great bare-knuckle boxing champion, and dreamed of becoming a prizefighter some day. Although he missed a great deal of schooling in the spring because of farm work, Frank managed to attend school fairly regularly in the winter months. He was usually an attentive student, but he reserved his greatest energies for the recesses, when the boys would gather in one corner of the school yard and test their "manhood" through various mixed bouts of wrestling, boxing and just plain fightin'. It didn't take long for everyone to discover that Frank, modest and unassuming in the classroom, stood head and shoulders above the others in the outdoor battles. And, as his reputation grew and word of his schoolyard victories made the rounds, Amelia grew more and more concerned. Lectures were plentiful at the Gotch supper table, with Amelia doing the talking and Frederick merely nodding, as if lending approval to his wife's arguments. But Frank always had the feeling his father, now forever slowed due to his injuries, was proud of his son's reputation as the best young grappler around.

Wrestling was a natural outlet for Frank. As a youth he had held dreams of becoming a famous scout, like Davy Crockett, or becoming a man of the mountains, like the legendary Kit Carson. But the frontier was fading rapidly, and the Indian war days had exhausted themselves by the time Frank was still a young lad. Hunting and trapping occupied his interest in his early years; foraging in the heavy timber and barging through the marshes around the Des Moines River helped put food on the table and was great fun. But, ever since the day he first wrestled and made a bully who was bigger and older say "uncle," young Frank was hooked.

He defended the sport to his mother, only to have her deny his every contention. He loved her and admired her far too much to treat her with anything less than strict respect, but he grew frustrated with her at times, so much so that he would often just shrug his wide shoulders and walk away from the table, leaving her voice trailing after him.

Now, he was in for another berating. The sun was setting over the back of the farmhouse as he made his way down the lane, past the chickens and roosters hunting for food scraps in the yard. The farm was not a very large one, but was not tiny, either. It was good in terms of yield; all Iowa land is great for farming, they say, maybe the best anywhere in the world. With money from his Civil War service, Frederick had purchased three hundred acres shortly after arriving from New York, in a section just south of town, and had struggled for nearly twenty years trying to pay it off.

The aroma of frying chicken tickled Frank's nostrils as he stepped on the porch, and he frowned as the boards moaned under the pressure of his one hundred and seventy-five pound frame, giving away his presence. Not that it mattered anyway, as he surely was expected by now. The yard was deserted, meaning the family - Frederick, Amelia and the other children, including Mary Fredericka and Millie Mable - were already seated and eating.

Frank swung open the door and barged straight in. Of those at the table, only his mother and father looked up, his father nodding quickly and returning to his meal. His mother stared after him as he walked to the wash basin. He could hear the sounds of eating and a few whispered comments - probably from Millie, the talkative one, to Mary - while he poured the water over his hands and soaped up, but it wasn't until he was drying his hands that the voice he had been dreading filled the room.

"Well, look at you, Frank Alvin," his mother's voice boomed. He heard her chair slide back and he turned just as she headed toward him, a cold look in her dark eyes. She was a short woman, whose appearance spoke of many hard years of labor. Her face was creased with lines - worry lines, she told the children - and her build was wiry and robust, necessary ingredients for survival in the rugged farming communities of Iowa.

She stopped short of bumping into her son, and looked sternly up at him, not at all intimidated by his bulk and size. "Obviously, you've been wrestling again," she said.

"And just as obviously, he lost," came a sweet voice from behind her.

Frank glanced over his mother's shoulder at his sister, Millie, eating again and pretending she hadn't said a word. He grinned at her, and she grinned back. Frank knew she hated to see him lose in anything, even a footrace, and that she had spoken not out of unkindness but as an attempt to try and soften the criticism their mother was sure to offer.

But Amelia wasn't about to be put off. She acted as though she had not heard a word, and kept her gaze steady on Frank, and his tattered attire. "This will take hours of mending, you know that," she said, fingering his torn shirt and trousers. Then, she noticed the blood stains for the first time, and the dark spots.

"In the name of the Lord," she said with a gasp, "what is this? What have you gone and done?"

"Aw, ma, it ain't much," said Frank, feeling guilty at the thought of his mother, already overburdened with work, having to mend his clothes. "We just decided to wrestle in some cinders instead of the grass and, well, I guess it did get a little rough."

"A little rough?" she repeated, still inspecting him. "I would think some of Custer's men looked better."

The comment brought chuckles from the table, and she turned and silenced it with one quick glance. Frederick ate away, apparently unmindful of all the carryings-on. At last, he put down his fork and looked at his son.

"Well, did you lose?" he asked.

Thankful to break away from the angry gaze of his mother, Frank neatly sidestepped her and headed for the table. He searched over the selection, realizing how hungry he had become from the wrestling and the walk home. He pulled up a thick chair and plopped himself into it, reaching for the big platter of chicken, the beans, potatoes and still warm pile of homemade bread.

Arranging the fixings on his plate, he looked up at his pa.

"Yeah," he said, "I lost. This guy said his name was David Jonas and said he was just passing through. We had quite a match and I thought I was going to beat him a number of times, but he was just a little too slick for me and kept getting away. Finally, he tricked me, or slicked me, I don't know which, and pinned me." He paused for a mouthful of chicken, and began chewing in earnest.

"But he came up to me afterwards and was real friendly acting," he continued. "Said I could be real good; no, better than that, he said I am real good, but that I need more polishing. He said that I should meet the Farmer...."

"Oh, no," said Amelia, walking quickly to the table. "That's just what you need. Farmer Burns is a no-account, traveling around wrestling everybody everywhere and neglecting his family. I don't know how he got the name of farmer; that usually means a fellow's hard working and industrious, not one that flits around the countryside taking on all comers."

"But ma," said Frank, after another mouthful. "Farmer Burns makes a lot of money. A guy can make maybe a hundred dollars a night by collecting bets with people who want to back their local hero. I heard tell once he even picked up one thousand dollars by beating a fellow in Des Moines."

"Hogwash," said Amelia.

"Well, now, Amelia, Frank has got a point there," said Frederick, rising to his son's defense. "I'm not saying Frank here could ever be good enough to make that kind of money, but I have heard, and from people who know, that the Farmer makes a pretty penny these days by his wrestling shows. And that's not something to sneer at when times is hard, like they are here now."

"Maybe so," said Amelia, "but it's still not a respectable trade. Let him get an occupation people look up to, like farming or banking. Besides, you said it yourself just now...Frank's not good enough to try and make money from his wrestling."

There was a long silence. The others had been paying attention to the discussion, but began to lose interest and, when finished eating, drifted away from the table. Shortly, only Frank and his parents remained. Amelia was taking care of the dishes and storing the left-over food, while Frederick was fooling with a cornpipe of his that had been stuffing up lately. The shallow light from the oil burner was growing dim, casting long, dark shadows over the interior of the small kitchen. Frank wolfed down most of his food, and was toying with the remainder, as well as what he was going to say next.

"You know this fella I wrestled with today," he began, not sure if either parent was still interested in discussing wrestling. "Well, I didn't tell you the all of it. He said his name was Jonas, but afterwards he took me aside and told me the truth. Said he used a false name when traveling, or no one but the Farmer would wrestle him. Said his name's really Dan McLeod, and that he's the American champ. Champ of the whole darn country."

If Frank was waiting for an enthusiastic response, he was disheartened. Neither parent said a word, but continued with their chores.

"So," Frank continued, after a short respite, "if I can do that well with him, and if he says I'm really that good, maybe I could earn some money wrestling. It would help us out here, and all...." His voice trailed off, and he slipped a quick glance at first his father, and then his mother.

"Dan McLeod," mused his father, taking his eyes off his pipe and looking at his son. Frederick stroked his long, graying beard, and ran his left hand through his thick hair. The right arm, not good for much work since the tree accident, rested on the table, holding the pipe. "I've heard of this McLeod fellow; they say he ain't too bad. Most folks think the Farmer could beat him, but folks around here are a bit prejudiced."

Amelia joined in, not content to let the conversation drift without her firm direction.

"You're not supporting this foolishness of Frank's, I hope. After all, we need all the help we can get around here. You don't go putting any ideas into his head, Frederick Rudolph Gotch. He's got enough crazy thoughts there now as it is."

She turned and walked out of the room, passing under the thick doorframe into the darkness of her bedroom, slamming the door behind her. Frederick and Frank sat in silence for a moment or two, then Frank spoke up.

"What do you think, pa?" he asked softly. He respected his father a great deal, and wanted his approval to pursue his interest in wrestling. If he could get his blessing, the path ahead would be much easier. Without it, he may never have the courage to leave the farm and strike out in search of his fortune, which he was beginning to believe more and more with each passing day lay in the field of athletics. There wasn't any money to be made in track and field, for sure. And certainly no one would ever pay to watch men run up and down the field in that new game of football. Baseball had an appeal to a certain group, but the money just wasn't there; and besides, Frank didn't really like baseball all that well though he could hit a ball a country mile.

And he had tried boxing. He had done all right at it; in fact, there was no one in Humboldt who could slip past his defense, or take too many of his well-aimed blows. But somehow, hitting a man didn't appeal to him near as much as grappling with one. In a real free-for-all fight he felt more comfortable wrestling than boxing. After all, most fights wound up on the ground, anyway, after a few blows had been struck.

Frederick Gotch stared hard at his son, taking in the handsome face, the dark eyes, the thick arm muscles and big shoulders. "Have you got the stomach for it....I mean really got the stomach?" he asked at last.

Frank nodded, his eyes fixed on his father's face.

Frederick raised himself from the table, stuck his cornpipe in his shirt pocket: "I think so, too," he said. He walked two steps, then turned around, facing his son. "Hear tell that Farmer Burns will be coming to Fort Dodge in a few days. Might be a good time for you two fellas to meet up."

With that, he turned and walked toward the bedroom, leaving his son alone with his thoughts.

CHAPTER 2

Situated some twenty miles south of Humboldt, Fort Dodge was a drawing card for many of the farmers in the northern portions of Iowa. As a much larger city, it had many more features available - like a wider variety of stores, taverns and sporting events - than did Humboldt. It was also a popular stop on the circuit traveled by the professional wrestlers of the time, a rough and hardy crew that moved from city to city challenging all comers. Word had filtered up to Humboldt that Martin "Farmer" Burns, one of the best-known and most respected of all the circuit wrestlers, would be in Fort Dodge for several days in December of 1899. And Frank Gotch, along with five of his friends, set out by horse and buggy to meet the famous wrestler.

The trip was not an easy one and took the better part of a day. The weather was cold, and the road wasn't in the best of repair. There were ruts and potholes everywhere, but at least it hadn't snowed in the several weeks prior to the trip. With a heavy snow on the ground, the Humboldt party would have been forced to wait at least 'til spring, a delay that would have sorely disappointed young Gotch, as he was fairly itching to take on the Farmer. An instant reputation would be the result of a victory over Burns, and thoughts of touring the area as a wrestler and bringing home money to his parents were dancing in the young Humboldt farmer's mind.

Traveling to Fort Dodge brought back memories of his first serious attempt at wrestling. Ed Kennedy was now the baggage master at Fort Dodge, but had been a Humboldt teacher several years earlier. Though Kennedy was much older and bigger than Frank, the two had been leaning toward an engagement for some time, and when it finally came about, the two wrestled in the snow outside the old schoolhouse where Kennedy taught and Gotch attended. Gotch had the better of the match, but Kennedy claimed the snow had hindered him, and challenged his pupil to a match the following summer. In the meantime, young Frank had become something of a hero to all the sporting minded folks, and there were plenty, in the Humboldt area. At the barn dances and husking bees, people sought him out to shake his hand and to talk about wrestling, and Frank, always shy and modest, appreciated the attention shown him. It was then that he first realized that to be a good wrestler would make him a celebrity of sorts, like Buffalo Bill, or even John L. Sullivan.

The rematch took place in front of the Gotch homestead, on a day when his mother was gone to Fort Dodge and was not home to make her displeasure known. A crowd of nearly fifty showed up for the long-awaited match, and the two battled on even terms for over an hour before the match was declared a draw. But Frank's reputation continued to grow until at last he was matched with the feared Marshall Green, known by the nickname of "the chicken picker" as the result of his occupation of preparing chickens for the supper table. Green was the uncrowned champion of Humboldt, and was a braggart to boot. The many friends of Gotch wanted to see their hero pluck the chicken picker in the worst way, and they talked Frank into taking the match in the Russell Opera House in April. Gotch was reluctant to agree to the winner accepting any prize money, realizing that to do so stamped him as a professional, and that word would eventually get to his mother. But the excitement of the moment prevailed.

When the match was set, Gotch arrived in overalls, with no thought of tights or sweat pants. His friends talked him into cutting off the legs of the overalls just above the knees before he climbed into the ring to take on the terror of Humboldt. Though Green was a much bigger and far more seasoned man, he succumbed to his younger adversary in three straight falls, all by strangle holds. Frank was ecstatic on the trip home and was proud beyond words when he laid the small bag of silver dollars - his take from the wagers his friends had made - on the dining room table. His mother had scarcely noticed the money, having received word that her son was in town facing the chicken picker and having been in fear of his life. But the money came in handy in the ensuing months. Still, the episode was little talked about in the Gotch household, and it was such a sore spot that Frank had not dared to bring it up at the time of the big discussion.

Riding to Fort Dodge, Frank figured he had nearly a hundred pickup wrestling matches to his credit, with victory in all but a handful. As a professional wrestler - he was beginning to like the sound of the term more and more these last few days - he had engaged in just two, beating the chicken picker and losing to McLeod. As he saw the outline of Fort Dodge, with its several buildings two and three stories tall and smoke curling up from hundreds of smoke stacks and chimneys, his heart began to quicken. This was a moment he had been looking forward to for years, a meeting with the Farmer. "Who knows," he said to himself, "this may be the moment when I find my fortune in life."

The three-buggy caravan slipped into Fort Dodge and the driver of Gotch's buggy, Elmer Smith, continually asked directions of passersby until at last they stopped at a large building on the southeastern edge of town. Along the way they had seen several signs proclaiming the presence of Farmer Burns, and of a wrestler advertised as "The Terrible Turk." The Humboldt boys all had a round of laughs as they read about the Turk, "recently imported from the Ottoman Empire, a terrible, fiendish wrestling machine." They all knew, from stories they had heard, that this sort of foreign wrestler was usually little more than an American matman trying some new gimmick to draw attention.

Standing in the night cold and before the building where they figured Burns must now be, the group grew silent as they studied a picture of Burns which showed him displaying his incredible neck power. It was said the Farmer could hang by the neck for several minutes with a thick rope around his neck, and not lose consciousness, so strong were his neck muscles. He had been seen walking into towns with an anvil tied around his neck and dangling behind him, held off the ground by the power of his neck. A stranglehold was virtually useless against him, because an opponent could not stretch his fingers all the way around the Farmer's neck; and if he could, it didn't matter much as all Burns had to do was flex the neck muscles, and fingers couldn't dent that knotted mass of tissue. The drawing of Burns glared back at Gotch and his friends, presenting an intimidating sight.

"He sure looks like a mean one, Frank," said Smith, fingering his slight beard and gazing wistfully at the picture.

"I'm sure glad it's you and not me that's gonna tangle with the Farmer," said another.

"Yeah, me too," said Frank, with a faint smile. "I wouldn't want you to get all the glory, and all that money, too." Gotch was pointing at the portion of the sign poster that had caught his attention: "Twenty-five dollars American money to any challenger who can last 15 minutes with Farmer Burns without getting thrown," it read.

The little group parked the buggies with a group of others and walked back toward the building, an old opera house that now played host to a variety of events, including wrestling matches. There were plenty of people milling about, waiting for the matches to start before paying to go in. Smith walked up to several men, well dressed and in light conversation, and asked where one could find Farmer Burns.

"Don't rightly know, young fellow," said one of the men, sizing Smith and the rest up. "Why, do have some business with the Farmer?"

"Well, sure do, as a matter of fact," said Smith. "We're down from Humboldt, and we have a fellow with us, Frank Gotch, by name, who plans to throw the Farmer and collect twenty-five dollars."

The rest of the men glanced over at the Humboldt party, and quickly picked out Gotch; he was far broader than the rest, and more powerful looking, with his bull neck and heavy shoulders. He broke into a grin, realizing he was being inspected.

"We've heard of Gotch," said one of the well-dressed men. "Hear he's a pretty fair country wrestler. But now this Burns, he's something special."

"Just direct us to him," said Smith, beginning to feel his oats. After all, he was representing Frank, and these fellows had even heard of Gotch. Things were looking up, he reasoned.

"Well, you can't talk to Farmer Burns until the show starts, in about another half hour or so," said the man addressing Smith. "Then, he'll be more than happy to accommodate you, I suspect." The others in the group nodded and murmured their approval, smiling slightly at Smith and the Humboldt boys.

Smith walked back to Frank. "Looks like we'll have to keep ourselves busy for a spell." The air was growing colder by the minute, and the group decided to go indoors, even though the festivities weren't set to start for some time. They all paid one dollar each for admission, declaring that it was a good investment, as Frank was sure to get their money back for them, and they figured to make a little extra on side bets with the members of the crowd, which certainly would back the Farmer. Burns was a legend in this portion of the state and was figured to be unbeatable. The Humboldt boys entered, and their mood was high and jovial after warming up and with the prospects of a big victory by their man.

There were several hundred seats available, and they were about one-third filled by fans who had also come in early to escape the harsh winter air. They moved about and chatted amiably, paying scant notice to the new arrivals. The Humboldt gang eased down front, where Gotch would be able to issue his challenge easily and gain the stage with little difficulty. Once seated they stared at the huge curtain in front of them, bright purple with a few spots where it was wearing thin, and speculated on what surprises the night held in store for them.

Within thirty minutes, the building was filled to capacity. Rustling sounds from behind the curtain made it obvious the show was about to begin. Then, with a blare of trumpets and a roll of drums, the curtain came jerkingly open, revealing a small ring. Standing inside it were two men...one thick and powerful looking, with a turban wrapped around his head and a sash at his middle. The other man was shorter and thinner, but well muscled, especially in the area of the neck and shoulders. Both men sported mustaches, and one other distinguishing mark: the ears on both men were thick and puffy, like pieces of cauliflower, giving away their professions. They were wrestlers.

The shorter man stepped forward. "Welcome to our wrestling program," he fairly exploded in a voice that seemed far too deep and powerful for its author. "I'm Martin Burns, known to most of you as Farmer Burns, and this is," he said, turning to his partner, "Ottoman the terrible, straight from Turkey, the greatest wrestling machine ever produced in that far off country, where men wrestle day and night, in pits and in gravel, and are recognized the world over for their prowess.

"As you know by our posters, we offer twenty-five dollars to any man who can last fifteen minutes with either Ottoman or myself. Of course, we reserve the right to decide which of us will wrestle any challengers." The Farmer was interrupted by a series of hoots and cat-calls; the crowd was very knowledgeable in this game, and knew that a challenger who posed a real threat would have to face Burns, while a lesser foe would get the "Turk".

Burns ignored the crowd and continued in his presentation, citing records and issuing a series of challenges to "the great local heroes" of the Fort Dodge area to come forward. Finally, several men left their seats and approached the stage. But Gotch remained rooted, assessing the challengers and watching every move with fascination. The Farmer was almost hypnotic in his delivery, Frank thought, and was indeed a magnetic personality. Gotch felt a sense of regret inside him when he thought of pinning Burns' shoulders to the mat, as surely he would. He liked and admired this crusty clever fellow, but he thirsted for his reputation. He was anxious to get into the ring with Burns, but by the same token he planned to wait until just the proper moment. Maybe Burns would wrestle one of these early comers, and Gotch would watch and learn more about his style of wrestling....

But luck wasn't on Gotch's side. It was Ottoman who took on the first three opponents, and he dispatched them with relative ease. The first man he bodylocked and threw in less than three minutes, dropping his two hundred and fifty pound frame on top of the one hundred and seventy five pound local with a fearsome thud, knocking the air from him and all but rendering him unconscious. Burns narrated the bout and helped the beaten man from the stage, returning moments later and setting the stage for the second bout.

It lasted even less time, and culminated with a strangle hold, which irritated the fans. The local contestant was rendered totally helpless when Ottoman slipped behind him and then tripped him to the mat. As the local wrestler was rising up, Ottoman clamped the man's head in a vice-like grip, his right arm up alongside the head and his left arm laying horizontally beneath the man's chin, along his neck, and the left hand catching hold of Ottoman's right arm at the elbow. In just a matter of seconds, the man's eyeballs rolled upwards under his eyelids and his body went slack. When Ottoman let go the man laid flat on the mat, as though asleep, and it took a solid swat on the back from Burns to bring him around. The crowd was strangely silent, not knowing how to react to the strangle hold. It looked suspicious and a few cries of "fake" were raised, but they died away when the man recovered, acting as though he was still in a trance of some sort. He needed help leaving the stage and staggered several times before disappearing from view to the stage's right side.

The third contestant, grown wary by the experiences of those who preceded him, was unduly cautious and tried to run in circles to avoid the Turk. The latter pounded steadily after his foe until finally trapping him on the ropes and lifting him bodily to the center of the mat, where he deposited him roughly in a body slam. The local matman tried to wiggle free of the grip of the Turk, but he was caught in a leglock and forced into submission in less than three minutes. The Turk had barely worked up a sweat in dispatching three men.

Burns addressed the audience again, asking for takers, and Gotch decided to make his move. Rising from his seat, he shouted, "I'm willing to try you or the Turkish fellow there, whoever's ready." He walked to the side of the stage and leaped up the four steps to the stage, walking to the center to meet Burns.

The Turkish fellow and Burns were watching him approach, and it was evident from their expressions that they sensed this foe would be far different from the first three. Gotch faced them and stuck out his hand: "Frank Gotch is my name, and I'm from Humboldt."

The crowd began to cheer, led on by the boisterous Humboldt contingent, small but suddenly full of life and very noisy. Burns lifted an eyebrow as Gotch said his name.

"Yes, I've heard of you lad," he said, and not without respect. The tone wasn't lost on young Gotch, and it made him proud, and all the more confident. He glanced at both Burns and the Turk, beaming with anticipation.

Burns turned from Gotch and consulted with Ottoman in a low whisper; the Turk nodded solemnly, keeping his eyes on Gotch. Then Burns turned to the audience.

"We have a challenger, young Frank Gotch from Humboldt. Ottoman is somewhat tired after facing three men, and because this will be your last chance to see me wrestle tonight, as there are no more takers, I will wrestle the Gotch lad."

Frank noticed the reference twice to him as "lad" and, though not angry, was upset. He planned to prove to Farmer Burns that he was far more than a lad, and he nodded quickly and walked off stage, where he proceeded to take off his heavy coat, shirt and overalls, leaving a pair of black tights covering his legs. His arms and torso were bare, though, and as he walked back on stage, he heard a small roar from the crowd. It was impressed by the young farmer's physique. Weighing almost one hundred and eighty pounds, Frank was heavily muscled, though still lean and supple. He walked to the ring and climbed in, swinging his arms vigorously to and fro across his chest. Burns had stripped to wrestling tights, but left his torso bare, revealing a body that was rippling with muscle, but not near the size of Gotch. Frank guessed Burns' weight at one hundred and sixty-five pounds, but noticed its rock-hard formation. While Gotch was anxious to begin, he stood and watched as the Farmer went through an elaborate stretching process, taking the better part of three full minutes.

Finally, the Farmer turned and approached Gotch. He stuck out his hand and the two touched for what would be the first of countless thousands of times.

"I won't wish you good luck, young fellow," said Burns, "as I'll wish that on me. But wrestle well; the crowd expects it of us."

"That I will, Mr. Burns," said Gotch. Ottoman, working as the referee, was holding a small gong. He instructed the two to release and step back, which they did. Then Ottoman, nodding to a time-keeper on the side of the stage, told the wrestler and the crowd that the fifteen minutes was beginning, and he would hit the gong twice, once to start the match and once, if necessary, to signify the fifteen minutes had expired without a fall. He looked quickly at both wrestlers, who were staring hard at one another, and gave the gong a resounding smash.

Supposing himself to be the far quicker man, Burns attempted a few feints at Frank's legs, hoping to make the younger, less experienced man commit a mistake and expose himself. But though Gotch fell for the fakes, Burns soon discovered his young foe was amazingly quick and could recover from a blunder in time to stop a true shot at a takedown. They circled each other after Burns' initial moves had failed to win him an advantage, and the crowd began to hoot: "He's afraid of you Frank," hollered one of the Humboldt boys. If the wrestlers heard the reaction from the crowd, they gave no indication. They were concentrating totally on the task at hand. Burns realized from his first hold on Gotch that he was up against an exceptionally powerful foe, and he was little less than amazed at the speed with which the strapping lad could move. "He shouldn't be able to move that quick, from the size of him," Burns told himself.

The Farmer finally grabbed hold of Gotch's head and pulled it down, wrapping an arm around his neck in a front headlock. He maneuvered left and right, front and back, trying to mix up his directions and confuse the young Humboldt strongboy. Then, he stepped forward with a quick movement and tripped Gotch straight to his back, landing on top. Only about five minutes had expired, and Burns had his man perilously close to a fall. But straining every muscle in his powerful body, Frank kept his back from the canvas mat. Burns switched his weight frantically, trying to fit himself into a position that would enable him to tighten his hold and pin the shoulders of Gotch, but Frank rolled to his stomach, ending the threat.

The two continued at a frantic pace for the next several minutes, Burns trying hold after hold, and Gotch dispatching them with his strength and speed. It was evident to most on-lookers, wise in the ways of the mat world, that Burns was far superior in skills, but Gotch was superior in speed and strength. Conditioning-wise, they appeared about equal. At last, Burns secured the feared double nelson hold, winding his long arms under Gotch's arms and bringing his hands together in a viselike grip on the back of the Humboldt lad's neck. It was a hold which, at the least, would produce a painfully sore neck.....

and, at the worst, could actually result in a broken neck. The crowd grew silent as the two wrestlers struggled, one to subdue the other by bending his neck down, forcing a submission or rolling the shoulders to the mat by the force of the hold, the other straining to break the torturous hold.

"Do you give?" asked Burns, applying more and more force by the second. Gotch didn't answer, but attempted to stand. Burns fought desperately to hold him, but the Humboldt farmer moved from his hands and knees slowly upward, until he was solidly on his feet, with the Farmer dangling in the air behind him, still holding on to Gotch's neck with the double nelson. Ottoman let out a gasp of surprise - and respect - at the show of force by Gotch, and even Burns was to admit later that he could hardly believe it when Gotch rose to his feet under such circumstances. Frank tried to shake Burns from his hold and the crowd, at first awed into silence by the show of strength on Gotch's part, roared and roared its approval. Most of the two hundred or so fans were on their feet screaming encouragement to their local hero. It was turning into the best show in these parts in years, and the fans were not hesitant to voice their approval and appreciation.

Burns managed to entangle his legs with Gotch's and tripped him to the mat once again. They fell heavily, with Burns landing on top, and the wind knocked from Frank's lungs. Taking advantage of Gotch's momentary plight, Burns shifted immediately to a half nelson and crotch hold, and propelled the still stunned Humboldt farmer to his shoulders. Ottoman slapped the mat hard, then slapped Burns on his shoulder, signifying the end of the match. It had taken nearly twelve minutes, but Farmer Burns had defeated Frank Gotch in their catch-as-catch-can style bout, saving the twenty-five dollar purse.

As the two men came to their feet, Burns reached out a hand and grasped Gotch's arm, helping him to stand. Frank shook his head in despair; it was obvious he had already recuperated physically from the desperate struggle, but there was the chance he would not be the same emotionally for some time. His pride had been dealt another rough setback, and he felt ashamed in front of his friends who had traveled to Fort Dodge with him in the hopes of sharing in a big victory...and of making some money, of course. Now, both hopes were gone, because he had let them down, or so he reasoned.

Burns was still holding on to his arm and talking to him in a whisper. The words came quickly, and in a hushed tone. Finally ridding himself of his own thoughts, Frank heard just the tail end of what Burns was saying, but it was enough to start him thinking heavily. The words "manage" and "big future" had struck home. Gotch was looking at Burns intently as the legendary Farmer strode to the footlights and addressed the audience.

"Ladies and gentlemen, I have never met an amateur wrestler the likes of this fellow in all my days on the circuit. I think this Humboldt lad could become, in time and with my direction, the champion wrestler of America. Who knows," he added, with a shrug of his shoulders, "maybe he could even be as good as the old Farmer some day."

With that, Burns held his hands aloft, and the audience began a wild and unrestrained cheering. It had been a good show, with a tremendous ending in the eyes of many. Ottoman had shown his mettle, and these two Iowa farmers had followed up with a display of wrestling prowess, courage and conditioning that would warm the hearts of those in attendance for years to come.

After the curtain was drawn shut, Burns turned to Gotch once again, extending a hand in friendship. Ottoman was nearby, talking to a small group of admirers, and the Humboldt contingent, having come on stage, was standing a way off, respectfully keeping its distance while Burns and Gotch talked. They were anxious not only to greet their comrade, but to stand near Burns and size him up, so they could tell their friends back home that they had actually been within an arm's length of the most respected sportsman in all of Iowa, and the Midwest, too, for that matter.

"I meant what I told them folks, Frank," said the Farmer, looking young Gotch square in the eye. It was the first time he had used Gotch's name, and it made him feel good. "You are good, mighty good. I heard tell of you from McLeod; he warned me against taking you on. Said I was too old and too light to tangle with your likes, but then I had to see for myself. I'd like to have you travel with me and the Turk."

Gotch was taken by surprise by the offer, and for the first time in his life grew suspicious and a bit standoffish. He could hardly believe that this man who had defeated him could be so impressed with him as a wrestler. And now that he knew the Farmer had talked to McLeod, Frank was doubly cautious. After all, Burns knew only that Gotch had wrestled twice, and had lost twice.

The Farmer sensed his discomfort; drawing on years and years of varied experiences, he knew the next few moments might be critical in gaining a friend or an adversary for life, and he knew one thing for certain: Frank Gotch, with training and tutelage, could become in time the finest wrestling machine America had yet produced. The Farmer wasn't about to lose the opportunity of getting in on the ground floor.

"Look, Frank," he said, throwing an arm about the brawny shoulders of the Humboldt strongboy, "let's go somewhere where we can talk privately."

Frank paused for a moment, then, remembering his friends, turned to search for them. He saw them standing several yards away, watching closely.

"But what of them?" Gotch asked, turning back to the Farmer and motioning to his friends.

Burns glanced in their direction, then called over to them: "Hey, fellas, come over here, if that be your mind." Immediately they approached, hands extended, anxious to meet Farmer Burns. After quick introductions, Burns told them what was on his mind.

"I want to spend some time with your friend here," he said. "Wouldn't you boys like to see him become a top-notch wrestler on the circuit, bringing fame to Humboldt and all of you good people up there?" The question was met by a chorus of affirmative responses, and Burns was pleased to note that even Gotch was loosening up and starting to smile once again. Burns saw the new manner overtaking Gotch, and was more than a bit pleased at the lad's ability to shake off adversity.

"That," Burns would say countless times in the years ahead, "is an invaluable trait for a professional wrestler, and goes a long way toward making a champion."

Two hours later, the small group came out of the opera house. Burns and Ottoman stood for a moment and shook hands with the others, and then departed in one direction, while the larger band left in the opposite direction. Among the latter group were Gotch and Smith, and they clamored into their buggy, with the remainder of the Humboldt crew climbing aboard their respective rigs.

"What do you think of all this, Frank?" asked Smith. The excitement of the night was quickly fading into exhaustion; it had been a long trip from Humboldt, and a night of energy-sapping developments. Now, the moon was riding high, and the Humboldt gang was determined to start out for home. There was plenty of work to be done the next day for all concerned, and it wouldn't pay to linger.

"I'm not sure, Elmer," replied Gotch. "It's all happened so fast. I sure like the Farmer, and I know I could learn a heap about wrestling from him. But, I don't know if I could earn a living, like he says."

The two were silent for a mile down the road, until Smith spoke out again. "What will your ma and pa have to say about all this?"

Gotch was lost in thought, and Smith had to repeat his question, speaking out to make sure his voice hadn't been lost amid the clippety-clop of the horse and the creaking of the buggy wheels.

"That'll be the hard part," Frank confessed. "I think the world of ma and pa, but I know there's more to life for me than just working a plow. It ain't that I feel I'm too good for that kind of life; heck, maybe I'm not good enough for it. Maybe I ain't the kind of person that has the stick-to-it-iveness or the gumption that one needs to work a farm and make a go of it. Maybe my brothers are just better suited to it than me. But I think I can wrestle with anybody, if given half a chance. The Farmer said he thinks I could beat McLeod, the champion catch-as-catch-can wrestler in all of America, with a year's matches under my belt. And I got to admit, Elmer, there ain't nothing I'd like better than to some day walk down the streets of Humboldt, and folks saying, 'There goes our Frank, the heavyweight wrestling champion of America....or the whole world.'"

Again, the two fell to silence, each lost in his own thoughts. It was Smith who spoke next.

"I think you can do it, Frank," he said. "But one thing's for sure...you'd be leaving Humboldt when you became rich and famous, and I wouldn't like to see that."

Gotch glanced at his friend in surprise. He squinted in the dark night, dropped a hand on Smith's shoulder, and gave a slight chuckle.

"I'll tell you this, Elmer," he said, his voice deep with sincerity. "No matter what happens to me, good or bad, I won't never think about leaving Humboldt. My roots are too strong. That's my home now, and always will be, whatever comes."

The sound of the horses' hooves striking the road eventually wore on young Frank's tired body, and he fell asleep amid visions of wrestling for the heavyweight championship of the world.

CHAPTER 3

The man striding across the wide-open camp could hear a coyote - or maybe even a timber wolf - howling long and plaintive in the biting cold. It was a more bitter cold than he had ever experienced in his twenty years of life. He had thought that Humboldt, not many miles from the Minnesota border, was prone to nasty winters, but this was far worse. The Alaskan air was dry, and the cold went right through a body, no matter how many layers of clothing one poured oneself into, he reasoned, shivering again.

Frank quickened his pace toward the big hall some two hundred yards ahead, the sight of the lights flickering through the windows and their promise of warmth spurring him on. The Farmer had tried to talk him out of this Alaskan trip, but the lure of the wrestling experience he would gain, and the hope of some big and quick money, were far too strong for him to resist. When Burns told him of the offer promoter Dick Butler had made to him, and why he had turned it down - after all, the Farmer wasn't a young man anymore and he did have a family and responsibilities in Iowa - Frank had seized on the opportunity for himself. He felt that Alaska, a region so exotic and far away, would be an ideal place for him to hone his skills and really learn his profession. He knew that in Iowa he would be facing pressures too great to overcome, at least starting out as a professional wrestler, what with his ma begging him to desist, and his friends expecting - and almost demanding - victory each and every time he competed.

Frank asked Burns to contact Butler on his behalf, and the Farmer had done so, if grudgingly. Ever since the match in Fort Dodge, Burns and Frank had kept in close contact, and Gotch had traveled to the Farmer's home in Big Rock, a dot-in-the-road village in eastern Iowa, for a series of long, exhausting - and highly informative - workouts. At first, they worked mostly on the basics - including leverage, conditioning and body position. But in short order, Burns began to show Frank some of the finer points of the sport, the submission holds known only to the upper lexicon of wrestlers. These moves were known as "hooks" and the men who used them were called "hookers," the most respected and dangerous of all wrestlers. True hookers, like Burns, were able to lock a man's joints - an elbow or an ankle or a knee - into a tight hold which, at best, was merely very painful and, at the worst, would result in a torn ligament, snapped tendon or a badly broken bone.

They often finished their wrestling with long discussions, which more often than not turned into lectures by Burns on the need to take perfect care of one's body. Farmer Burns was nothing if not a fanatic on physical and mental fitness. He touched no liquor or tobacco, carefully mapped his workouts, ate nourishing, well-planned meals, and believed wholeheartedly in the benefits of hard labor in the outdoors.

"Clean air, hard work, good habits and an optimistic outlook on life will get ya where you're going," he would say repeatedly.

After one long workout, Burns and Gotch discussed at length the pros and cons of Frank moving to Alaska for a while. Burns was interested in keeping his young, eager protégé near him for another six months, at least, so that he could continue in his development. But when he saw Frank was bound and determined to try the Alaskan market, he capitulated. He admitted it had taken some talking on his part to interest Butler in this new and untested wrestler, but Burns was not a man to be taken lightly, and his opinion of Gotch eventually persuaded Butler to take a chance with the Humboldt farmer.

Prior to Gotch' s departure, he spent several weeks in hard training with the Farmer, working for hours in the old ring which stood a hundred yards to the rear of the Burns house. Each morning they rose at dawn for several miles of roadwork, running through the quiet Iowa farmland. Returning home, they took a light breakfast of eggs, toast, sausage chunks, and juice, made by the Farmer's wife, Mary, and then retired for a strategy session, endlessly discussing various moves and counter-moves. Then it was on to hours and hours of wrestling, with the emphasis on drills and learning various holds and techniques, culminating with a session on hooks and hooking.

Gotch was always surprised at the emphasis his tutor placed on stretching prior to workouts; sometimes the Farmer would spend up to fifteen minutes in twisting and loosening up before he would consent to wrestle. At first it irritated Frank, always eager to exchange holds, but the Farmer would pretend not to notice Gotch's impatience, muttering that the stretching "keeps the muscles loose and prepares you against tearing one of 'em, about the worst thing that can happen to a wrestler." Eventually, Gotch joined in rather than wait idly by as his mentor went through the paces.

Burns spent most of his workout on drilling, going over basic moves and counters time and time again, until Gotch would grow impatient and begin to wrestle hard. But the Farmer would stop at that point and back away, hands on hips. "Frank," he would say, with that straight-on look he always gave to those he was talking to, "we're going to do this my way. It takes more than brute strength to win in this game day after day. Shore, you're plenty strong, too strong for the boys around here, that's certain. But if you want to beat the likes of Tom Jenkins from Cleveland and that bunch, you'll need more than just strength. Why, Jenkins is a millwright and powerful as the day is long. He's bigger than you and stronger. You won't beat him by playing his game. You gotta learn to wrestle....I mean really wrestle....those boys. Now, we're gonna drill, and drill, and drill some more."

They were lessons Gotch would forget from time to time, but ones he would always return to. In time, drilling and conditioning would become the main ingredients of his success.

But approaching the hall in the frozen wastelands of Alaska, shivering in the darkness, he could only wish he had remained in Iowa. Sure, the pickings had been good here in Dawson, where most of the men were strong and hardy, though short on wrestling know-how, but he missed his family, friends and the Farmer. Besides, changing his name had upset him, even though Butler and Burns had agreed that it was the best idea. As a matter of fact, Butler insisted he do so. It was hardly likely that any of the men had heard of him from his miniscule feats in Iowa, but the gold prospectors and miners intensely hated a ringer - a boxer or wrestler who came north with a world of experience, intent on taking their hard-earned dollars in matches that were too lopsided. Of course, Gotch hardly qualified as a ringer with his meager background, but the Farmer's reputation was known far and wide in pugilistic circles, and Butler wasn't taking any chances.

Under the name of Frank Kennedy, Gotch passed an uneventful first month in his mining camp near the town of Dawson, and he actually went into the streams with others, panning for gold. But events moved ahead quickly after his first run-in with the camp bully. Challenged by a bulk of a man named Conner, young Frank had thrown him to his back and made him yell "uncle" with a wrist lock that threatened to break Conner's arm, one of the hooking moves Burns had taught him. Word spread quickly, and he was offered a bout with Billy Murdock, the camp's champion wrestler. It was supposed to be a finish match with no time limit, but Gotch ended it with another wrist lock in just five minutes, setting the entire camp to talking about the new wrestling wonder.

Two more matches were quickly arranged with champions of neighboring camps, and the young man from Iowa was almost speechless when, after less than thirty minutes of wrestling and two victories, Butler poured nearly two thousand dollars into his hands in gold coins and Canadian paperbacks. Miners were nothing if not betting men and gamblers, and the stakes ran high whenever one of their own was challenged to a test of manhood through boxing or wrestling. Butler was concerned that Kennedy's alias would be uncovered, but Gotch took to the mines each and every day with the rest of the workers, and they continued to accept him as one of their own. Even the tremendous payday in Dawson, when Gotch threw a miner named White three times in an hour and pocketed eight thousand dollars, didn't harm Kennedy's standing in his own camp. And it was that match which set up the biggest bout of all.

Silas Archer was a huge, barrel-chested man who weighed well over two hundred and twenty pounds. Working in Dawson, he had defeated every man who had dared test him during the past five years, and was uncrowned - and undisputed - wrestling champion of the entire Yukon Territory. He had heard of Kennedy's triumphs and even witnessed the decisive victory over White, but remained in the background, content to rest on his reputation until the time, and price, for his appearance was right. At Butler's urging, Kennedy issued a challenge to Archer through the Dawson paper, but there was no immediate response. When Butler also leveled a challenge in Kennedy's name, Archer stepped forward. He announced he would wrestle for a five thousand dollar purse, winner takes all. Gotch came back with an offer of ten thousand dollars, shaking Archer's confidence somewhat, but forcing him to wrestle, lest he lose his considerable reputation as a man who faced all challenges head-on. The match quickly developed into the single largest event to come along in the territory for years, and was scheduled August 13, 1901, in the old Savoy Theatre on the outskirts of Dawson.

It was toward that very theatre Gotch was now making his way. The coyote - or wolf, he had never learned to tell them apart - howled again and a blast of wintry air struck at him just as he climbed down the creaky steps on the backside of the theatre. The "Savoy" sign dangled over head, as though ready to come tumbling down any second after years of struggling against the arctic winds. Pushing open the door, the freezing Iowa farmer hurried inside, slamming the door against the vicious night. He was behind and under the stage area on the bottom floor, but he could feel the heat already, and heard the hushed sound of hundreds of voices coming from above, where the miners were already gathering in anticipation of a great night of wrestling, betting, drinking and fighting. Maybe Kennedy and Archer were the main antagonists, but there was no way that so many tough and hardy men, most of them a long way from home and their families, would get through the night without contesting their own skills against anyone within shouting distance. It would start good-naturedly, enter into the challenging stage, and end with broken noses, dislocated shoulders and a few arrests. The next day, most of them would be side by side in the mines, or ankle deep in the waters of various streams, digging and panning for their fortunes. Few would find it here, or anywhere, during their turbulent lives.

Frank moved toward a dressing room Butler had reserved for him, and found the one with his Kennedy name tacked to the door. He opened the door, stared in at the austere room, and shut it behind him, moving to a small locker against the far wall. There was a pair of woolen tights, black and heavy, laying on the chair before the locker, and two thick boots at the foot of the chair. He couldn't repress a grin as he recalled his first matches back in Humboldt with his teacher, Ed Kennedy, and the chicken-picker. He felt like he had come a long way in just three short years of wrestling, and he wondered if he would ever face a bigger match than this one tonight. Before he could really reflect on the matter, the door slammed open behind him, and a thick, short man flew in, chattering in his excitement.

"Wow, what a crowd, what a crowd, Frank!" gasped Dick Butler, rubbing his thick hands together in anticipation, a big grin peeking out between his mustache and bushy beard. He was attired in a dark suit and wore a black stovepipe hat. He carried a fancy cane in one hand and his long winter coat was draped over the other arm.

Frank, stooping to take off his boots, glanced up at Butler and smiled.

"Getting kinda fancy on me there, ain't ya, Dick?" he asked, continuing to tug at his boots.

"Naw," said Butler, shrugging. "Yeah, yeah, I guess I am," he reconsidered. "But what the hell, Frank, what the hell...I mean tonight we leave this place as millionaires. Oh, the Farmer was right, bless his heart, when he said you'd win us a fortune up here with these dumb miners."

"I ain't won it yet, Dick," came Gotch's reply, and Butler stiffened. He knew his man was anything but cocky before a match, and always had respect for his opponents. Yet, he had never heard Gotch express any doubts about his ability to win, and this new approach flustered him.

"What's wrong, why'd you go and say something like that?" said Butler, inching forward nervously, and scrutinizing the young man upon whose abilities he had just bet nearly ten thousand dollars. He squinted at Gotch, still dressing. "Tell me," he pleaded, "are you sick or something?"

"Naw, it's nothing like that," said Frank, straightening up and staring down at Butler. He had his shirt off, and his hairy chest was thick with muscles developed behind the plow, pushing it through the rich Iowa soil for years. The oil can light in the corner left much of the room in shadow, and Butler, looking up at Gotch, was struck again, as he had been on several other occasions, by the incredible width of Gotch's shoulders.

"It's just that anyone can lose, and I don't think we should count on anything til the wrestling's over."

Butler smiled faintly. This was the serious side of his young friend, and he appreciated it. The fun-loving aspect was gone now that the competition was about to begin. Butler appreciated the mental preparation necessary for a big match like this, and knew Gotch was getting himself ready. It promised to be a grand and rewarding night.

In ten minutes, Gotch had finished dressing and had completed a short loosening up period. Though the Farmer wasn't with him, his training principles were. Butler, assured that all was well, left to check the crowd and the final preparations, and Gotch remained in the room alone. His thoughts reverted back to Iowa as he finished his stretching and moved into his drills. He ducked low and moved quickly, as though searching for a leg to grab and then stood up abruptly, twisting his body and dumping his imaginary foe on the wooden floor. He duck-walked, stretching out his thighs, and did a series of rapid pushups to get the blood flowing to his arms, then rose and quickly shook his arms vigorously as they dangled at his side. He planted his right foot on the floor, and swiveled at the ankle time and again, hoping to loosen up the area and thereby avoid a crippling ankle injury, then repeated the exercise with the left foot. He placed both palms on his forehead and pushed back roughly, flexing his neck muscles and resisting the pressure. The veins stood out in his neck and his teeth ground together as he strained.

Butler re-entered, looking more excited than ever. He had his two brothers with him, and they were grinning in a silly fashion, nodding toward Gotch in greeting.

"I never seen anything like it, Frank," Butler said in a high-pitched voice. "There must be a thousand miners up there. They's hanging from the rafters, and still pouring in through the doors. And everybody's in a betting mood and they brought plenty of gold dust with 'em. Best of all, they's betting on Archer. They think he's gonna whup you, Frank."

Gotch smiled quickly. "Let's find out," he said, nodding to Butler and his brothers, and they quickly backed out of the room as he came toward them, dressed in the black uniform which covered his legs and chest, but left his big arms bare. Together, they walked down the corridor and to the stairs in the back, climbing them and emerging at the rear of the stage. In front of them was a large ring, with a padded gray mat, bright red ropes boxing it in. The large green curtain at the front of the stage was drawn tight, but they could hear the tremendous noise being generated by the large throng. The clinking of glasses and the scattered laughter of women filled the air, and piano music rolled in from somewhere in the building.

Across from them stood a group of eight men, regarding them in silence. In the middle was Archer, decked out in a bright red robe. He stared hard over at Gotch, then smiled, weakly. It was an attempt at showing his confidence, Frank knew, and he offered no salutation in return. Instead, he turned to Butler.

"How much do I stand to gain on this one, Dick?" he asked.

Butler dug into his pocket and pulled out a wad of paper, and began thumbing through it. "You'll get about ten thousand just for winning, and another five thousand in side bets," he said. Smiling, he patted Frank on the back: "A good night's work, right, son?"

Gotch nodded. One of the men from the other group started forward and walked over to them. He and Butler shook hands, having met several times when setting up the match. He turned to Gotch and sized him up.

"So you're Kennedy," he offered. "Glad to meet ya. I'm Lind, Archer's trainer...and sponsor. You look like a nice young fella. Too bad you're gonna get roughed up tonight. But maybe we'll be able to scrape up enough money to get ya back to....where is it you're from, anyway?"

Gotch wasn't taken unaware by the man's question. He had been schooled carefully by Butler, and told to avoid any reference to Iowa or Farmer Burns, just to avoid suspicion. He nodded slightly at Lind, and said that he was from the States.

"Which one?" asked Lind, arching an eyebrow and staring hard at his man's opponent.

"What's it matter, Lind?" interjected Butler. "Hell's bells, we come here to wrestle, not to conduct a geography lesson, right boys?" Butler's brothers voiced their agreement, and Lind, with one last long look at Kennedy, changed the subject. Addressing Butler, he stated the terms again, "just so's there'd be no confusion at the last minute."

"They'll wrestle for sixty minutes or for two falls, whichever occurs first," he said, and Butler nodded his agreement. "A pin means one man's entire back and shoulders being flat for three seconds, not just one or the other. A man can quit anytime, but that's a fall, too. And no choking, or gouging or punching. This ain't no boxing match, it's a wrestling match. You got your money, Butler?"

Butler turned to one of his brothers and motioned for a black bag he was carrying. Opening it up, he pulled out several thick wads of greenbacks and some gold powder bags. He counted out ten thousand - five thousand covering Kennedy's end of the purse, and five thousand for himself.

"Where's O'Keefe?" he asked, glancing about and suddenly acting suspicious. "I don't see him nowhere, and this thing don't come off until he shows up."

"He's been sent for and he'll be along any minute," said Lind. "What's the matter, don't you trust me?"

Butler glared at Lind in response, and then demanded to see his ten thousand. A man from the Archer party was summoned and counted it out to Butler's satisfaction. Meanwhile, Gotch continued to loosen up, twisting his arms and doing a series of deep knee bends, and torso twists. He didn't want to tighten up before the match even got under way. He reckoned that the Farmer would be proud of him if he could be there to see him employing his own tactics of preparation. Archer, on the other side of the ring, stood motionless and sullen, watching Kennedy warm up - "wearing his stupid self out," is what

Archer called it - and talking quietly with his friends.

A slim dignified appearing man came up the back stairs and approached Lind and Butler. He was Thomas O'Keefe, the town banker, and the only man either party trusted with the money. He was to hold it until after the match was over. And just to make sure everything was on the up and up, the town marshal and two deputies came with him. Dawson was as rough a town as one could find anywhere in the Western Hemisphere, filled with miners, prospectors, criminals and thugs of every description and temperament. On several previous occasions, during a big match, the house had erupted in total pandemonium, and the banker was knocked cold, the money stolen. The principals involved this time around - notably, Butler and Lind, Gotch and Archer - were determined to forestall any such eventuality.

"Let's get going," Lind said, after speaking briefly with the banker and the law officers, merely three men who had tired of the uncertainties brought on by the drudgery of mining, and had turned to toting a badge just so they could draw a salary, no matter how meager, and have some guarantee of an income for their wives. Listening to the growing noise from beyond the curtain, they grew restless and fingered their rifles nervously, glancing about.

Lind walked to the edge of the stage behind the curtain and gave the word to two men, who began drawing on the heavy ropes. Slowly, the dark green curtain retreated and a prolonged cheering erupted from the audience, tired of waiting to see this great match that had been ballyhooed around the various camps for more than a week. After the curtain had been fully opened and the cheering subsided, Lind stepped to the center of the stage and held his hands out wide, asking for complete silence. It took a while, but it finally came, and he addressed the crowd.

"Tonight, we have the most eagerly-awaited wrestling match ever to take place in Dawson, or the whole of the Yukon for that matter," and he paused for dramatic effect.

"Yeah, we know that....just get on with it, big mouth," someone shouted from the back of the house. Lind grimaced, and continued.

"You all know Silas Archer, a great and undefeated wrestler from right here in Dawson. He's big and mean and ready to wrestle, and to defend his title as the champeen wrestler of the Yukon. Ladies and gentlemen, let's have a hand for Silas Archer."

Lind turned and held an arm out in the direction of Archer, who stepped forward to Lind's left, and faced the crowd, which roared its approval. He was a big, thick man, with a handlebar mustache and dark hair which hung over his ears and halfway down the back of his neck. He stood over six foot tall, but a goodly portion of his two hundred and twenty pounds was now sagging to his waist. He hadn't been able to round up any matches in recent months due to his reputation as a fearless and unbeatable matman, and he had taken to drinking lots of beer and eating heartily, unconcerned about his shape or conditioning. He smiled at the cheers, and finally held his arms up in response, and the crowd cheered all the harder. He was their favorite, it was plain to see.

When the noise subsided, Lind continued.

"His opponent is that fearless prospector only recently arrived from the States in search of his fortune. You have seen him wrestle, or heard of his wrestling, as he's been whipping a few of the lesser boys around here as of late. His name's Frank Kennedy, and he's bitten off more than he can chew tonight."

Butler jumped forward at the words, but Gotch reached out an arm and held him back. "That dirty, no-good bastard!" spit out Butler, his eyes burning with rage, "I'll get him for that."

Frank smiled for the first time. "No, Dick, I'll get Archer for that," he said, and then walked to Lind's right side. The crowd was laughing at Lind's last remark, and there was a mixed portion of booing and cheering when Kennedy stood before the crowd, and bowed slightly. Lind leaned toward him, his hand by his mouth, and whispered, "Sorry about that, kid; but facts is facts."

"Don't mind a bit, Mr. Lind," Gotch retorted. "I just hope you're still laughing when this whole affair's over and you're ten thousand dollars poorer."

Gotch reached across the front of Lind and held out his hand to Archer, who stared at him coldly before finally accepting the handshake. The crowd hooted its approval, and began shouting to get the match under way. Lind introduced the timekeeper and the referee, a man named Wilkins, and the two wrestlers stepped to their respective corners of the ring. Butler acted as Kennedy's second, while Lind did the same for Archer. The referee walked briskly to each corner, saying he wanted the "boys to keep it clean, or we'll stop this thing, by shooting if we have to." Archer threw off his red robe, displaying a white, large body that had plenty of hard muscle to it, covered by a layer of lately-increasing fat. He wore black tights, but no top piece, as Gotch did.

The miners came to their feet, raising mugs of beer into the air and screaming support for their choice as the two men circled one another warily, searching for an opening. Archer moved first, grabbing hold of Kennedy's arms and attempting to shake him. But instead, Gotch threw the Alaskan from him with a show of strength that impressed the miners, and sent reservations into Archer's corner. Archer frowned and circled some more, with Gotch, suddenly, the pursuer. Just in that fleeting exchange, the tempo was established. Archer would be the pursued, Gotch the pursuer.

They clinched again, grabbing one another behind the neck and attempting to bull the other man down. Archer grunted heavily as Gotch pushed his head down and came over the top with a long right arm, reaching for a front facelock. It was a dangerous hold to be caught in, and Archer struggled to break free from the grip, and did at last, but only with a mighty effort which left him somewhat drained, and not a little discouraged. He backed away as Gotch advanced smiling, and Archer saw with dismay that his younger opponent was brimming with confidence. Several more times they came together, only to break apart when neither could gain an advantage. But Gotch knew, could actually feel, that the match was his. Burns had told him many times the look in the other man's eyes would give him away. It could be part of man's strategy to back away or to appear tired, then to erupt in an explosion of power and movement. But a man's eyes, said Burns, never lied. It was a lesson the young Humboldt farmer recalled here in Alaska as Frank Kennedy, and a lesson that would come back to him many years later in Chicago, when he was wrestling the most feared matman of his generation for the world heavyweight championship.

Now, there was no denying the young Iowan. The prospect of great wealth never entered his mind as he pursued the man in front of him; it was, instead, the excitement of the competition that forced him on. He truly loved to wrestle, to pit his strength, skills, quickness and competitive heart against other men in the ringed arena, to see who would survive. He began mauling Archer relentlessly, darting in and out with his attacks and leg dives, forcing the other man to back up repeatedly, and to ward off his continuous advances. He could hear Archer breathing heavily, and saw his chest heaving up and down in an effort to catch his second wind. Gotch clutched the older, bigger man in a vise-like grip near the ropes in Archer's own corner, then ducked underneath the outstretched arms and behind the tired man, lifting him easily from the floor. With his arms about his waist, Gotch carried him kicking and writhing to the center of the ring, the miners screaming wildly. Lind's face was beet red as he hollered at the top of his lungs for Archer to escape, while Butler was beating on the ring post and shouting for Kennedy to end it now.

Gotch slammed Archer heavily to the mat, and fell on top of him. He worked an arm under Archer's right arm, bringing his hand up on the flattened man's neck, in a half nelson. With all the power he could summon, he bore down on the neck, forcing Archer to burrow his head into the thick and mushy mat. Then, Kennedy moved to Archer's right side, holding him flat with the one hand and with the immense pressure on the neck, worked his other arm between the man's legs. Grabbing hold of Archer's left thigh, he drove his shoulder solidly into his ribs and at the same time pulled in on the thigh and pushed down even harder on the neck. The concentrated force flipped the exhausted Archer to his back in a pinning position. He squirmed and kicked to free himself, but Gotch's head was now buried deep in his rib area and the incredibly strong arms held Archer helpless. The first fall was over, the referee slapping the mat hard to signify a pin.

Gotch arose amid a deafening roar from the spectators. Archer lay flat, unable, it seemed, to rise. He had five minutes to recuperate for the second fall, but he appeared totally done in. Lind scrambled through the ropes and was at his side, yelling obscenities at him and coercing him to win the next two falls. Butler was at Gotch's side pounding him on the back, drooling in his excitement. The referee stood calmly by, glancing apprehensively at the audience, which was on its feet and throwing money into the ring.

Gotch returned to his corner and gazed out at the audience. It was the most exciting moment of his entire life. He had just defeated the champion wrestler of the Yukon without breaking more than a mild sweat, and he was about to earn ten thousand dollars. He knew that even if Archer would consent to wrestle the second fall, it wouldn't last as long as the first.

Archer struggled to his feet and to his corner, but he looked in no condition to continue. Finally, the referee walked over and consulted with him. Archer, head hanging low, shook his head several times and Lind, in exasperation, slammed his fist into the corner ring post. The crowd, sensing that Archer wasn't going to contest the second fall, broke up into a number of short, violent exchanges, with fans of Kennedy and Archer going at one another, in an attempt to collect money or avoid paying off bets. Gotch walked across the ring.

"How about it, Silas," he offered. "Can we go again?"

Lind looked up and shouted at the top of his lungpower: "You're a ringer, Kennedy; you beat him too easily. We'll have your hide for this."

But Archer held out his hand. "Don't pay him no mind, Frank," he said in a husky voice. "My day is done, that's all. You're the best around here, maybe anywhere. I can't go with you again. You're too strong, too quick. Maybe I couldn't beat you at my best."

Gotch felt a sudden affinity for Archer; the battle was over now, and he had won not only a great deal of money, but also a great deal of respect. The praise coming from Archer meant a great deal to him, and he offered his hand. "It happens to all of us, Silas, and it'll happen to me, some day." He was surprised at his own philosophical assessment of the situation, and thought of the moment many, many times in the coming years, and smiled inwardly.

The referee asked a final time if the Archer corner was surrendering, and Archer nodded that he was. Grabbing Kennedy by the wrist, he walked to the center of the ring and asked the crowd to quiet down, but to no avail. Finally, the sheriff fired three shots into the ceiling, and the miners and prospectors gave him their attention.

"Archer can no longer continue," said the referee in his most powerful voice, "and so the winner of the first fall is the winner of the match. The new champion wrestler of the Yukon is Frank Kennedy. Gentlemen, pay your bets."

With that announcement, bedlam broke out. Frank hurried back to his corner, slipped between the ring ropes and hustled down to his room with the Butlers and law officers close behind. After toweling off, he changed into his clothes while the Butler boys divided up the spoils, chuckling the whole time. When Frank was dressed, Butler handed him a heavy pouch, containing a total of ten thousand dollars in paper money, both Canadian and American, and gold and silver coins. Gotch figured he had at least another five thousand coming to him in side bets, to be collected in the following days at the campsite. He and the Butler boys shook hands, and one of the law officers agreed to accompany him back to his shack, though Gotch wasn't sure that he liked the idea of a man he knew nothing about - except that he wore a badge of some kind - carrying a rifle and following him anywhere. Still, he decided to accept the escort and the group of men disappeared into the night, while the uproar in the theatre continued unabated.

Despite the adulation heaped upon him, the following days and weeks slipped away slowly for Frank, who began to grow more and more lonesome for Humboldt. He made a decision that he wold never leave Humboldt again for any length of time, no matter how tempting an offer he would receive. "Yep," he told a fellow miner-prospector one night, "I'm just an Iowa farmer at heart. This here Alaska's okay, and I'm sure there are plenty of other great spots in the world to live in, but Humboldt, Iowa, will always be my home." It was a promise he would never break.

Everyone wanted to share time with the new champion wrestler, and Frank gave up trying to work the streams and mines at all. He certainly didn't need the money, and was too tired from staying up all night recounting the big match. For the first time in his life, he began to drink too much. It seemed everyone in Dawson, men and women, wanted to have a beer with the new hero of the Yukon, and Frank couldn't find the will power to resist. It was a combination of homesickness and bravado which kept him going night after night, into the wee hours of the morning...and led to a painful setback that put everything back in perspective for him.

Two weeks after the Archer victory, Butler approached Frank with another idea for an immensely profitable venture. There was a boxer in town from Australia by the name of Frank Slavin, a real dandy with his fists in the style of former heavyweight boxing champion Gentleman Jim Corbett, who had taken the title from the legendary John L. Sullivan. Butler said the town was just itching to see the two get in a ring and mix it up, and that betting was already running high even though the two hadn't even met, let alone agreed to fight.

Frank was reluctant to box, having done very little of it since the days of his schoolyard matches, and Slavin flat out wouldn't wrestle. Finally, Butler convinced Frank he could win any style of contest; but it proved to be a disastrous mistake for the young Iowan, and a severe lesson in humility. Before a large crowd, Slavin boxed him bloody, feinting Frank out of position then peppering his face with stiff jabs, and wracking his body with mean hooks. Frank pursued the faster man doggedly, grunting as the mitted fists slammed into his ribs and face. Finally, in the fifth round, frustrated and exasperated beyond measure, Frank resorted to his own style of fighting. He forced Slavin into the ropes, wrapped him in a bear hug, then lifted and shoved him over the top rope and into the audience, where he lit on three miners, breaking a table and two chairs. Though nearly unconscious, Slavin struggled back to the ring apron and slipped between the ropes into the ring, where Frank stood glaring at him from two swollen eyes. The referee stepped between the two battered warriors and raised Slavin's hand, giving him the bout on a foul.

"I learnt a good lesson," Frank told a glum Butler in the dressing room, an ice pack on the right side of his face, trying to suppress the swelling. "I'll fight anyone in a mixed match, where anything goes - but I'll never wear padded gloves again." It was a promise made in good faith, but time would erase some of the bitter memories and Frank would eventually forget his vow.

Several more wrestling matches followed with easy wins for Frank, including a win over Colonel John McLaughlin, a legendary collar-and-elbow style wrestler from faraway Vermont. McLaughlin was a small man, but was regarded as the king of wrestling on the Eastern seaboard. Frank simply overpowered him, using a hooking wrist lock Burns had taught him. It soon became apparent that his reputation would preclude any other bouts. No one dared to step into the wrestling arena with the seemingly unbeatable Kennedy, and he made plans to return to Iowa.

He booked passage on a vessel named the Skagway, and was set to board late one evening when the Butlers caught up to him. They were determined to celebrate with him one last time.

"We owe you too much to let you slip away without a big farewell," shouted Dick Butler as he and his brothers led Gotch to the grandest saloon in town. They celebrated so long and hard that the Skagway sailed without Frank. He was angry at missing the boat - until word came back ten hours later that it had sank in the Yukon River, and all aboard had drowned.

"I guess we're even now," Frank said solemnly to the Butlers as he prepared to board the next ship, six days later. "I made a few dollars for you boys, but you saved my life by causing me to miss the Skagway."

When he boarded the vessel which would take him from the shores of the Yukon, Frank had over thirty thousand dollars with him. But as much money as he carried, it was only a tiny fraction of satisfaction compared to the feeling which was swelling up inside of him. He was committed now, he knew, to one goal: he wanted to be the heavyweight wrestling champion of not just the Yukon or Iowa, but the entire world.

CHAPTER 4

Times were always difficult in the Gotch household, but the past few months had been even worse than usual. It had been a bad season for crops and Frederick's lame arm and leg were acting up more than ever; to the point, in fact, where he was nearly incapacitated. And money was a continuing problem. The Gotches owned three hundred acres - or, rather had purchased three hundred acres some time ago and were still making payments on it - and there was the prospect of foreclosure looming its ugly head constantly. Finances were so bad that at times the family went from week to week with absolutely no money in the home at all.

As if that weren't enough, Amelia couldn't shake the empty feeling she was experiencing day after day, and which was growing steadily worse. When her youngest son, Frank, had come home from his encounter with Farmer Burns in Fort Dodge wanting to be a wrestler, she felt sure her life had reached the lowest point possible. She had argued and fought against the prospect of his becoming a professional wrestler with all the strength her body could summon, but when he announced he was journeying to Alaska for one year to wrestle she had nearly collapsed with despair.

He had written three times while in Alaska, and she had been delighted beyond measure when she received the last letter, stating he would be returning home soon. He had written nothing about his wrestling, and she supposed the trip had been a failure in all respects, and he would now forsake wrestling and take up the respectable - if not always profitable - profession of farming. Heaven knew Frederick could use every bit of help on the farm, even though Frank's older brothers were working from sunup to sunset, as well as farming their own eighty-acre plots.

Frank had written that he had booked passage on the Skagway, a vessel which would bring him all the way from Dawson to Seattle, Washington. He would take the train to Fort Dodge then, and travel the rest of the way by horse and buggy. She had been elated, only to be crushed by the news that the Skagway had sunk in the Yukon River just one hundred miles out of Dawson. She and the other members of the family had feared the worst at first, but then received information that Frank had actually missed the ship at the last moment, being detained by friends. Thirty-six passengers drowned in the icy waters, but Frank lost only his trunk of clothes.

The Gotch house was dark when Frank walked up the lane, the light of the moon his only guide. He had debated whether to stay overnight in Fort Dodge, but he had decided to push on for home. He had missed the farm and the simple, four-room house perched on a gentle hill six miles south of Humboldt. Though Iowa farmland was acknowledged to be the most fertile in the world, the particular section owned by his family was hilly and rough to plow.

Approaching the farm on the road from Humboldt, he had recalled the years of backbreaking work he had put in on the land, and smiled, knowing it was the backbone of his wrestling success. It was the strength developed here on this farm that had held him in such good stead when he stepped on the mat to face other hardy men in the truest test of one's manhood that he knew of. He had missed the farm almost as much as his family, and he knew Humboldt would always be his home, no matter what direction success may lead him in.

The steps creaked under his weight, and he stopped on the porch to glance inside, through a window. There was a small oil lamp burning in the far corner of the kitchen, which meant someone should still be awake, for his mother would never allow a lamp to burn throughout the night for fear of fire. Frank turned his eyes on the interior of the house, noticing the familiar sights, but saw no one. He figured it to be nearly midnight. He hadn't been able to rent a horse and buggy in Humboldt, and had run into no one he knew from whom he could ask a ride, so he had walked the six miles, carrying his large bag of valuables with him. Now, even his strong and youthful body was tired, and he sat down heavily on the front porch. He wanted to see his family, but he didn't want to wake anyone; sleep was too precious during the fall season, when farm life revolved around early risings and the hard, exhausting toll of harvest. He laid his head down on his bag, soft with the clothes it contained, and stretched his nearly six-foot frame out on the wood floor. Clasping his hands on his chest, he took one deep sigh, and fell fast asleep.

He couldn't believe he hadn't heard the rooster crowing, a "song" which had awakened him faithfully for many years. But he hadn't. The first sound he was aware of was that of his mother opening the screen door to the porch. He opened his eyes and stared up, while Amelia just stood in the doorway, mouth agape, staring down at her son.

"Hi, ma," he said tiredly, a smile breaking onto his lips. "I'm home."

Amelia was a strong woman, reared in hard times and living in hard times. But she wasn't without emotion, and she gasped, hands flying to her face, and then broke out crying. Frank leaped from the porch floor and reached out for her, enfolding the small, sturdy body in his powerful arms. She buried her head in his chest and sobbed, while he held her tight.

"Hey, everything's okay," he said. "There's no reason to cry...."

The door opened again, and Frank looked up to catch site of Frederick William, his oldest brother, who grinned sheepishly and reached for Frank's hand. Frank stood holding Amelia, shaking his brother's hand, and in moments he was surrounded by his family - two sisters and three brothers. Only his pa was missing.

After much hugging, Frank held his mother at arm's length and looked at her: she wore her usual black dress, which dropped all the way to the floor, and her hair, grayer than Frank had remembered it being just a year earlier, was tied in a neat bun at the back. Her face was lean and hard, and there were more lines marking it than a year ago. She looked troubled.

"Where's pa?" asked Frank, looking first at his ma, then the others.

"He didn't come home last night," said Amelia, her voice trembling a bit. "That's why I left the lamp burning....waiting for him to come home. Then, this morning, when I opened the door and saw a body lying here....well, at first I thought it might be your father. It scared me a little, and then when I saw it was you, well, that gave me a start, too. You've been gone so long."

Everyone laughed nervously, including Frank.

"Aw, I haven't been gone all that long, ma," he said. "I thought I'd be away for a whole year when I left, but it's only been about nine months, or so."

"Well, we was shook up a plenty, Frank. When we heard about the Skagway going down, and all them people drowning up there," said Charlie, his second oldest brother, and the strongest member of the family, after Frank. He was a big man, even bigger than Frank. He could have been a fine wrestler, Frank felt, according to his physical talents. But wrestling took something that Charlie never had, a certain mean streak from time to time, Frank reasoned. And Charlie was just a big, good old boy. He never liked to pit his skills and strength against another man. "No need for, it," Charlie had said once, the only time the two brothers had ever discussed Frank's career as a professional wrestler. "I just work my farm, don't bother nobody, and don't expect nobody to bother me."

"It gave us a horrible fright, Frankie," said his sister Millie Mabel; Amelia nodded her head in agreement.

"Well, I must admit I've thought a lot about it, and decided the good Lord must be watching out for me....and have something special for me to do with my life, by keeping me off that ship," said Frank. He looked quickly at his ma to see if she would suspect something by adding the last phrase, but she had a far-away look in her eyes, as though she was not really listening to the conversation at all.

"But, where's pa?" Frank asked again.

"He went to town yesterday to see about getting a loan to keep us going," said Amelia, looking down the lane. "I can't figure out what's keeping him, unless he had some ill luck...." Her voice trailed away.

"We've sure had our share of that lately," said Millie Mabel, a note of despair in her voice.

"Have you eaten yet, Frankie?" asked Amelia, referring again to his boyhood name. Frank winced; he had never liked the name and felt it was a concession to his manhood when his mother stopped calling him Frankie in favor of Frank about four years ago. But now, for some inexplicable reason, she was calling him Frankie again. He guessed it was because she was under such mental and emotional strain lately, and he shook his head.

"Haven't actually eaten for almost twenty-four hours," he said.

"That's some sort of record for him, isn't it?" said Mary Fredericka.

Frank and the women moved inside while the men looked to their chores. Frank wanted to tell Frederick, Charles and George that he would sit with them later and describe his adventures up north, but watching them trudge across the farmyard toward the barns, he realized it probably didn't matter. They were blood kin, as close as could be in that respect, but they were worlds apart in their hopes, desires and interests. Frank loved the farm as much as they, but in a different way. He wanted to be around it always, but could never, he knew now, earn his living on it.

His mother toiled at the big, iron stove, preparing his favorite meal of flapjacks and sausage. Times may be hard on a farm money-wise, but there was always plenty to eat. After breaking his fast, he waited for his sisters to leave before initiating a conversation with Amelia.

"Ma, how bad has it been?" he asked. He waited patiently while she finished cleaning up the stove, took off her long, red apron, and settled at the table with him.

"We're down to the last nickel, Frankie," she said, "and payments due in three days. We could lose the whole farm, I suspect. And I don't know what we'd do, I just don't know." She looked down at her hands, folded together on the white tablecloth, and began wringing them. Frank felt the despair swelling up in him, like a hard punch to his stomach. Then, his mind snapped back to the heavy bag outside. He leaped to his feet so quickly that his mother looked up with a start.

"Land sakes, Frankie!" she said, clasping a hand to her breast.

He was gone but a second and flew through the door on his way in from the porch. He swung the big bag around twice and slammed it hard on the table in front of his mother, giving her another start. She slid back from the table and stared up at her son as though he had suddenly gone mad. She'd heard how gold fever can strike a man, robbing him of his senses, and she was afraid some such terrible calamity had befallen her youngest son up in that great frozen wasteland. It was just about the last straw for her, and she was on the verge of collapse.

"Look, ma," he said, grabbing the bag and holding it upside down so that the contents spilled out on the table.

Dirty clothes, sweat shorts of heavy cotton, socks, wrestling shoes and a pair of black wrestling tights spilled out first. But on top of them tumbled several heavy bags that made a heavy jingling sound, and several more bags that landed with a thud. His fingers worked nimbly as he pulled the strings loose and turned the bag upside down. Dozens of gold and silver coins fell out onto the table, many rolling across it and falling to the floor. But before they had settled, he was untying a second and a third bag, with the same results. Then, with his mother sitting wide-eyed and disbelieving, he untied still another bag and pulled out a thick wad of bills - Canadian and American green-backs - and flipped them on the table. And still he wasn't done. He grabbed another bag, and winked at Amelia.

"Gotta be more careful with this stuff here, ma," he said. He worked silently, then very lightly laid the bag down, its open end toward Amelia. He nodded at her, then motioned for her to investigate its contents, but she sat rigidly, as if tied to the chair.

"Go ahead, ma," he said. "Look inside."

Slowly, she reached out a weathered hand and touched the bag. Her fingers probed inside, then withdrew. They were covered with a light, yellow dust and she was about to blow it from her hand when Frank grabbed her hand and held it tightly.

"Ma," he said affectionately, looking down at her, "be careful what you blow away! That's pure gold dust."

Amelia Gotch was at a loss for words. Her first thought was that her son had joined up with the remnants of that infamous gang of a few years back, but then she remembered the James boys were mostly in prison, or dead. But there was still that Wild Bunch out in Wyoming some where. Dark thoughts flooded her mind, and she grabbed at her head with the pain of it all, the gold dust settling into her graying, dark hair.

"What's wrong, ma?" Frank asked, puzzled by her reaction. He thought she would be beyond words with joy, perhaps, but he wasn't at all prepared for the expression she turned toward him now.

"You've stolen," she whispered, in a voice he had never heard before from this woman who had reared him. It was as though they were to be her very last words, so deep was her shame and humiliation.

Frank stood for a moment, searching for a comeback, and then he burst out laughing. He rolled his head back on his massive neck, and laughed and laughed, slapping his thick hands on his thighs. He gained control of himself, and moved to where his mother sat, now staring at him with a blank expression, lost in the happenings of the past minutes. Frank kneeled by her side, his eyes looking into hers straight on.

"No, ma," he said, suddenly grown very solemn. "Ma, it's nearly thirty thousand dollars here, and it's money I earned in Alaska. By wrestling, ma. That's how I got it. Honestly. Fairly. Struggling with other men, often bigger and older and heavier. Men who wanted to whip me, ma, but men who I whipped instead. Most of it's from side bets, but a lot if it is from the gate receipts themselves.

"But it's money I earned, and money that come to us because of the long hours of hard work I put in on this farm, work that made me strong enough to be a professional wrestler, ma. And because I got it through my work here with you and pa, I'm giving it to you, because you deserve it. You can tell pa when he comes home that he doesn't have to worry about a monthly bill; he can just pay off the whole darned farm now, if'n he wants to, ma."

The two - woman and son - continued to stare into one another's eyes. Amelia couldn't repress the tears that came to hers, and Frank had to blink hard several times to stop his own tears from flowing. Amelia stood and walked away from her son, staring out the door at the farmyard, and beyond; Frank stayed at the table, kneeling, but watching his ma.

When she turned to him, her tears were gone.

"I thought you'd given up on this wrestling, but I can see that you haven't," she said somewhat sternly, and Frank felt a keen stab of disappointment in his stomach. "But what you've done for your family, Frank, is a wonderful, kindly thing. I don't know how your pa will feel about all this, but let's wait for him to come home. Then, we can have a good, old fashioned family powwow."

Frank rose and nodded. He knew he had won.

With his father's arrival late that afternoon, Frank's homecoming was complete. He had heard the horse and buggy approach, and watched from the window as his father hitched up the horse, using just his good hand and arm, and watered him. Frank walked to the door and met his pa, who stopped cold in his tracks when confronted by his son's huge frame in the doorway, and then limped forward with arms outstretched.

It was a joyous family dinner, with Mary's fiancé, a young local farmer, showing up, as well. Frank entertained well into the night with his tales of Alaska, and even Frederick, Jr., and Charles seemed interested beyond Frank's expectations. The family roared when Frank told of his battles with Billy Murdock and Silas Archer, but Amelia sat in her rocker by the fireplace, rocking gently and showing no expression whatsoever. They asked questions about the territory, the mountains and the weather. George was most interested in the bear and elk Frank saw, while Millie Mabel questioned him about the wild camp women she had heard stories about, drawing a gentle rebuke from Amelia and a confession from Frank that he had been far too busy to pay attention to women of any sort.

Not a word was spoken about the fortune Frank had returned with, though he mentioned he had picked up "a few greenbacks" through his wrestling. He noticed that Amelia stopped rocking and glanced at her husband at the mention of the money, but Frank continued on with his stories until all save his folks said their goodnights and slipped away to their beds.

Then Frank and his ma and pa gathered around the small kitchen table and discussed the bags of money and gold dust. At first, Amelia and Frederick were adamant in their refusal to accept any money - Frank couldn't tell if it was because it was earned by wrestling, or if they were just too proud - but by the time they were ready to turn in, Frank had gained his way. Some of the money would go to pay off their farm, to buy eighty acres of prime Iowa farmland for Frank, and the remainder would go into the Humboldt bank for security against hard times in the future. Reluctantly, Amelia and Frederick agreed to his proposal. Then, Frank turned to the subject of his career.

"Ma, I just have to wrestle," he said, holding her bony hands in his thick, muscular, fingers. His dark hair, parted down the middle, and his heavy, dark brow framed his face, which she noticed with pride was very handsome. His gray eyes probed her face, searching for a sign of understanding and compassion for his position. He hated to dictate to his ma, but he had no choice. He knew he could never be happy without trying his luck at professional wrestling.

"The Farmer says I can be the best, ma....the best in the whole country and maybe some day in the whole world. I want to do it, ma, and not just for money or for me. I want to do it for you and pa, for the Gotch name, for Humboldt, and for Iowa. I want people to know who we are, and what we are....good, hard-working, God-fearing people who know what it means to struggle and overcome and still reach for something. Can you understand that, ma?"

She tried to understand, as best she could. She loved her children, all of them, and perhaps this one more than the rest, though she refused to entertain that thought for more than a second, chasing it from her mind. Still, she despised the idea of her son wrestling for a living, despite the good fortune which had accompanied his wrestling in Alaska. She tried to give him the support he pleaded for, but she failed.

"No, Frank, I can't understand it," she said gently, and his head dropped. "But I won't stand in your way," she added quickly. "Don't ask me to condone it or to flaunt it, or to talk about it, but I will accept it."

Frank looked up again, then glanced at his pa, who was smiling back at him. Frederick Gotch said little these days, except with his eyes. And Frank knew that he saw more than approval there; he saw pride.

"I'll make you proud of both me and wrestling some day, ma," said Frank. "I promise that to you."

CHAPTER 5

Frank Gotch sat at the window of the hotel and looked out into the street below him, where a large crowd was gathering. He ran a hand through his thick, black hair, and shook his head, a smile growing on his face. He continued to gaze out the window, even after the knock on the outer door and the conversation that cropped up in the other room. When the door to his room was knocked on, he rose to answer it.

"Frank, this here is Robert Sanders from the Bellingham newspaper," said Emil Klank when the door opened. "He's here to interview you, like you promised him."

Frank had caught the irritation in Emil's voice at the last statement. Klank had been his manager for nearly a year now, ever since Frank had defeated him in a match at Bellingham, Washington, in 1903. He had worked Klank over desperately in that bout, hurting his right arm to the extent that it had never really been the same. Frank felt bad about the injury and liked Klank well enough that the two became partners, with Frank doing the wrestling, Burns supervising the training, and Emil the managing. It had worked out well for the most part, and Gotch and Klank had almost always seen eye to eye. Except on certain occasions like today. Here it was just five hours before the most important wrestling match of Gotch's career - maybe the most important wrestling match ever to take place in America, for that matter - and Frank was granting an interview.

Klank had tried to talk his charge out of it, but Frank was unbowed. He had given his word, he reminded Klank, and that was that. Besides, Frank knew and recognized the value of the news media in creating interest in his career and in wrestling in general, and he felt obliged to spend some time with this fellow.

Sanders was a short, rather distinguished looking man who sported a short mustache and chewed on a big cigar. He wore a derby hat, and a dark gray suit. His hands, with short, thick fingers, clutched a pad of writing paper and several pencils. He shifted the pencils into the left hand with his paper pad, and he stuck out his right hand to Gotch.

"Glad to meet you, champ," he said in a high-pitched voice that surprised Frank. Gotch smiled quickly and extended his own right hand, which engulfed Sander's. The writer had a strong handshake, which impressed Gotch somewhat, and he felt a bit more at ease, supposing that Sanders was perhaps a writer who was strong and hardy himself, and who would understand more of what wrestling was about than most writers.

"I'm not the champ yet," said Frank, still grinning slightly. "That title still is held by Tom Jenkins. But, I hope to do something about that later today."

"Well," said Sanders, "you are the champion of Iowa, are you not? And any man who has beaten Farmer Burns certainly deserves to be called a champion of some kind."

"Yes, that's certainly true," said Gotch. "Beating the Farmer is no easy task, that's for sure. He's the toughest man I've ever wrestled....sorry about that, Emil," he said, winking at Sanders, who turned to Klank, standing in the doorway.

"Oh, yes, you've also wrestled Mr. Klank several times, I recall," Sanders began making notes in his pad.

"Just once is all," said Emil, dourly.

"Yes, just once," said Frank, still smiling. He knew the memory of that battle was painful to Emil, who had always known he wasn't a world beater, but who had taken great pride in his ability to give any man a fair exchange. That had been the case, until he met Gotch.

Gotch and Sanders moved to the center of the room, and took chairs, while Klank hung around a table at the far end, looking out the window where Gotch had been moments before.

"That's some crowd out there," Klank murmured.

"Yes, they're real sportin' fans in this part of the country," said Sanders. "There's not much out here in Washington that can attract the fancy of the sporting crowd, but they do love their wrestling matches. And you in particular, it seems, Mr. Gotch. They are quite impressed with your style of wrestling. That's why my editor has dispatched me here to talk with you. Our readers want to know more about you."

Gotch squirmed a bit in his chair. This was the part of wrestling - the public life - that he had been unprepared for when he first hooked up with the Farmer after returning from Alaska two years earlier. After his short visit to Humboldt, he had set out for Burns' home in Big Rock, about a hundred fifty miles east of Des Moines, and spent several months on the Farmer's farm, working hard on the techniques of wrestling - and hooking - that he would have to learn to be a success. Then, the two had spent nearly one full year touring the state of Iowa, and venturing into some nearby states for a few quick matches. He won the Iowa state title from Orem Wassem in Burlington in March of 1901, and won a major match against a two hundred and eighty pound matman who called himself the champion of Rumania. That bout had been held in Davenport, and convinced Burns it was due time to head out West. He defeated the French star Carl Pons on January 10, 1903, in Seattle, becoming an immediate hit with the fans of the great northwest. Pons, much taller and heavier than Gotch, had been on a rampage through the area until Gotch put the clamps on him.

Gotch won six more straight matches in Bellingham, Washington, including two classic bouts against Burns.

The first came October 5, and ended with Gotch taking the first fall, Burns the second and Gotch the third and final fall with a half nelson and crotch pin. The three falls had taken nearly one hour, and Gotch's youth had been the deciding factor. Burns' vast experience balanced out the fact that Gotch outweighed him by nearly thirty pounds, and they were even in quickness. There had been some rumbling in the crowd that Burns might have let Gotch win, since they were known to be training together and that Burns had a strong interest in the budding career of Gotch. Frank had been irritated when word of a possible fix had reached him and he was eager to talk to the Farmer to discuss what they should do to counter such talk.

"There's nothing we can do," said Burns. "Folks are gonna believe what they want to believe, no matter what the truth is, or what we say. Let them talk. You and I will just wrestle."

They wrestled again just a month later, with the same results. After the match, Burns stood tall and addressed the audience, stating Gotch was now the finest wrestler in America and ready to take Jenkins' title from him. And his victory over the giant Indian, Chief Two Feathers, was still the talk in every tavern and barbershop in the Seattle area. But in between all the successes had been a disturbing loss to Tom Jenkins, the American champion from Cleveland. And Gotch knew that match was really what Sanders had come to talk about.

Still, the newsman wasn't about to leap into the subject of Jenkins without warming his subject up to it. He asked questions about Gotch's background and life on the farm in Iowa, raising his eyebrows occasionally at Frank's comments, and nodding encouragement from time to time, as well as grinning at the little asides that Frank injected. Sanders found himself warming to the hulk of a man who sat before him, nattily attired in a three-piece suit and speaking, for the most part, with the clarity of a schoolteacher. Sanders found Gotch to be a handsome man, and one who was very considerate of others, constantly asking if he was talking too fast for Sanders to keep pace with his pencil.

"Wrestling those matches with the Farmer was both good and bad, fortunate and unfortunate," said Gotch. "Defeating him meant that I was learning my profession and learning it well, but yet it caused me a certain degree of mental anguish. We had become friends, of course, through our training. Yet, we always knew that some day we could wind up on the mats facing one another, as that's the nature of our sport. You know, he defeated me back in Fort Dodge, Iowa, four years ago, in just my second - or, I guess my third - professional match. I was keenly disappointed that night, but I made up my mind then and there that I would defeat him some day.

"Well, we trained together for nearly two years and I've learned most of my wrestling from that man, so I'm greatly indebted to him. But, that doesn't hold me back when it's time to wrestle. You see, I learned a long time ago that you have to be two different people if you want to be a good wrestler. First, there is the out-of-the-ring person. I try to like everyone. But inside the ring - that's totally different. I have learned through experience to never hold back once I step into the ring. I'm all business then."

"I can vouch for the fact that Frank don't hold back none, ever," said Klank, rubbing his right elbow. "This old arm ain't ever been the same since he snapped a ligament in it with that darned bar lock he uses."

Sanders paid little attention to Klank's remark, but went right on.

"I've got some clippings from our paper about the Burns match, and the one with Two Feathers," said Sanders. He pulled two long pieces of paper from inside his vest, opened them carefully, and started to read:

"The Indian was an unknown quantity. As he stepped out of his gorgeous blanket, his great height and sparseness stood out in contrast with the powerful build of his white opponent. In less than a minute the Indian had the white man down on the mat and to the wonder of the spectators that long, lithe creature kept Frank Gotch under for a straight fifteen minutes, defending the most desperate efforts of Gotch to free himself. The friends of the local favorite were scared and did not hesitate to say so. Was the wonderful wrestler who had defeated the great Farmer Burns and between whom and the American championship only one man intervened, to go down to defeat before this Indian from a Montana reservation? It looked that."

Sanders laid the paper down beside him, and looked back up at Gotch, who had been listening with undivided attention. Gotch leaned back in his chair, and heaved a sigh of relief.

"Whew," he breathed again. "It sure sounds as if I was in serious trouble doesn't it?"

"Yeah. Well don't forget who won that match, and won it easily," interjected Klank, standing at full attention across the room and glaring at Sanders. He didn't like this writer, and he was taking no care to hide his feelings.

"I - and our readers - would be interested in knowing how it was that you were able to defeat this Indian, Frank, considering the rather slow start you got off to. Can you tell us?"

"You're darned right he can," said Klank, moving forward with one hand outstretched, pointing at the writer. "But why should he? He's got a pretty big match coming up here, and why should he give Jenkins any last-minute information?"

"Hold on, Emil, it's okay," said Frank reassuringly. "It doesn't matter what we say here now. The paper won't come out before the match, will it, Mr. Sanders?"

"No, Frank, it won't," said the writer. "This story will only be printed after the Jenkins about is over."

"Well, then, there's nothing to worry about, and here's your story, Mr. Sanders. Wrestling consists of strength, endurance, speed and skill. And a lot of brain work. Two Feathers was strong and fast, but he had very little skill or endurance. He took me down and held me for a spell, all right, but I could hear him breathing hard up there on top of me after a bit, and I knew that I could wear him out. When he got tired, he quit thinking even more, and it was easy for me to slip around him and take control. And that's just what I did, winning both falls."

"And don't forget what Two Feathers said afterwards," said

Klank. "He said Frank was the best he's ever seen, and far too good for him or anybody else."

"Apparently, Mr. Jenkins doesn't agree with that assessment, though," said Sanders. "He's the champion of America, and has already beaten you once. How will you, then, defeat him tonight?"

"Maybe he got the decision in Cleveland, but he didn't beat Frank," said Klank, obviously angry and threatening in mood. "He used the strangle hold, and everyone knows that's illegal. He strangled Frank."

Sanders had turned toward Klank with the latter's outburst and turned again toward Gotch, who was still sitting back in his chair, apparently at ease. He had been taking it all in with his usual quiet manner and he seemed deep in thought. Sanders felt a reluctance to interrupt this powerful man's thinking, but did nonetheless.

"Tell me, Frank, how that match went, if you would be so kind." He sat poised with pencil.

"It's like Emil said, he used a strangle hold. I've used 'em myself, but not since I really began wrestling for serious. I can remember beating the Chicken Picker - a man named Marshall Green from Humboldt - with one, but just because I didn't know any better."

"But Jenkins knows better," yelled Klank. "He's the American champion; he shouldn't have to resort to strangle holds."

There was a moment's silence. Sanders felt obliged to break it.

"According to my records, Jenkins won both falls, the first in one hour and fifty-five minutes, and the second in just twelve minutes. How do you explain the great disparity in times between falls?"

"I didn't recuperate after the first strangle hold," said Frank, rubbing his neck. "Actually, he was far more aggressive than I was the entire match. I wasn't ready for Tom Jenkins that night, but I sure will be today."

The memory of that first match with Jenkins was now coming on all too strong for Gotch. He had wrestled just 21 official matches - winning 19 - when he had met the feared American champion in his hometown of Cleveland, Ohio, on February 22, 1903. Jenkins had reigned as American champion for nearly six years at the time, and while Burns was the most respected matman in all America, the rough and ready Jenkins was the most feared. A former ironworker, he was incredibly strong, and thought nothing of mixing it up in the roughest fashion possible. His style was wide open at all times, with plenty of elbow shots to the face and body mixed in with his wrestling. He was cagey, a veteran of hundreds of matches. It was Jenkins who had taken the American title away from Dan McLeod, who had defeated the young Gotch four years earlier in the gravel in Iowa.

Jenkins had been the aggressor from the outset of their first match. Gotch had taken the bout merely to see how he could stack up against a matman of Jenkins' caliber. In truth, he had never expected to win. And he had taken a fearful pummeling for nearly two and one half-hours. When he returned home to Humboldt for a short break between matches, his face had been so badly swollen and bruised from Jenkins smashing an arm across it that his family hardly recognized him. Once again, his mother had sent up a plea that he discontinue in the barbaric sport, but he had, as always, resisted. He spent hours each morning running through the Iowa countryside and many more hours with Burns, Klank and other sparring partners in endless rounds of wrestling. He had wrestled once in Des Moines before returning to Washington, where he had rattled off eight straight victories, including those over Burns and Chief Two Feathers. He knew he was now ready for Jenkins.

"Are you, in any way, afraid of Jenkins after the mauling you took in your first match?" asked Sanders, fidgeting in his chair as though he expected the worst from such a question.

"Hey, what kind of question is that, for crying out loud?" yelled Klank. "Of course, he ain't afraid. Didn't you hear what Farmer Burns said after Frank whipped him up here a couple of months ago? He said Frank ain't afraid of no man, of any nationality, and that's the truth. Wait til you see what Frank does to Tom Jenkins tonight."

Gotch rose from his chair and stared out the window again. After a moment, he nodded down toward the street.

"That's why I won't lose tonight, Mr. Sanders," he said quietly. "Those fans down there have come out to see me, and to wish me luck. I won't let them down today. Or my friends, either."

Klank paced nervously in the dressing room, while Joe Carroll and Duncan McMillan, two of Gotch's wrestling partners, and Farmer Burns milled around, trying to look busy. Frank had been in his black wrestling tights for nearly thirty minutes, and had finished his limbering up exercises over fifteen minutes ago. The arrangement was that they would be told to enter the ring at three p.m., but it was already twenty after three and they had received no word. The delay was working on everyone's nerves, except for the Farmer, who sat contentedly in a corner munching on an apple.

The door banged open and George Kennedy came hustling through, causing everyone to stop what they were doing and look up.

"What the hell's going on out there, George?" demanded Klank, the irritation ringing in his voice.

"Jenkins wants more money, seeing the size of the crowd," said Kennedy, a big, blond man who wrestled with Gotch when the latter needed to work against size and strength. "People is everywhere out there," continued Kennedy, gestulating backwards. "There must be two thousand of 'em, and they're getting up to twenty-five bucks for some seats."

"He's got a guarantee of five thousand, twice as much as us," said Klank. "What's the man want, anyway?"

"Seems he wants another two thousand on guarantee," said Kennedy.

Klank muttered a blast of obscenities, though he was not a man given to swearing, causing the Farmer to glance up sharply with a look of disapproval. Burns didn't swear, drink, smoke - or think much of those who did. It was, he said, a sign of weakness when a man couldn't exercise control over his habits, and his mouth.

Klank barged through the door, slamming it behind him, and returned fifteen minutes later, as angry as when he left.

"Okay, Frank, let's go," he said as he entered, his face flushed with anger. "He got his money, damn it, now let's give him the beating of his life."

Gotch slipped on his long green robe and the entourage moved out of the small dressing room into the main lobby of the Bellingham pavilion, the largest such structure on the entire Pacific coast. The crowd was spilling out into the lobby and many were still at the gates trying to get inside. When Gotch was sighted, a huge roar went up for the man who had become the town's favorite. Bellingham fans admired the calm restraint and the quick smile Gotch always showed, while Jenkins had remained aloof and surly since his arrival two weeks earlier.

Klank led the way, with Kennedy right behind, parting the crowd and shoving their way to the main entrance. They took a left turn, and headed straight toward the ring, a mat sitting on a five-foot platform and encircled by red ropes, some hundred feet ahead. The thousands of fans who were already seated came to their feet as the Gotch party approached, and shouted their encouragement. Men reached out to touch him and to pound him on the back, while Carroll and McMillan tried to protect him as best they could. Gotch showed no emotion as they worked their way to the ring, climbed the four steps up to the apron, and moved between the heavy ropes into the ring itself. A referee, dressed in all white, came forward and talked to Klank, then came over to shake Gotch's hand.

"I'm Tom Davis," he said in a deep, rough voice. "I'll be your official today, Mr. Gotch. Best of luck to you. And remember, no strangle holds today."

"Tell that to Jenkins, will you," said Frank, with a quick half smile. Davis nodded, and walked to a far corner, where he spread his arms out on the ropes and waited.

"Where's that damn Jenkins?" asked Klank, searching across the arena in the opposite direction they had just come from. "He's going to keep us waiting, you can bet on that."

Burns slipped behind Gotch and began massaging his shoulders, starting softly and quickly increasing the pressure on the Humboldt farmer's thick trapezius area. The Farmer kept up a steady, but low toned, stream of words, offering encouragement and reminding Gotch of their training strategy.

"Remember, stay away from him early; he's too strong to go right at. You gotta wear him down, Frank. That's why we ran those ten miles a day back in Iowa....we want to tire him out, then do our stuff, right?" Frank nodded silently, and continued to stare across the arena, where he knew Jenkins would first appear.

Within three minutes of the Gotch arrival, the crowd began to whoop and holler again, signaling Jenkins' entry. At first, Klank could see nothing other than a movement in the surging crowd, but soon he could make out the features of several of Jenkins trainers, and then the Cleveland millwright himself. They came quickly down the aisle as the crowd gave forth with a mixture of cheers and jeers. Though Jenkins wasn't as popular a man as Gotch, he was still the American champion and the most feared wrestler of the past decade.

The party clamored up the steps and two men held the ropes open for Jenkins, who slipped gracefully between them and bounced into the ring, his long, red woolen robe jiggling with the movements. It was held in place by a thick and luxurious leather belt, with a huge buckle in the middle. It had a figure of two wrestlers and the words "American Heavyweight Wrestling Champion" on it. The belt had been fashioned for Jenkins six years ago in Cleveland, and was officially recognized as the championship belt. It was to be worn into the ring by the champion, and Jenkins had agreed to surrender it should he ever lose. Slowly, with loving care, he unbuckled the belt, removed it from his waist, and handed it to one of his assistants.

Satisfied that the match was going to be held - he had some doubts after the long delay - Gotch turned to his corner. The feeling which was becoming normal now each time he wrestled was overtaking him. He could remember the first time it took hold of him, and how it had shaken him deep down inside. He was by nature a friendly, compassionate man.... but ever since his first bout with Jenkins, he now experienced a transformation when he was about to wrestle.

He felt the frenzy welling up inside of him, and he allowed it to run its full course. He was learning to use the anger and anticipation as a weapon, but he knew he had to control the emotion rather than let the emotion control him. He wanted to dispense with any formalities and all introductions and tear into Jenkins. Instead, he held his urge in check, and glared down at the ring floor, grabbing hold of the top rope and shuffling his black shoes back and forth on the hard canvas that covered the sawdust mat.

The ring announcer was asking the crowd for quiet, and it responded with a great hoot, and then held its collective voice.

"Ladies and gentlemen," he began, in a loud baritone, almost as if singing, "this is the long awaited match for the American heavyweight wrestling championship."

The voice droned on, issuing several proclamations, but Gotch heard nothing until the sound of his own name. He turned and held up a hand to acknowledge the cheering of the crowd, and then turned quickly and discarded his robe, leaving it with Klank, who was screaming instructions into his ear from close range.

Gotch stared across at Jenkins, who had stripped to the waist and was standing in the middle of the ring. He raised both hands straight above his head, clenching his fists, as he was introduced as the heavyweight wrestling champion of America. He cut an imposing figure, Gotch admitted - with his black, handlebar mustache and heavily muscled torso. He was built like a hero of ancient Greece, with thick muscles rippling beneath the thin skin. He was a handsome man, but his mouth was always turned down in a hostile smirk, and he gave the impression of a man about to explode in a blast of violence. He sneered at Gotch, and Frank smiled back; inside, Gotch was seething, burning for action.

The referee called them together for a few words, mentioning again that the strangle hold was illegal. Neither man showed any expression. They shook hands, and the bout was on.

Two hours later, Klank sat in the dressing room, his body dripping perspiration, as though he, himself, had been a contestant.

"This match wasn't a scientific grappling match," he muttered half aloud, as reporters hastily scribbled notes. "It was the fiercest battle in wrestling history. If I live to be a hundred years old, I never expect to see a mat struggle the likes of this one."

Gotch and Jenkins moved around the squared area under the bright lights, feinting one move after another. Several times they embraced in the tried-and-true style of the catch-as-catch-can wrestler, called elbow and collar, with one man grasping the other behind his neck and at the elbow of his extended arm, and the other doing likewise. From this position, they attempted to pull or shove one another off balance, permitting the other to make a move that would result in an advantage. The object was clear to each man, and to the audience, adept at watching such contests: the purpose was to throw the foe to the mat in such a position as to gain a submission hold, or to pin the other man's shoulders securely to the mat, thereby gaining a fall. The bout would be contested until one man could gain two falls, with no time limit under enforcement save the midnight curfew, some eight hours hence.

For nearly fifteen minutes the two men circled, tied up, shoved and heaved, with neither gaining any sort of an advantage. Gotch was reminded of the fearsome strength of this mighty man from Cleveland, while Jenkins found himself once again considering the amazing speed with which Gotch moved. Though they were nearly equal in strength, the edge was to Jenkins. In speed, the clear-cut decision was in Gotch's favor. Endurance and conditioning would probably be the telling point, considering their knowledge of the game was similar, though Jenkins had nearly a decade's more experience than Gotch, who was a quick thinker and a rapid learner, studying under the best teacher of all in Farmer Burns.

Suddenly, the pace began to quicken, with Jenkins showing less caution and resorting to his roughhouse tactics. He jammed an elbow into Gotch's face, shoving him into the ropes; Frank attempted to maneuver away, but Jenkins caught him on his hip, with one arm under Gotch's left arm, and threw the Humboldt farmer heavily to the mat, leaping for him. But Gotch rolled away and sprang to his feet in an instant, and shot back at Jenkins, grabbing his right leg in his vice-like grip and standing erect with Jenkins' feet completely off the mat. Gotch deposited him roughly on the mat and moved behind him, controlling his arms and keeping the Cleveland millwright spread out on the mat, his face burrowed deep in the thick folds. Frank dug his chin into the broad muscles on Jenkins' back, and Jenkins grunted in pain. The crowd roared its delight and Klank nearly climbed into the ring, screaming instructions at Gotch.

"Break his damn arm off," shouted Klank, eyes wide.

The two men struggled, one attempting to escape and the other fighting to retain his position of control. Finally, agonizingly, Jenkins pushed himself to his hands and knees, straining with every ounce of muscle in him. His arms bulged, the thick veins popping up and standing out rigidly along his biceps and forearms, Gotch clinging to his backside. Jenkins struggled to his feet; but as he did so, Gotch shifted with lightning speed, inserting a half nelson with his right arm and ramming his left arm between Jenkins' legs. Straining, he lifted Jenkins clean off the floor, then cranked down hard with his right hand, turning Jenkins upside down.

With a ferocious grunt, Gotch slammed the heavier man to the canvas with every bit of strength he could command. Jenkins groaned heavily as he smashed into the canvas; dazed, he made an attempt to gain his feet again, not realizing he was playing into Gotch's game plan. Gotch resumed his hold and let Jenkins reach his feet, then continued to lift the champion, and repeated the slam again....and again....and for a fourth time. The last time, Jenkins let out an agonizing scream, as Gotch followed him to the canvas, dropping the full weight of his shoulder deep into Jenkins' midsection. Clamping down hard at the neck and pulling up a leg, Gotch pushed his chest into Jenkins'. He heard the heavy gasping, and the referee's pounding on the mat. He heard Davis' flat palm strike the mat hard, and then Davis patted Gotch on the shoulders, signifying the pin. The fall had taken twenty-three minutes.

Gotch rose from his battered foe and walked to his corner, where Klank and Burns were going slightly mad with the excitement of the moment. The crowd was on its feet to a man, cheering wildly. Gotch looked back over his shoulder and saw Jenkins' seconds lifting him from the mat and escorting him to his corner. He was gasping badly for his breath and clutching at his chest, as though nursing cracked ribs. His legs were unsteady beneath him, and he could not have made the short trip to his corner without the strength of his comrades.

"We've got the son of a bitch, we've got him!" Klank bellowed almost hysterically. "He can't continue, he can't go on...."

"No, you're wrong," said Burns quietly. "He'll continue....and he'll work for the strangle hold, Frank."

Gotch sat in his corner, facing Jenkins' corner, and nodded. He knew Jenkins would never quit, and that the loss of the first fall would merely make him more desperate, more dangerous. His conditioning was tremendous, Gotch knew, and so was his heart. He could not count on Jenkins quitting, nor did he want him to. What he wanted was a clear cut, decisive victory. Anything less would not satisfy the burning hunger within him, a hunger that ravaged him every time he took to the mat ever since the loss to Jenkins the year before.

The start of the second fall occurred in just ten minutes time from the conclusion of the first, and Jenkins held his body to one side as he advanced. Gotch saw pain and anger in his foe's face, but no sign of resignation, or acceptance of defeat. Jenkins drove at Gotch in a surprising show of force, and backed him into the ropes. He went for a headlock, and secured it, but Gotch powered out of it and tossed Jenkins from him, and advanced himself, causing the ex-millwright to back up for the first time all night.

Gotch smiled calmly: "Come on, Tom," he said in a low whisper. "The match is just now getting fun. Let's see what we're made of, you and me."

With a roar, Jenkins stormed after his challenger, and managed to wrap his powerful arms around Gotch's neck. He began squeezing with his huge arm cutting across Gotch's windpipe, but the referee was having none of the strangle hold, and pulled the two apart. They clashed, and once again Jenkins secured a strangle hold, with Davis separating them and issuing a warning.

"Once more, Jenkins, and I'll throw you outta here, whether you're the champ or not," Davis shouted.

Jenkins was gasping once again, evidence that he was in pain and running short of breath. Gotch was smiling, and in no discomfort. The long, torturous daily runs in the Humboldt hills had paid off handsomely. He began to pursue the rapidly tiring Jenkins, tossing him about the ring as though it was no effort at all. Finally, in total frustration, Jenkins aimed a blow at Gotch that would have knocked the big farmer flat had it landed, and Davis stopped the bout.

"You're all through, Tom," said Davis. Turning toward Gotch, he grasped his right arm and raised it high.

The pavilion, noisy all during the match, erupted. Policemen tried to keep the ring clear, but to no avail. Klank and Kennedy grabbed Frank and hoisted him to their shoulders, while Burns moved over to the Jenkins corner to seek the championship belt he had worn into the ring. But he failed to negotiate the small area between the corners, so heavy was the crowd, and he followed Gotch and Klank from the ring.

They battled their way to the dressing room, and it took nearly fifteen minutes, with every man, woman and child trying to shake the hand of the new American heavyweight wrestling champion. Gotch, in his usual good-natured manner, tried to shake each hand and respond to each offer of congratulations, but it was hopeless.

Reporters were waiting for Gotch at his dressing room and they squeezed into his tiny quarters with his entourage. Klank directed Kennedy and a policeman to guard the door and keep all others out, a nearly impossible task. Sweat ran freely down Gotch's body as he pulled the black wrestling top away and tossed it in a corner. He plopped down heavily in a chair. His big chest, covered with hair, also had specks of red on it, from a nosebleed. Other than that, he was unmarked.

"You're the champ, Frank, how does it feel?" asked one reporter, pushing close to hear the answer.

Frank smiled, and shrugged. "It's what I've dreamed of for over four years," he said, "but it doesn't feel as good as I had thought it might."

"That's cause you're disappointed that Jenkins couldn't give you a tougher match," said a voice from the back, and everyone laughed.

"No, Tom Jenkins is plenty tough, all of you know that - and me for sure," said Frank. "But his day is over, and mine is just beginning. I'm ready for anyone now."

"How about Hackenschmidt, the Russian Lion?" asked a man sitting in the front row.

Gotch turned a quick eye on him, then nodded. "Yeah, anyone," he said.

The referee, Davis, burst into the room, carrying the championship belt with him. He pushed through the throng and approached Gotch.

"This is yours, Frank, you sure earned it." He placed the thick belt, eight inches high at the front and studded with bright and glittering stones, with the huge buckle in front, into Gotch's hands.

"Tell us officially why you stopped the bout," said Sanders. "The readers will want to know your explanation."

"It's simple," said Davis. "Jenkins deliberately fouled Gotch three times with a strangle hold, which was barred by the articles governing the contest. I saw that he was all in and that he was trying to force me to call the match against him on a foul instead of taking his medicine and being thrown twice, so I refrained from calling the fouls, as I saw that Gotch was wrestling strong and easily breaking his holds.

"Seeing that I would not call his lesser fouls, Jenkins deliberately aimed a vicious swing at Gotch, which everybody could see, and seeing that there was no use in further prolonging a contest which was too one-sided to be otherwise than brutal, I gave my decision."

It was nearly dark outside by the time the Iowa contingent was ready to leave the arena. They walked down the dimly lit hallway and headed for the main exit, where a single doorman stood vigil, waiting for them. Stepping into the cool northwest air, they were greeted by a small crowd of faithful fans - perhaps one hundred - who let out a whoop when they saw Gotch. They encircled him, asking for autographs and offering their congratulations. Weary and anxious to begin the long trek back to Iowa, Frank stood his ground and smiled warmly at his fans.

"Thank you, thank you," he murmured time and again, signing blank pieces of paper and then ticket stubs extended toward him. Finally, the small group disbanded and Gotch and his group headed for the horse and buggies that were waiting to take them to the train station.

"You know, it's late, Frank," said Klank, somewhat weakly. The day's events had drained him as much as Frank. "Maybe we should just stay here a couple of days and head back then."

"No," said Frank firmly without breaking stride. "I want to get home. I feel the need to be back in Humboldt, Emil, to be with family and friends."

After stowing their trunks and belongings on back, they entered the three buggies waiting for them. Burns climbed in next to Frank, who was sunk back in his seat, and seemed, to the Farmer, suddenly much smaller in the dim light.

"You okay, Frank?" he asked. There was a note of concern in his voice. Even the Farmer, who had been through nearly four thousand matches - counting the various county fairs, and such - was to admit later he had seldom seen such a rough bout from start to finish. He knew the strain it could put on a man, both physically and emotionally.

"Sure, Farmer," he said quietly.

The driver offered his congratulations, and the horse pulled away into the night, leaving the darkened pavilion behind.

The next morning, they all sat at the dining table in the hotel. Klank held the Seattle Times paper in his hand.

"Listen to this, Frank," he said. He began to read: "There is a new star in the sporting world. His name is Frank A. Gotch, his home is Humboldt, Iowa, and if he so chooses he can register 'heavyweight champion catch-as-catch-can wrestler of the world' after his name.

"The right to do this he earned last night in one of the most terrific mat battles ever seen in America. It seems preposterous to the average man who has followed athletics to be told that there exists a man twenty pounds lighter than Tom Jenkins, for six years the undefeated world's champion, who can make him quit like a dog, but that is just what Frank Gotch made him do last night.

"So after one fall had been taken from Jenkins, which left him a hopelessly defeated man in the center of the mat, so dazed that he had to be lifted to his corner and restoratives applied, he deliberately fouled Gotch four times in the second in order to force the referee to give the decision against him on a foul."

Finally, Frank spoke.

"Champion of the world? Those are nice sounding words, for sure. But the reporter, in his excitement, is forgetting all about a fella named Hackenschmidt. Shoot, he's beaten Tom twice already. He's the world champion. Tom was just the American champion."

Frank paused before continuing.

"So, Farmer....am I ready for the Russian Lion?" he asked.

He was greeted by a long silence, but he didn't push. He knew the Farmer was thinking, weighing all factors carefully.

"Almost," came the response. "Almost."

It wasn't the answer he had wanted, but he knew it was a truthful response. He could always count on the Farmer for that. The Russian Lion would have to wait. But Frank Gotch would not be too patient in his quest.

CHAPTER 6

If the new American wrestling champion had expected Humboldt to change much, he was disappointed. It had taken him four days to arrive from Seattle by train, though they had stayed an extra day in Cheyenne, Wyoming. Cheyenne was a town that held special appeal to Gotch, as it smacked of the wild and wooly frontier. Walking the streets and watching the cowboys, he felt an exhilaration of youth, and remembered the dreams he had nourished then. Maybe Jesse James had strolled these very same streets, he told himself, or Wild Bill Hickok.

He had been startled in one store to find his own name staring back at him on the front page of the Cheyenne paper. "Gotch new champion," the headline said, and the drop headline proclaimed he had beaten Jenkins easily to win the title. He stood and read most of the story, then picked up the paper - and two additional ones - and purchased them. He didn't let on who he was, even when the storekeeper looked at him strangely, as though he might recognize him. Frank's picture wasn't in the paper, though, and he knew the chances of anyone in Cheyenne, Wyoming, knowing him were very small.

He was recognized in Fort Dodge, though, and a small crowd gathered as he and Klank, and Burns and the others were saying their good-byes, promising to keep in touch and to start planning their next move. They figured Jenkins would be demanding a rematch, and they knew a considerable amount of money could be made with the bout.

The ride from Fort Dodge to Humboldt was as rough as usual, and far nosier than he was accustomed to, as the driver insisted on carrying on a conversation with the new American champion the entire way. It wasn't every day that he got to tote a celebrity, the driver assured Frank, and he wasn't about to let the opportunity pass without a good deal of conversation.

Humboldt was bustling when the carriage rolled into town. Moving onto the main street, it crossed over the bridge on the Des Moines River and entered the business section. It wasn't until then that Frank realized there was a crowd assembled in front of the courthouse; and it wasn't until the carriage pulled up in front that he realized the reception was planned.... for him.

A small band struck up a song as the carriage approached, and Frank recognized the mayor standing in front of the crowd. He also recognized many friends, men like Elmer Smith, who had been with him the night he had wrestled Burns in the Fort Dodge Opera House, and Marshal Green, the "chicken picker" who had lost to Gotch several years earlier. Gotch smiled and waved to those two, as well as to Ben Barth and other farmers who worked near the Gotch homestead. He also caught a glimpse of several of his old school chums, boys who he had once tumbled through the grasses with when he was just learning his trade.

He waited for the carriage to come to a full halt, and then he climbed out, accepting the hands stuck in his direction and shaking all of them. The mayor, a somewhat round man named Martin, read a short speech, welcoming home "Humboldt's favorite son, the greatest wrestler in America," and presented him with a proclamation which declared him the most famous person in Humboldt's history. The ceremony ended abruptly, but Frank's fans were not about to let the day end without a bit of celebration. With Smith leading the way, Frank was coaxed into retiring to the local saloon for a round or two of toasting. Though he subscribed to Burns' philosophy of a sound mind in a sound body and was generally opposed to drinking liquor, he was not above having a beer from time to time, especially when he wasn't in serious training. And he relished the prospect of spending time with these old friends. The worst part of being a sports champion, he admitted, was the travel. Even though he enjoyed visiting various parts of the country, he missed the camaraderie of Humboldt.

Smith, Barth and several others led Gotch to a table in the saloon, and all eyes followed them. Big Jim, the bartender, a man who had the size but not the heart to be a top-flight wrestler himself, came over with a round of beers, and proudly proclaimed it "was on the house, in honor of the greatest wrestler in all of America...and maybe even

Humboldt, if you can whip your brother, Charlie."

Everyone joined in laughing, including Frank. He knew full well what Big Jim meant; a lot of folks in Humboldt thought Charlie might be stronger and rougher than Frank, but knew he would never leave his farm to prove it. And Frank didn't mind that sort of talk, or thinking. He was secure in his own ability and accomplishments, and was pleased people still remembered Charlie and the potential he harbored in that powerful body.

But Frank knew far more than anyone in Humboldt that it took far more than just power to make a good wrestler. Jenkins was as powerful as any man who lived in the entire United States, and yet he had lost his title to a man who was strong, but was more than "just" strong. Skill and cunning were just as important as strength, maybe even more so; and, above all, Frank reasoned, was endurance. More and more, the contests were coming down to a test of staying power; the man who could continue to keep up the pace for an hour, and sometimes much longer than that, was the one who, in all likelihood, would emerge victorious. Burns had stressed the need for long, arduous runs, and Gotch was a believer, more and more so with each passing match.

"What's next for you, now that you're the American champion of wrestling?" asked Smith, downing his fifth beer, and slamming the empty mug on the oak table. There were six men at the table, and all leaned forward, eagerly waiting Gotch's pronouncements. They were men whose lives centered around Humboldt and the surrounding area. A big trip to them was to Fort Dodge, and to trek all the way to the state capital in Des Moines - some hundred miles south - was a real ordeal. And yet they were sitting in the company of a man who had, in the past year, wrestled in such cities as Davenport, Omaha, Cleveland, Tacoma, Seattle and Bellingham - to say nothing of Alaska.

"Well, I don't rightly know at this point," said Frank, sipping on his beer. "Emil Klank, who's my manager now...."

"What happened to the Farmer?" injected one of the men, puzzled. Most had assumed that Gotch wrestled exclusively for Burns, and the name Klank was still somewhat new to them.

"Farmer's my trainer," said Frank, trying to explain the various roles his associates played, "while Emil's my manager. Farmer helps get me ready for the big matches by training with me and discussing strategies and the like, while Emil takes care of the business aspects. You know....setting up the various bouts and arranging for the press coverage and accommodations, and things like that."

"And picking up the dough, too, right, Frank?" asked Smith. Everyone chuckled. They had heard, and read, how much money their friend was making these days, and they were not a little awe-struck. For a man to earn up to five thousand dollars - more than a year's salary for most of them - for just one match was almost beyond their comprehension.

"Yeah," laughed Frank. "That's a big part of it, too. And you need a wise fella to represent you when you're dealing with some of those city slickers, I can tell you that."

"But what's next, Frank?" asked Smith again. He was anxious to know where his friend would be off to soon.

"We might go out east," said Frank, rolling the beer mug between his thick hands. "Emil's not sure what would be best. But I got to give Jenkins a rematch, that's for sure. He's deserving of it, being the former champ; and besides, he did me a big favor by giving me one after he licked me that first time."

"Yeah, and I'll bet he's wishing he hadn't," volunteered one of the men. "You really gave him the what-for this time."

Everyone raised their glasses at that, and offered a toast to Frank. He felt a glow growing inside, to be able to bring this much joy and glory to Humboldt and his friends. When he and Smith left several hours later, they were alone, the others having drifted off one by one til the two old friends were the only ones left. Together, they walked down the main street of Humboldt. It was late afternoon, and both harbored thoughts of getting home.

They halted in their tracks as a woman came hustling toward the two with a look of concern on her face. They stopped abruptly as she approached, her plumed hat bobbing in the slight wind, her floor length dress swishing as she walked.

"Are you Frank Gotch, the famous wrestler?" she asked. Frank nodded, but held his tongue, not knowing what to expect from this woman, who looked hard-set upon some mission, the object of which he could not fathom a hunch.

"I'm Mrs. Oestrich," she said with an air of importance. "My daughter, Gladys, is involved with a contest to raise money for the new Catholic church we plan to build here in Humboldt. We aren't Catholic, mind you," she said, pointing a gloved finger at the two men, "but it's a civic responsibility to help out whenever it's for the good of the community....don't you agree?" The two men nodded their agreement, and exchanged quick and puzzled glances.

"Well, Gladys is trying to raise money for the project. It's a popularity thing, actually, Whoever can raise the most money receives a watch, but that's not important. What is important is that the money all goes toward the church. And I think it would be lovely if you, Mr. Gotch, would contribute something. After all, we all know you're a millionaire now, thanks to your wrestling exploits."

"Hardly a millionaire, Mrs. Oestrich," said Frank, with a chuckle. "But I'll be glad to donate something to such a worthy cause. Where is your Gladys now?"

Mrs. Oestrich grimaced, as though in pain.

"She won't come out and work for herself," she answered. "She's embarrassed to solicit help for herself in a popularity contest. But I told her it's the fund-raising that matters, and she shouldn't give the popularity matter a second thought. Still, you know how young ones are about such matters." She smiled prettily, confident that Humboldt's most famous citizen was about to contribute to her daughter's fund. Frank stuck his hand into his pocket, then left it there for a moment.

"I'll strike up a bargain with you, Mrs. Oestrich," he said. "I believe in what your daughter's doing, but I also believe in a person standing up and being counted for themselves. If you'll have your daughter come to me personally, I'll give Gladys ten dollars for each hundred votes she has."

Mrs. Oestrich quickly agreed. "That's a fine idea, Mr. Gotch. And I'll tell Gladys to ask you when she sees you." With that, she said "Good day," her shoes click-clacking on the boarded sidewalk as she hustled away. Gotch and Smith watched her disappear around a corner, then burst out laughing.

"You handled that just right," said Smith. "You'll probably never hear from either of them ever again."

"I hope I do," said Frank quietly. "If the daughter's as pretty as the mother, I may want to get to know her."

The two men stopped in at several stores on main street, exchanging greetings with the various merchants and shoppers, all acquaintances. Frank was posed the same questions over and over - questions pertaining to his future plans, and others which sought his opinion of Jenkins, a name well known in Iowa, a bastion of wrestling and sports fans - but he didn't mind. He was pleased to share his experiences with the hometown folks.

After yet another hour of talking in the various shops, Gotch and Smith decided it was time to head for home once and for all. Frank had built a little house on his eighty acres south of town, not too far from the family home, and he was now more than anxious to spend some time there. But leaving Down's Hardware store, they were amazed to find an attractive girl waiting for them. She had been sitting at the long bench in front of the door, and rose quickly when they neared her. She had dark hair and long dark lashes, and was dressed in a long white dress and pink shawl. Gotch couldn't assess her age at first glance, and was considerably surprised when she at last told him.

"Are you Mr. Gotch?" she asked, somewhat shyly, but yet with an air of confidence, as though she knew something he did not.

"Yes, I am," he answered. "And who might you be?"

"I'm Gladys Oestrich," she replied, with a short curtsy, which brought a quick smile to Frank's face. "I believe you recently talked with my mother about the prospect of raising money for the new Catholic church."

Gotch glanced at Smith, who was smiling broadly, then back at the girl staring him straight in the eye.

"Why yes, that is so," Gotch said. "Have you come to collect?"

"Yes," she answered straightforwardly, and Gotch found himself admiring this little lady who was standing before him, staring up at him. She was only five feet tall, and surely weighed less than one hundred pounds. And she was very young, not over sixteen, he surmised. He dug a hand into his pocket, and pulled out his wallet. "I had promised ten dollars for each hundred votes. How many do you have?"

"Three hundred and thirty," she said, "but I hope to get even more."

Gotch let out a low whistle. "You must be a very popular girl to have so many votes already. How old are you?" he asked suddenly, and realized just as quickly that he felt foolish for asking such a personal question.

"I am twelve," she answered.

Smith smiled, then chuckled, and Gotch looked stunned; he could hardly believe this attractive young lady was just a girl of twelve. He opened his wallet, peeled out four ten-dollar bills, and handed it to her.

"Here; this is more than I agreed upon, but I'm sure you will be gaining many more votes."

She looked at the bills, then at Gotch. "But not that many more," she protested handing it back.

"No, you keep it," he said, holding both hands up in front of him in protest.

She smiled sweetly, unloosened the bag from her arm, slipped the bills into it and snapped it shut. She smiled, gave another small curtsy, and stepped briskly away. The two watched her, as they had her mother only an hour or so earlier, until she also turned a corner and disappeared.

"There goes a real cute little girl," said Smith, scratching his head. "Hard to believe she's just twelve years old, though."

"It sure is," said Gotch. The two resumed walking down the sidewalk.

"Gonna marry her some day, though," muttered Gotch, half-aloud.

Smith stopped, and placed a hand on his friend's arm. "What was that?" he asked, studying the face of the best man he knew, or would ever know.

"I'm going to marry Gladys Oestrich some day," said Gotch, staring his friend squarely in the face.

"But, she's only twelve. It'll be years until she's marrying age," countered Smith, surprised at Gotch's infatuation. Frank was a popular fellow with the women at the dances they attended as youth, he knew, but Frank had never shown much interest. Besides being somewhat shy and retreating, Frank had always been too busy with farm chores and sports in general to pay much fuss to womenfolk.

"I know that," said Frank. "I'm not ready to settle down now, either. Got some business with a lion from Russia first. But when the time comes, that's the woman I'm marrying," he said firmly. Smith knew Frank Gotch just well enough to believe him, no matter how improbable any proposition may seem.

CHAPTER 7

E mil Klank dropped the newspaper and turned to Frank Gotch, who was sitting across the room lost in thought. Klank waited for Gotch to speak, but when he didn't he spoke out himself.

"Do you want to hear what else it says, or is that enough?" said Klank, who had been reading a newspaper account of Jim Jeffries' latest plans. "And while I'm asking questions, how come you're so interested in Jeffries all of a sudden?"

Frank didn't answer immediately, and so Klank fell to silence, brooding over Gotch's silence. At last, Gotch spoke.

"Ever hear of Kid McCoy?" he asked.

"Sure, he's the former prize fighter. Pretty fair boxer, I hear tell."

"Well," said Frank, standing up and stretching, "He's going to start training with me a bit."

Klank looked startled. "What for?" he asked. "He don't know nuttin' about wrestling. What more do you need than me and the Farmer?"

"You and the Farmer don't know anything about boxing, though, Emil," came the reply.

Klank left his chair, too. He walked over to Gotch, staring him straight in the eye. They were about the same height and age, but Gotch was about fifteen pounds heavier.

"So what?" he asked.

"So, I'm thinking about doing a little boxing, maybe taking on Jeffries for the title."

"So, you read that piece in the Chicago paper, too," said Klank.

"Well, I think you're crazy. I think you might just as well forget the whole thing. You're a wrestler, not a boxer. Or have you forgotten all about a fella by the name of Frank Slavin."

Gotch turned from Klank and left the room, but was back in a moment. He had a stack of papers with him, and set them down on the table in front of him. Klank watched silently as Gotch sifted through them. He smiled when he found the one he wanted, and held it in front of him, preparing to read from it.

"Just listen to this, Emil. This is a story about Jeffries in the Chicago American.

"After carefully scanning the pugilistic field, Jim Jeffries has about come to the conclusion that there is prospect for but one good heavyweight battle before he relinquishes the championship crown, voluntarily or otherwise. Jeff has picked out from his group of challengers, for there are many ambitious to fight the champion, as the three most deserving of attention - Bob Fitzsimmons, who has twice met defeat at his hands; Marvin Hart who is about matched with Jack Johnson, the Negro champion, and Frank Gotch, the champion wrestler.

"Let these men fight it out and I will take the best' says Jeff."

Gotch put the paper down and looked at Klank, but his manager said nothing.

"Did you read what Joe Walcott, the former welterweight champion, said? And don't forget, he was a wrestler before he became a boxer."

"Maybe so," said Klank grudgingly, "but he wasn't a very good wrestler."

Gotch dismissed the statement with a sweep of his hand, and pulled out another newspaper clipping.

"Listen to this," he said, and began reading aloud: "Gotch is the fastest man for his size on his feet I ever saw. He is as nimble as Jim Corbett. In brute strength, I doubt if champion Jeffries surpasses Gotch in any point. I do say that he frames up the best of anyone I know at this time as possessing the qualities which must be possessed by the man who defeats champion Jeffries."

Gotch put down the second clipping, and searched Klank's face for a sign of submission. But he was disappointed; Klank stared ahead, unmoved.

"Aw, c'mon, Emil," said Frank, his hands raising in the air in a sign of frustration. "There's good money....big money....to be made in this kind of a venture. Think of it, the American wrestling champion against the world's boxing champion. You know, there's a report out of Australia that Hackenschmidt has been doing some glove work, that he's thinking about boxing, too. He's down there on a tour and can't find any good wrestling competition."

"But what about the world's wrestling title which everyone says belongs to Hackenschmidt?" said Klank. "We still haven't got that out of the way yet. Wouldn't it make more sense to shoot for that now? You've been wrestling for six years; don't you want the shot?"

"Sure I do, Emil, more than anything. But the Russian Lion - if that's what he is - isn't going to give me a chance. He's just not going to. And I just can't keep wrestling the same Americans over and over and over. The public is getting tired of me against anyone else who isn't the world champion."

"He's scared...." said Klank, his voice trailing off.

"No, I don't believe that," said Frank. "I don't think Hackenschmidt is afraid of any man. He's won too much....he's never lost. Heck, Emil, he doesn't know what defeat is, so how can he be afraid of it? Naw, he just doesn't want to make another trip over to America. He was here three years ago and whipped everyone easy. Even Jenkins wasn't much of a match for him."

"So why's he thinking about boxing? And, why are you?" demanded Klank.

"The money...and the thrill of being both a boxing and a wrestling champion," said Gotch. "It's never been done before. Not even John L. Sullivan could wrestle well enough to win the title."

The two men sat in silence. Klank was beginning to regret the trip he had made in from Omaha. Every time he visited Frank on his own farm, he seemed to come out on the short end of any discussion they had. He felt there was something about the Iowa air, and what it did to Frank, that made him impossible to argue successfully with. Not that it made sense; Klank didn't think Iowa air was so special, as did Gotch and Burns - especially Burns. But still, the two men always seemed different, more full of ideas and more obstinate, in Iowa. There must be something different about Iowa air, Klank conceded to himself.

"Emil," Gotch began. "Listen, I've wrestled twenty-three match-es this year, as opposed to just ten in 1904. I've beaten Dan McLeod four times, and that's enough revenge for the time he defeated me in the cinders back in Luverne, in my first pro match. I've beaten Jenkins twice more, Jim Parr twice, and Yankee Rogers twice. There's no one left to wrestle here. And Hackenschmidt doesn't seem inclined to come across the water again. He's safe in Europe, where he can draw big crowds, make good money and beat nobodies. So what's to be done? Who am I going to wrestle? Heck, Emil, I might as well try boxing.

"And as for Slavin.....shoot, I was young then, just past nineteen, with no sense about boxing. I've studied it a lot since then, and done a lot of sparring with some good men. Even done some sparring with Sailor Tom Sharkey, when we met up in Chicago that time. He couldn't touch me, I was just too fast. And he fought Jeffries to a standstill before losing in the twenty-fifth round.

"It's about money, darn it. Boxers are making more money these days than wrestlers. Jim Corbett said I could probably get $15,000 for a fight with Jeffries. Heck, Emil, I'll have to wrestle ten times this year to make that much."

"Or move to the East," said Klank quietly, knowing how Frank felt about that prospect.

Gotch walked across the room and out onto the front porch, where he stood gazing out across his eighty acres. He took several deep breaths. Yes, he admitted, he loved this Iowa air and land more and more each passing day. Ever since winning the title from Jenkins in Bellingham in January of 1904, he had been besieged by offers, requests and even demands from the nation's leading sport's promoters to move to the East. There was more in the way of opportunity for him, he was told, out East, where the big business people were.

The door slamming behind him broke his train of thought. Klank's hand fell on his right shoulder.

"Look, Frank, anything you want is fine with me. I've got all the confidence in the world in you. If you want to box, then go ahead. But I still think we should go after Hackenschmidt. And there are still some Americans left to wrestle. That doctor in Seattle, what's his name.... Roller....wants a go with you, and there's that smaller guy in Wisconsin, Fred Beell. Then, you and the Farmer can always draw a full house any time you two decide to tangle, anywhere. There's money and prestige, and eventually Hackenschmidt will have to wrestle us. He can't duck you forever."

"Maybe he can, maybe he can't," said Frank. His voice sounded weary. He had wrestled hard the last year, taking his title across the continent. He had endured three more brutal matches with Jenkins, winning the first rematch in Cleveland, but losing to the fired-up mill-wright in New York City March 15, 1905, in front of nearly ten thousand fans. Frank had been sick prior to the match, and left the ring in a dazed and weakened condition after losing the title. Just two months later, slightly improved physically, he lost to Jenkins again, and was so embarrassed that he refused to return to Iowa without the title. Instead, he stayed in the East and trained with a new fervor, winning the title back in a brutal match in Kansas City. Again, nearly ten thousand fans showed up, with thousands more turned away at the door. The Kansas City writers called it the greatest sporting spectacle ever seen in that city.

He felt he needed the match with Hackenschmidt, or he would have to go into boxing in order to get a crack at a world title, his ultimate goal. One or the other, and at the moment he didn't much care which.

It was while having supper at his parents' home several weeks after his discussion with Klank that the decision was almost made for him. Amelia heard an automobile draw up, and left the table and went onto the porch. She was gone for several minutes, then returned, with a somewhat pained look on her face.

"It's for you, Frankie," she said, and resumed her seat at the table. Frank glanced at her for a sign, then at the other faces around the table. Nothing further was said, and he left the room.

Elmer Smith was on the porch, fidgeting nervously; he gave the appearance of having done something wrong, yet he was obviously excited.

"What's up, Elmer?" asked Frank suspiciously. He glanced back in at the kitchen, then at his longtime friend, who seldom journeyed out to the Gotch household. In all the years they had known one another, Smith had probably been to the farm on just five occasions.

"I'm sorry to barge in on ya at home, Frank," said Smith. "I know your ma doesn't like it much."

Frank shrugged: "It's okay, Elmer....she just doesn't understand a lot of things that are happening to me, and the family, since I became a wrestler. And she's still not used to hearing the sound of an automobile pulling up, rather than a horse and buggy. But what's got you in such a tizzy?"

"You'll never guess who just sent word that he wants to meet with you, Frank. I was down at the telegraph office, when the message came in, and Mickelson asked me if I would come out and give you the message."

Gotch shrugged again, somewhat amused by his friends' excitement. He didn't know who the telegram was from, but he knew he would not be as excited as Elmer was, even if it was from President Theodore Roosevelt himself, direct from the White House in

Washington, D.C.

Smith was obviously waiting for Gotch to take a guess. But when he didn't Smith blurted it out.

"Jim Jeffries, that's who," he said, searching Gotch's face for a reaction. When there wasn't much of one, Smith acted disappointed.

"Frank, that's the heavyweight boxing champion of the entire world. The Old Boilermaker....the Rocky Mountain Grizzly Bear...the man who defeated both Corbett and Fitzsimmons, like they was nothing. And the man who whipped Tom Sharkey just as easy."

"Hardly easy, Elmer," said Gotch calmly, his mind already hard at work, wondering what Jeffries had in mind. "The sports writers say it was one of the most brutal matches ever contested, and that both men were nearly dead after it was over."

"Well, yeah," said Smith, "but Jeffries is still the champ. He won. And he wants to meet with you, Frank."

Gotch held out his hand, and Smith pulled out a piece of paper from his back pocket. Frank took the yellow, thin paper, and read it carefully. It was from Jeffries, sent from San Francisco. He was going to be in Burlington, Iowa, in two weeks, and he wanted to meet Gotch, to talk over some business potentials, the telegram said. Gotch read it again carefully, then folded it up and stuck it into his back pocket. He thanked Smith for bringing it all the way out to the farm, knowing that he must have taken some little time from his chores, searching for Frank on his own eighty acres first before heading to the older Gotch farmstead.

It took several more minutes of conversation to calm Smith down, and when he finally left, Frank faced the task of informing his parents of the telegram. His mother was even more against boxing than wrestling, if that was possible, and she left the room when Frank began discussing his future plans. Frederick listened attentively, and seemed interested, but it was hard to tell about him these days. He couldn't understand the world Frank was living in now, though he was proud of his son's accomplishments. After all, Frank had his own acreage, a nice house, and all paid for. In addition, he had paid off the Gotch mortgage, and had bought some other adjacent land, which he was renting out to other farmers. He was rich and famous, and someone to be proud of, though boasting was never his way.

When Frank left his parents' home, he knew the next several weeks would be the most important in his life since he decided to make the trip to the Yukon territory six years earlier. There, he had earned enough money that he could just about do whatever he pleased for the ensuing years. Now, he would soon know whether he would give up wrestling for boxing.

CHAPTER 8

Built like a sturdy Iowa barn, the world's heavyweight boxing champion was a formidable fellow in both appearance and reality. James J. Jeffries had his first boxing match in 1896, knocking out Hank Griffith in the fourteenth round in Los Angeles. In the years which followed, Jeffries crawled in the ring twenty-two times, winning each match, including sixteen by knockout. At six foot and one-half inches tall and two hundred and twenty five pounds at his fighting best, he was held in awe - if not outright fear - in the ring. He won the world title from Bob Fitzsimmons, the crafty blacksmith who had defeated Gentleman Jim Corbett with the solar plexus punch, by an eleven-round knockout in Coney Island on June 9, 1899, and defended it eight times. On May 11, 1900, he gave Corbett a shot at his old title (which he had taken from the legendary John L. Sullivan back in 1892 in New Orleans) and knocked Corbett senseless in the twenty-third round. He scored three more wins before kayoing both Fitzsimmons and Corbett in return bouts, and by 1905 he was thinking seriously of retiring. His toughest battle had come in a twenty-five round decision over rough and ready Tom Sharkey in 1900, and now there was a lack of suitable challengers to keep Jeffries busy.

Besides, the public was not overly attracted to the personality of the quiet and shy Jeffries. He lacked the flamboyance of earlier champions - such as John L., who used to boast he could whip any man in the house, and Gentleman Jim, who attracted fans with his dashing style and sharp attire.

Jeffries hated the public eye, and he had gone to great pains to keep the meeting with Gotch out of the newspapers. Apparently, he had been successful, thought Gotch, as he moved through the lobby of the hotel where he was to meet the boxing champion. Frank had wired to San Francisco that he would be happy to meet Jeffries, and Jeffries had sent back another wire giving him specific instructions on the time and place of their meeting. He requested Gotch come alone, and Frank agreed.

Gotch heard his name, and turned to see a small man standing against the far wall, motioning to him. He was nattily attired in a three-piece suit, sporting a narrow black mustache and a brown derby. He was carrying a small silver-headed cane, which he tapped nervously on the floor as Gotch approached.

"You are Mr. Gotch, I presume?" he asked politely, smiling slightly. When Frank nodded, he stuck out his hand.

"I am William A. Brady....Jack Brady, Mr. Jeffries' business associate. Would you be so kind as to follow me?"

Gotch nodded again, and followed the much smaller man around two corners, down a hallway, and to a room at the end. Brady held up the cane, rapped smartly on the door three times, and smiled when a gruff voice said to enter.

The room was pleasantly decorated, large and comfortable, with two beds, several chairs, a writing table, and a sofa. The drapes were large and flowery, bright pink with chartreuse flowers....not a room one would associate with the heavyweight boxing champion of the world. Yet, there was no mistaking the man sitting in a large chair, staring at them. He was huge...maybe weighing as much as two hundred and fifty pounds, Gotch thought, and his face was large, with a square jaw and close-cropped hair. He sported a massive neck, and huge shoulders which squared off abruptly. He was wearing a white shirt, with the sleeves rolled up several folds, exposing thick, hairy forearms. He stared at the newcomers for a moment, then rose from the chair - Gotch thought it looked as though the exertion was laborious, so huge was the body, thick and round - and came forward.

"Mr. Gotch," said Brady, turning so he was flanking both men. "May I introduce Mr. Jeffries. And Mr. Jeffries, Mr. Gotch."

The two champions shook hands, holding the grip for a moment longer than might have been the normal custom between men just meeting. But these were not ordinary men....each knew that, today perhaps more than ever. One was the undefeated heavyweight boxing champion of the world, the other the top wrestler in America.

Suddenly, Gotch smiled. He didn't know why exactly, but he

liked this man; it was a feeling he seldom experienced so quickly. And Jeffries, taking the cue, smiled back, exposing a wide mouth and a set of crooked, jagged teeth. He was not a handsome man like Gentleman Jim, but he was a man who commanded respect and admiration, of that there was no doubt.

"Pleased to meet you, Mr. Gotch," said Jeffries, his voice gruff and somewhat hoarse, as though he were fighting a cold. It was, Gotch would come to learn, his normal voice, cold or no cold. It came from deep in a cavernous chest, and always had a raspy edge to it, one that made many men uncomfortable, but one to which Gotch took a strange and immediate liking.

Their hands released, and Gotch responded in turn, expressing his pleasure at meeting Jeffries.

Jeffries gestured for Gotch to take a seat.

"Can't stay on my feet too long sometimes," said Jeffries, resuming his spot. "Old groin injury, or something like that," he said, making a face, and rubbing a big, thick hand along the inside of one of his massive thighs. "Acts up at strange times, hurts like the devil."

He looked at Gotch.

"You ever have that problem?" he asked, genuinely interested in hearing the answer.

"Nope," said Gotch. "Had a lot of ailments in my time, but guess that's not been one of them."

Jeffries nodded.

"You're lucky then, Frank. Stops you from running hard, from training like you should."

There was a moment's pause, and Gotch was about to comment on the weather when Brady cleared his throat. Gotch looked at the dapper little man who had also taken a seat. He had almost forgotten he was still in the room.

"Mr. Gotch, we understand that you are having troubles arranging a bout with Hackenschmidt, that Russian Lion fellow, and are considering other avenues of competition. If that is indeed correct, we would be interested in discussing some possible arrangements with you....ones that might be of benefit to both you and to us."

"A little boxing, perhaps?" said Gotch, smiling slightly.

Jeffries cut in.

"Heard you was interested in doing some boxing," said Jeffries, "and also heard that you would probably be pretty good."

But Brady cut him short.

"That, however, is not what we wanted to talk to you about, Mr.

Gotch. What we have in mind is some barnstorming across the country, you and Mr. Jeffries taking on all comers, in either boxing or wrestling. Mr. Jeffries would, of course, handle the boxing, and you the wrestling."

Gotch was taken by surprise, on two accounts. He had supposed he was being considered as a possible boxing foe for the champ, first of all, and he had not considered even in his wildest imaginings that Jeffries thought enough of him, or any wrestler, to consider going into business with one.

Brady and Jeffries were watching him, studying his face for a reaction. Gotch shrugged, not knowing what to say, and smiled.

"We've surprised you, I can see that, Mr. Gotch," said Brady. "But let me fill you in on our situation, and perhaps you will see the enterprise much clearer.

"Jim has been the heavyweight champion of the world for five years now, and there just aren't any more challengers left....no disrespect to you, Mr. Gotch. We've heard reports of your fistic abilities, and Tom Sharkey, who Jim greatly admires, is a big fan of yours. Sharkey uses a lot of wrestling in his training, and even wrestled some matches several years ago. But we think your future is in wrestling, and we'll expand on that later, if you'll just bear with us."

Gotch was watching Jeffries, who was now gazing out the window as Brady spoke, apparently lost in thought. Gotch couldn't decide if Jeffries was listening to his partner talk or was far away, dreaming of streams thick with trout and forests of bear, deer and badger. Jeffries' love of the great outdoors, and hunting and fishing, was well known. Several years earlier, he had even lived among a tribe of Indians in the Rocky Mountains of Colorado for a spell, forsaking the pleasures of white society for a fling at the primeval world he apparently longed for. Gotch found himself admiring this great boilermaker of a man more and more with each passing moment.

"....already beaten Fitzsimmons twice and Gentleman Jim twice," Brady continued, with Gotch missing several words due to his own reflections. "He's knocked out the last five men in a row, with ridiculous ease. Corbett lasted until the eighth round - no, make that the tenth - in Frisco, but he was on the canvas a dozen times or so, it seems. And when Fitz went down in the eighth back in `02 from that punch to the abdomen....well, I was afraid he would never get up again. Then, there was that second round knockout of Jack Munroe in San Francisco last year, in August.

"The fact of the matter is, Mr. Gotch, the public thinks Jim is unbeatable now. They won't pay top dollar to see him fight any more, so sure is everyone that there will not even be a contest. Even Sharkey, the greatest brawler this country has ever seen, is done with Jim now. That last fight, in Coney Island, was enough to teach even old Sailor Tom that he can never beat Jim."

Gotch recalled reading the account of the brawl. It had taken place in 1899, and was the first to ever be filmed at night. In order to insure acceptable moving pictures, huge lights had been installed directly above the ring, and the heat from the low-hanging lights was incredible. Sharkey's aides had foreseen the problem, and came to the fight with two huge electric fans, which were placed behind his corner and used to cool him down between rounds. The two men battered each other unmercifully for twenty-five rounds. Jeffries entered the fray with a swollen left arm and it became almost useless as the fight wore on. Sharkey, on the other hand, suffered cracked ribs from the pounding right fist of Jeffries, and fought much of the last fifteen rounds gasping for breath, in too much pain to straighten himself up. His left eye began bleeding and swelled shut in the middle rounds, and a butt in the face from Sharkey's forehead knocked out one of Jeffries' front teeth. The heat had been so bad at ringside that many of the spectators had stripped to the waist, and one person in the back rows fainted. The intense heat from the lamps had even caused long range problems for the fighters, as both began to suddenly lose hair in blotches. Looking at Jeffries closely, Gotch could see a series of scars on his face, and he wondered which were the result of the memorable battles with Sharkey.

"Now, we're looking for new fields to conqueror," said Brady. "We've tried the acting route (Gotch recalled, with a smile, the rough reviews Jeffries had received for his stage efforts, which even included a role as legendary frontiersman Davy Crockett). But we feel our best possibilities at the moment lie with barnstorming, essentially the same type of entertainment you and Farmer Burns are so well acquainted with. We have heard of your exploits in Alaska, and of the Farmer's successes on the fair circuit, challenging all comers."

Brady was making a strong case for barnstorming, and he continued on for nearly an hour. All the time, Gotch sat merely nodding or injecting a word or two, while Brady discussed the various possibilities of Jeffries and Gotch campaigning together. Jeffries would offer a thousand dollars to any man who could last five rounds with him, with Gotch offering five hundred to any man who could avoid being thrown in thirty minutes of wrestling. The idea was certainly not a new one - even John L. Sullivan had barnstormed for a season, and, of course, barnstorming brought Gotch and Burns together for the first time in Fort Dodge in December of 1899, the same year Jeffries won the world title from Fitzsimmons at Coney Island.

The more Brady talked, the more Gotch became aware of a yearning deep within. The attraction of big money and touring with Jeffries held great appeal, but he was after an even bigger, more important dream: Here was Jeffries, the heavyweight boxing champion of the world, not just America. He had traveled abroad, had sparred with the best men the European continent had to offer. He had been greeted enthusiastically by royalty, and had been courted by princes and dukes, because he was the champion of the entire world, not just America. Sitting in the hotel room in tiny Burlington, Iowa, listening to Brady talk and watching Jeffries stare out the window, Gotch knew more than ever that he was not going to rest, or go on any kind of a tour, until he had become world champion, too. No, boxing was out for now....he would spend his energies and time concentrating on what he did best. And he would not rest until he had lured the Russian Lion into a ring, with the world title being the prize.

When Brady finished his presentation - for that's precisely what it was - Gotch responded as politely, and as firmly, as he could. The invitation was tempting, and he was flattered to be so considered. He wished the enterprise well, but it was not what he was searching for at the moment. Neither Brady or Jeffries, who had left the room for a short spell and had returned in the final minutes of Brady's pitch, expressed any great surprise at Gotch's decision, and left Gotch wondering if Jeffries ever showed much feeling about matters, one way or another. He seemed to be a giant of a man somewhat lost in a world that idolized him, but didn't care to know him. Gotch felt a great deal of sympathy for Jeffries, though he did not know exactly why.

He was surprised, and pleased, to be invited to dinner with the two men, and Jeffries genuinely warmed up as they left the hotel the back way. Jeffries was almost obsessed with avoiding crowds, and the three men slipped away to a small, but delightful, restaurant Jeffries and Brady had been frequenting ever since their arrival. The proprietors, a jolly Greek named Nick and his wife, Penelope, greeted Jeffries and Brady with big hugs and a bottle of the best Greek wine available, and took them to a secluded table at the very rear, showering them with attention and service, but being careful not to intrude. It was obvious they were aware that these men desired privacy.

Halfway through the meal, Jeffries asked Gotch about his family, particularly his parents. When Gotch told him about the objections toward wrestling he had to overcome, the champion nodded, a sad expression on his face.

"I know the same feeling, the same experience," said Jeffries in his gravelly voice, wiping his mouth with a napkin and clearing his throat heavily before continuing. "I was born in Ohio, but we moved to California when I was quite young. I got involved with track and wrestling" - he paused and looked at Gotch for his reaction, and, for the first time since the two had met, grinned at Gotch's expression of amazement - "yes, I considered myself quite a wrestler at one point.

"But I leaned more toward boxing when I had trouble finding fellows to wrestle with. They were all afraid of my bear hug" - he held out his two enormous arms, then slowly brought them together, his hands clenching, in the form of a bear hug - "and wouldn't consent to grapple. But I never had trouble finding anyone to race with, or to box with. Everyone assumed I was too slow and too clumsy to be any good in those sports."

"Including Jim Corbett and Bob Fitzsimmons," interjected Brady, who had spent the greater part of his last few minutes sipping wine and attacking a huge piece of steak prepared expertly by Nick.

"Yeah, they never did respect my boxing ability too much," grunted Jeffries. "Course, you know I used to be a sparring partner for Jim Corbett, and he used to make a lot of fun of me."

There was a moment of silence, as Jeffries seemed to dwell on some unpleasant moments in his past. Gotch continued to reflect on the man's native shyness, and an inferiority complex, and was amazed to realize the heavyweight boxing champion of the world, the bear-like Jim Jeffries, was really shy and insecure, despite his fame and fortune.

"Anyway," continued Jeffries, obviously warming up to the prospect of discovering a new friend whom he could feel uninhibited with, "I was talked into fighting this negro, Hank Griffin, when I was just nineteen years old. He was a professional, I found out later, but I didn't know it at the time, even when it was announced the winner would get seventy-five percent of the fighter's purse, and the loser the rest. I still just thought it was a fun fight, sort of. And my friend insisted on it.

"Well," he said with a chuckle, "this Griffin fellow made a fool of me for about ten rounds. He was so fast and so clever that I never even touched him after we shook hands. But long about the tenth round, I realized something. There was just no way this fellow could hurt me, no way at all. And, in the fourteenth round, I got in my one and only clean blow of the fight."

"And Griffin fell like he was shot by Wild Bill Hickok," laughed Brady.

"Right," said Jeffries, chuckling himself, and slapping a thigh. "But my ma read in the paper the next day that I had been in a fight, and she was furious. Why, boxing was little better than train robbing, as far as she was concerned."

"It was almost the very same thing for me, except I lost my first wrestling match," said Gotch, feeling right at home with this big hunk of man and his personable manager. He told about Dan McLeod coming to Luverne and slicking him into a wrestling match, and how the two grappled for hours in the cinder path, and the supper at home that night. Jeffries listened intently all the while Gotch was talking, and the two shared many another story back in Jeffries' hotel room, talking long after Brady excused himself and retired.

A bond had developed between the two men, and when it came time to part company the following morning, after a breakfast, each was sad. They promised to keep in touch, and Gotch added that after he won the world title from Hackenschmidt, he would relish the thought of barnstorming with Jeffries. Brady and Jeffries drove Gotch to the train station, and they shook hands. On the train ride back to Humboldt, Gotch knew he would always be friends with the Rocky Mountain Grizzly Bear. He also realized something else; he could never climb into the ring with Jeffries and slug it out for the championship, no matter how much he might covet the title. Throwing a man in a wrestling match was far different than hitting him in the face with all your might, even if you were wearing a padded glove. Gotch knew once and for all that he was a wrestler, and not a boxer. But it had taken an evening with the heavyweight boxing champion of the world to convince him.

CHAPTER 9

Swinging wildly at the small ball as it raced past him, Frank stomped his foot in frustration. He chased the ball off the court, picked it up and began squeezing it as he walked back to the court. Handball was a great game for his reflexes, he mused, and the running and quick stopping was ideal for building wind and endurance. In addition, he liked squeezing the ball and watching his forearms work, the muscles jumping and wiggling as he squeezed and relaxed. All in all, he reasoned handball was quite a sport.

"Hey, Gotch, quit taking it out on the ball, it wasn't its fault you can't hit it."

He looked up at the familiar voice, and smiled at Farmer Burns coming across the yard. Then, he stopped dead in his tracks. The whole camp was buzzing now, with all eyes turned on the same sight as were Frank's.

Farmer Burns was legendary for his neck strength; no man had ever been able to choke him with a strangle hold when he flexed those mighty neck muscles. Once, even, he had allowed himself to be hung by a rope from a scaffold, and had dangled for three minutes flexing his neck and showing no signs of strangling or choking. But this trick was too much.

The Farmer was moving slowly across the training area, complete with a ring in the middle, and handball courts off to the side. He was without a shirt, and was flexing his neck so mightily that his face was twisted into a grotesque shape. The cause for the exertion was trailing along behind him, about a foot off the ground; there, bobbing up and down slightly as the Farmer shuffled forward, hung a fifty-pound anvil. It was secured to a rope which hung tight around his neck.

"I don't believe my eyes," said Gotch after overcoming his speechlessness. He ran to the Farmer's side, ready to untie the knot or lift up the anvil and take the pressure off the neck, which was thick with veins ready to pop, all bright red and puffy.

"Stay back, stay back," said the Farmer in a gruff voice. "Ain't reached my goal yet."

Gotch moved aside as the Farmer edged past, his legs now in a slight squat, tiring from the pressure on his neck, which was working its way down, apparently. He looked as though he were in dire need of relieving himself.

Half the camp was trailing along behind now....ten men scratching their heads in puzzlement, and not just a little concerned for their friend's well being. Finally, at the side of the ring, Burns clutched the apron, and tilted his head far to the side, allowing the anvil to rest on the ground. He gave a huge sigh of relief, then reached up and untied the knot; he had difficulty in doing so, and Gotch came to his aide.

"You gotta be half nuts, Martin," said Frank, using the Farmer's real name for one of the very few times in their nine-year relationship. "What was this all about, anyway?"

"Wanted to impress you fellas," said the Farmer, rubbing his neck and then rolling it from side to side. "Figured you boys would think I was getting soft if'n I didn't prove to you that the old Farmer still had some grit left in him despite advancing years."

They all were gathered around him now, and began laughing, nervously at first, and then with unrestrained joviality. It had been a ridiculous sight, to be sure...a man walking through a camp with an anvil tied to his neck. And even Burns joined in the laughter as the preposterous nature of the act struck home with full force.

They all took a refreshing dip in the farm and then sat in the grass drying out. The camp was beginning to draw many spectators each and every day. They were accustomed to the routine Gotch and his stablemates went through....long runs through the countryside, bouts of handball, pulley work and the hours of wrestling in the big ring. But they seemed to never tire of the activities, especially on a boiling hot summer afternoon. Young boys could be found hanging around the camp at all times, night and day, and Gotch usually had time for all of them, chatting amiably after the workouts were over, and buying ice cream on a number of occasions for every boy present. But the last several days he had been on edge, waiting for Burns. Now, they were together, and he knew what Burns had to say would go a long way in determining his future.

The last two years had been good - very good, in fact, to Gotch. He had invested money in good Iowa farmland, and owned several hundred acres. He had a comfortable home built on his original eighty acres, replacing the one he had constructed himself shortly after returning from Alaska. He was a gentleman farmer of no little substance, and the best known man in all of Iowa. He had business opportunities constantly available to him. At age thirty, it was true that his home life was found lacking by some - his mother, for instance, wanted to know constantly why he had not yet married, but he didn't dare tell her that he was, in fact, waiting for a little sprite to grow up into a woman, that he had committed his heart to Gladys Oestrich some time ago. Whenever he saw her or her parents - her father was a lawyer - in Humboldt, he would go out of his way to exchange pleasantries with them, and he had been over to the home for dinner on several occasions. He was careful, though, not to show too much attention toward Gladys, lest her parents perceive there was an unnatural interest there. He was, after all, many years her senior. But Frank was a patient man, and even though he had dated quite a few glamorous women around the nation, including the famous actress Ida Emerson, he had no time for a serious relationship at this point in his life. Training for a bout with the Russian Lion was the most important aspect of his life. Nothing else mattered nearly so much as climbing in the ring some day opposite George Hackenschmidt.

It had been over two years since the meeting with Jeffries in Burlington. They had seen one another on just one instance since, but had immediately taken up where they had left off, talking of old times and exchanging plans to get together in the future. Jeffries had officially retired since they first met, but the sporting public was not about to forget him, and he spent a great deal of his time in public appearances, traveling the country to referee bouts and, from time to time, to box a few rounds with the local champions.

Frank, meanwhile, wrestled twenty-four times in 1906, and even had one boxing match, kayoing a burly Canadian named Sam Williams in the fifth round of a bout in Buffalo, New York. It had been a mistake, Gotch knew, from the outset, but he just didn't seem able to walk away from boxing completely. He didn't feel comfortable with gloves on, throwing jabs at a man's face rather than trying to take him down to the mat. He had controlled the bout from the outset and Williams had been exhausted from the pace Frank had set.

What's worse, the bout triggered more talk of a match between him and Jeffries, with sportswriters clamoring for Jeffries to come out of retirement and take on the grappling champ of America. Currently, the boxing title rested in the hands of Tommy Burns, a small, five-foot-seven slugger who took the title from Marvin Hart with a twenty-round decision in Los Angeles in February, of 1906. Jeffries, upon retiring, had refereed a fight between Hart and light-heavyweight champion Jack Root, and proclaimed Hart - the winner by a knockout in the twelfth round - the new champion of the world. But everyone who followed the fistic sport knew the greatest heavyweight in the world, now that Jeffries was out of the picture, was one of two black men, Jack Johnson or Sam Langford.

The Buffalo Express newspaper had compared Gotch in strength to the legendary strongman, Eugene Sandow, who toured years earlier with the Ziegfield Follies, and declared he was as quick as a lightweight, and a bundle of tricks, as well. There were reports out of Buffalo that Gotch had already been installed as a ten-to-four betting favorite over Jeffries, should the two ever meet in the ring. But Gotch knew that would never happen; even if Jeff would come back, Frank would not crawl between the ropes to swap punches with a man he liked and admired so much.

Gotch's thoughts these days were reserved almost exclusively for Hackenschmidt. The stories which came across the Atlantic portrayed the Russian Lion as an invincible matman whose equal would surely never be seen in the immediate years ahead, and maybe ever. He breezed through tournament after tournament, regardless of style. He overwhelmed the opposition, whether they wrestled the above-the-waist only style known as Greco-Roman, or whether it be the nearly-anything-goes catch-as-catch-can style that was quickly gaining popularity. His strength was considered unapproachable, and nearly every week one could pick up a Chicago or New York paper and find a new account of some exploit or accomplishment. His physique was said to be the best ever seen anywhere, including Sandow, and there were those who said he was superior to any man who had ever lived in just about any area of physical expertise.

But Gotch still hungered for the chance to test this adonis from Russia, who was also one of the top weight lifters in the world. He was running long miles through the Iowa countryside, and wrestling as long as four hours a day on some occasions. He played handball to sharpen his reflexes and improve his quickness, and worked with pulleys and weights to increase his strength. He had something to prove, something that meant the world to him. Even here in Humboldt, his hometown, where he was loved and respected, few people thought he could defeat the Russian Lion. After all, they would point out, the story was that Hackenschmidt had never lost in his entire career, while Gotch had now tasted defeat six times in one hundred and five matches. He hadn't lost for nearly three years, except for the strange match with Fred Beell of Wisconsin, where he had slammed his head into the ring post and had wandered around the ring the next several minutes dazed and bleeding, an easy prey for the cunning Beell. But in three subsequent matches, he had toyed with the Wisconsin grappler en route to three crushing pins.

Just when Gotch had began to believe he would never be given a chance to wrestle Hackenschmidt for the world title, electrifying news arrived in the form of a telegram. He was called down to the Western Union Station in Humboldt, where the message was waiting for him. It had a New York dateline, and he had torn it open in haste, noting it had come originally from Germany. It was, in fact, a message from C. B. Cochran, Hackenschmidt's personal manager. It was short and to the point: "Interested in world title match with Iowan Gotch. Please send Burns to New York, June 2, to work out details. Wire C. B. Cochran, Suite 336, Roderdam Hotel, Munich, Germany, if interested."

"If interested!" Gotch said, shouting the words over and over. Timothy Mickelson, the telegrapher, looked up with a startled expression, and laughed when he saw the expression on the Humboldt farmer's face. Gotch leaned across the counter and grabbed Mickelson, nearly knocking his glasses off and crushing the man in a bear hug.

"Tim, do you know what this message means?" He hardly waited for Mickelson to shake his head that he didn't. "It means," continued Frank, "that Humboldt is finally going to have a champion of the world in something....wrestling."

Gotch immediately dispatched a telegram to Burns informing him of the good news. It hadn't surprised him that Cochran had asked to do business with Burns rather than Klank, even though Cochran undoubtedly knew that Klank handled most of Gotch's business affairs. Still, it was Burns who commanded respect worldwide. Though the Farmer had never actually won an official world title, he had gained the respect of a world champion. And besides, Klank had a reputation for being a difficult man to do business with. Burns, it was well known, was stern, but wrestling was his great love and money matters were never as close to his heart as they were Klank's. In short, Cochran knew the financial arrangements would go much smoother with Burns representing Gotch than with Klank negotiating.

Burns wasted little time in responding to the telegram, and within seven days he was in Humboldt. The two men spent all day at the table in Gotch's living room, making plans and discussing strategy for the meeting with Cochran. They had not invited Klank, for fear he would be too demanding, and would hinder their plans for the titanic match. Both Burns and Gotch were concerned with the financial dealings, but not near so concerned as they were with the actual match. They considered it a monumental stroke of good fortune that Hackenschmidt was now, suddenly, willing to come to America and wrestle Gotch, and they were not willing to make any move which might endanger the match itself. Money matters would have to be secondary.

When Gotch and Burns parted company near sunset, they shook hands firmly on Gotch's porch.

"This is it, Farmer," said Frank solemnly, his jaw muscles tight and flexing as he stared into the face of his friend of many years. "This is the moment we've been waiting for."

Burns nodded grimly.

"We'll get the Russian Lion here, into our den, one way or another, my friend," he said. "And when we do...." His voice broke off, and the two men stared at one another. Burns swiveled and walked away. Gotch watched him climb into the small black automobile. Burns turned the ignition, and Gotch stood on the porch and watched until the auto disappeared from sight. He entered the house, went to his closet, and pulled out his running gear. He came back to the porch, limbered up briefly in the cool air, and started jogging down the very path Burns had departed on just minutes earlier. He ran his eyes over the Iowa landscape, the fields of corn gently stirring in the breeze, waiting to be harvested, and dreamed of facing the Russian Lion.

That had been two months ago. Sitting on Frank's front porch again, Burns described the New York trip, his dislike for the big cities, and the ordeal of traveling across country by train. He threw in colorful stories, and wrinkled his face for effect as he talked, and Gotch laughed politely at all the expected points. But his thoughts were far away. Finally, he could contain himself no longer.

"Let's have it, Farmer," he said straightforwardly. "What did the

Russian Lion have to say?"

Burns stared at his friend and pupil intently, recalling the night they had first met. He had been impressed from the very start with the young farmer from Humboldt. He thought, even back in Fort Dodge eight years earlier, in 1899, that some day this Iowa farm boy could become the greatest wrestler in the world. Now, he allowed himself one of his rare smiles, and Gotch stared at him all the more intently.

"We're on our way, Frank," said the Farmer. "Cochran has agreed to our terms, and you will meet Hackenschmidt next spring."

In anticipating this moment, Frank thought he would jump up and down, run in circles, and pull his hair, acting like a man gone mad. But, he did not feel like that at all. He smiled, then reached out a hand and laid it on Burns' shoulder.

"I knew you'd do it, Farmer," he said affectionately. "Where do we meet? Do we have to cross the water, or will it be here in the United States?"

"Chicago," said Burns. "Hack likes America, and enjoyed his first visit over here several years ago. Besides, Cochran thinks the American public is eager to see the Russian Lion again, and will turn out by the thousands to watch him everywhere he goes. Cochran says they will come to America at the end of this year, or very early next year, and begin their training, starting out in New York and working their way westward. They plan to draw thousands of fans to his work-outs alone."

"And the money," said Gotch, even though deep down he didn't even care about the purse. "How about that?"

"The lion's share to the Russian Lion," said Burns, with a chuck-le. "They are expecting a crowd of ten thousand, they say, and demand a guarantee of twenty thousand dollars for them. Their expenses are far greater than ours, of course, and so I agreed to that, and said we would take just ten thousand."

Burns paused, and Frank nodded his agreement.

"Let's get ready," he said, clapping his hands together. "Line up some bouts for me, Farmer."

He started to rise, but Burns reached out and firmly grabbed his arm. Gotch turned his gaze on his old friend.

"Frank, we must talk strategy," said the Farmer, his voice con-veying the seriousness. "The Russian Lion is....well, I've learned a great deal about him. He is a very, very formidable foe. The men I talked to in New York, who have seen him, say his strength is incred-ible, that it knows no limits.

"I went to see Muldoon at his health farm. Even he stands in awe of Hackenschmidt."

William Muldoon, America's first great sports hero, had learned how to wrestle as a young man in the Union camps between battles of the Civil War and returned to New York City to become a policeman. Muldoon continued his wrestling exploits, and soon was making more money by wrestling on weekends than by serving as a cop during the week. He gave up his police beat and became world champion in Greco-Roman wrestling. He retired undefeated and eventually trained John L. Sullivan as a boxer, and was now running a health farm. Muldoon was called "the solid man of sport" because of his impeccable reputation as a straight shooter, and was perhaps the most respected sportsman in the entire nation.

Gotch settled back down into his chair, ready to listen. He knew from years of experience that Burns never took a foe lightly, but Gotch detected a new, never-before-seen concern in his friend's tone, and in his eyes. The Farmer had never said much about Hackenschmidt, and now Gotch knew why. Perhaps this was the only man in the world Burns held a touch of fear for. Burns had crawled in the ring on thousand of occasions, and had wrestled against men far larger and younger. Still, he always emerged unscathed, and almost always the victor. But Gotch sensed that even Farmer Burns would hesitate before climbing into the ring to face the Russian Lion.

"You've wrestled just once this year, and here it is summer already. I want at least ten more matches before you tackle Hackenschmidt, and we want a couple on the East Coast, so we can train with Jack Carkeek. He's wrestled Hackenschmidt several times, once here and twice in Europe. Of course, he lost, and lost badly, but he can be of great help in our planning. He says Hackenschmidt is the most marvelous physical specimen he has ever seen, and he has enough strength in his massive muscles to tear you apart, Frank, but he also says he has one big weakness."

"And that is....?" asked Gotch, his gray eyes probing Burns' countenance, searching for an answer.

"He can be made to lose confidence if things go against him in the early going," said Burns. "He doesn't like to run, and his wind and endurance are not the best. But, then, they seldom need to be, as he finishes all of his matches very quickly. Carkeek says he either overpowers his opponents with his great strength, or he frightens them with his appearance the moment he disrobes."

Frank sat for a minute in silence, and then broke into a big grin.

"Well, we won't let him frighten us, will we," he said with a chuckle. He rose to his feet, and the Farmer did likewise.

"We'll train for a long, hard match," said the Farmer. "You'll have to do more running than ever before to build your endurance."

Gotch nodded.

"It's like that river in town, Farmer," he said. "Look at how it rolls along so peacefully and steadily. But further down, it erupts into violence as it breaks over the rocks and works its way through the narrow bed it has carved for itself. It may be peaceful here, but it will erupt soon enough.

"And that's how I'll wrestle the Russian Lion. At first, it will be peaceful enough. I will flow along just smoothly enough to lull him into complacency. And then, I'll erupt, just when he has grown confident....and tired."

Burns smiled, briefly.

"A good plan," he said. "Let's be about our business, for the Russian Lion will be about his at this very moment, I'm sure of that."

CHAPTER 10

Jack Carkeek walked the width of the room and extended his hand. He was a wiry and sinewy man, and his black mustache made him look like a leaner version of Tom Jenkins, though he was not nearly as handsome as was the Cleveland brawler who surrendered the American title to Gotch. But when Carkeek broke into a large and friendly grin, Gotch took his hand and knew he would like this man right off.

"Glad to meetcha, Frank," said Carkeek. "I've heard a lot about ya, out here in the East, but I haven't had a chance to see ya wrestle....since Butte, that is...and that was plenty enough that night."

The two men shared a quick laugh. It was September of 1905 when the two had tangled in Butte, Montana. Gotch had just lost to Jenkins, and was in a foul mood. Carkeek had been promoted as a former world champion, but in reality, he had been the European champion the year previous, before losing that title to Hackenschmidt. Gotch took out his frustration on Carkeek, exhausting him with a series of moves and tosses and then applying the toe hold in such fashion that Carkeek had begged for mercy.

Frank remembered the night well, not so much because of the man he wrestled but because of the toe hold. He had used it sparingly for several years previous, but that was the night he discovered just how devastating it could be. Since the strangle hold had been made illegal, the toe hold - at least Gotch's version - had become the most feared move in all of wrestling. Other wrestlers could apply it, but none could come close to matching the ferocity of Gotch's toe hold. It wasn't just in the strength Gotch could apply - it was also in the way he slipped it on, twisting his leg between that of an opponent, and the manner in which he gripped the foot of the foe and twisted it. The pain was almost unbearable, and Gotch had made many a wrestler limp away from a match in fear he might never walk correctly again. That wasn't the case, though; the effect always wore off, even if it did take awhile.

"Are you going to be using the toe hold on Hackenschmidt?" asked Carkeek, a gleam in his eye. "That I would like to see, for sure."

Gotch patted his old foe on the back.

"I will certainly use the toe hold, if I get the chance," said Gotch. They were standing in the middle of a large gymnasium, surrounded by athletes of assorted types and sizes working out. Some were engaged in fencing, while others were lifting weights. Overhead, more sped by on a big circular track, with the long iron railings alongside the track to prevent runners from falling off onto the main floor below. From the far corner of the gym came the rat-a-tat-tat of the speed bag being tattooed by flying fists, and the heavy thud of boxers working on the heavy bags trying to develop punching power. Pulleys squeaked, and men grunted as they tugged at them. It was the busiest time of the day for the New York Athletic Club, where Gotch had come with Burns for some special training.

"Where's the Farmer?" asked Carkeek as he and Gotch moved to a quiet corner and sat down on a thick wooden bench.

Gotch, attired in heavy sweat clothes, wiped the perspiration from his brow. He had been in the ring in the center of the room, going through some calisthenics, and had broken a good sweat. He had attracted a crowd of about fifty men as he went through his paces, but when they saw he wasn't sparring, they slowly drifted away, glancing over from time to time to see if he was about to engage in some sparring, either boxing or wrestling. He had been in the city for a week and had been using the gym twice a day, and had become a familiar sight to the regulars. As of yet, the press hadn't found out the champion from Iowa was on the scene, and Gotch preferred it that way. He wanted to get in some serious training before the reporters showed up with their questions.

"He should be along," said Gotch, lifting up a heavy black shoe to the bench and retying the laces. He glanced long and hard at Carkeek, who seemed guarded.

"What's wrong, Jack," he asked. "Are you worried about something?"

"No, not really," said Carkeek, avoiding Gotch's gaze. "No, not at all."

There was an awkward moment of silence, and they caught sight of Burns moving quickly across the gym toward them. He shook hands with Carkeek, and took a seat. He immediately sensed tension in the air.

"Hey, what's with you guys?" he asked, shrugging his shoulder, and looking at first Gotch and then Carkeek.

"Got me," shrugged Gotch back. "Jack seems a little upset, though,"

Both Iowans stared at the former European champ. He glanced around nervously, then turned toward Burns.

"Look, Farmer, don't take this wrong. I'm all for you guys. I'm on your side all the way. But...."

"Well, what is it, man?" asked the Farmer, quickly losing patience.

"I don't like saying this," he said, "but I had forgotten how small Frank is. I mean, Farmer, it don't look good. The Lion, well, he's just so damn big, so damn powerful...."

There was another awkward silence. Gotch laid a hand on Carkeek's shoulder.

"Jack, is that all that's bothering you?" When Carkeek nodded, Gotch broke out laughing, and so did the Farmer.

"Hell, Jack, you ain't no different than anybody else, is he, Farmer?" said Frank. "Why, no one, not even my closest friends back in Humboldt, think I have any kind of chance at all."

Burns nodded.

"So don't let that get you down," said Frank. "It sure ain't bothering me none."

Carkeek seemed genuinely relieved.

"Frank, Farmer, I'll tell you all I know about the Russian Lion, and I sure wish you the very best. But I got to tell you now, I got to keep it up front, I don't think you can beat him. I think he's unbeatable, that's all."

"Well, you just tell us all you know about Mr. Hackenschmidt," said Burns, "and you let Frank and me do the rest."

The three men adjourned to a back room, and Carkeek took over the conversation. He painted a chilling portrait for Gotch and Burns, describing in full detail the many and incredible feats of strength attributed to Hackenschmidt, who was generally regarded as one of the strongest men in the world, as well as the world's champion heavyweight wrestler.

"Gentlemen, he's as strong as any man who ever lived; certainly stronger than Sandow or Lurich," began Carkeek in the quiet of the room. He reached out and picked up a light piece of luggage he had set at the front of his couch. He leafed through it, and pulled out several pieces of crisp, heavy paper. He stared at them, then handed them over to Burns, who looked at them curiously. He shuffled through them - there were a dozen - and handed them to Gotch, a strange expression on his chiseled face.

Gotch raised an eyebrow when he saw the first. It was a photograph of an incredibly muscled man. He had a light, almost skin-colored cloth about his lions, and dark stockings that came up halfway on his calf. His head was bent, and turned toward his right, making his facial features impossible to see clearly. But there was no mistaking the physique....the muscles bulged everywhere. He was grasping a rope, his arms sporting the biggest muscles Frank had ever seen. He glanced over at Burns, who was staring back at him, expression unchanged, and then at Carkeek.

"This is our man?" asked Gotch, a touch of surprise in his voice. He had seen blurry newspaper photos of Hackenschmidt in action, but nothing this detailed.

Carkeek nodded, and Gotch turned to Burns. Slowly, Burns's stern expression faded away, and a grin overtook his features. Gotch grinned, too, and suddenly they both broke out laughing. Carkeek was puzzled.

"I'm sorry," said Frank, seeing Carkeek was puzzled. He remembered Carkeek was a German immigrant who had come to America just ten years prior. He was a European, and physique men were far more acceptable there than in America. Until the advent of the great Eugene Sandow, who toured America the decade previous with the Ziegfield Follies, few Americans had ever heard of men who exhibited their physique.

"Why would he want to pose like that?" asked Burns, turning his gaze on Carkeek, and trying to refrain from smiling and more outright laughter.

"Because," said Carkeek, very seriously, "it is an art, a way of expressing oneself. Besides, Hackenschmidt is far more than just a physique man, a flexer of muscles. He is incredibly strong."

Gotch thumbed through the remaining pictures, and found himself admiring the man he was looking at. Truly, he was a muscular phenomenon the likes of which he had never seen. Yankee Joe Rogers, whom he had defeated on a number of occasions, weighed around two hundred and fifty pounds, and was bigger than Hackenschmidt, but not nearly as muscular. He guessed Hackenschmidt was very, very powerful. He found himself listening intently to Carkeek's every word.

"Hackenschmidt was actually born in Estonia, but was discovered by the renown Dr. Krajewski and moved at age twenty to the doctor's mansion in St. Petersburg to train there. The doctor has a very well-equipped gymnasium, with all the best equipment of the day, and many of the best athletes of Russia train there. Dr. Krajewski was once the personal physician of Czar Nicholas II, and was the founder of the St. Petersburg Athletic and Cycling Club. He saw Hackenschmidt perform when he was just a youngster, and pronounced there on the spot that, with training, he could become the strongest man and the greatest athlete in all of Europe, at whatever sport he chose.

"He began competing in all sorts of weightlifting meets, and soon was the very best in Russia. They say he has lifted two hundred and ninety-one pounds overhead - and with just one arm, in a form of lifting called a bent press." Carkeek came to his feet, and bent over at the waist, throwing one arm up over his head, demonstrating the move. "He has lifted over three hundred and thirty pounds over his head in the continental clean and jerk, where you push the bar overhead with both hands, using your legs to help push. Then, believe it or not, he has taken the position of a wrestler's bridge, on his neck, and pulled three hundred pounds up to his chest and then pushed it straight overhead, as well."

Carkeek paused to let the effect of his words sink home, and he knew by the silence of his listeners that they were impressed.

"Most of his early wrestling was done in the continental style of Greco-Roman," he continued, and then waited patiently while Gotch told briefly of a Greco-Roman match he had entered in Canada. Gotch didn't bother to mention he had breezed through the competition, nor did Carkeek ask. He continued once Gotch had completed his story.

"That's where his upper body strength is so important. In that form of wrestling, where no holds are permitted below the waist, he is totally unbeatable. No man in all Europe, or the entire world, for that matter, can touch him here. He became the Greco-Roman champion of the world in 1901 in Vienna, where he defeated most of the top matmen in the world in a three-day tournament, without a close match. Then, he switched to the catch-as-catch-can style because it's so wide open in style, with a lot more moves and excitement. He defeated everyone there just as easily, and became the catch-as-catch-can champion of the world, as well."

Burns interrupted at this point: "That's where he first met Jenkins, in London, if I'm not mistaken."

"Yes," replied Carkeek, leaning forward in his intensity. He was very interested in discussing Hackenschmidt. Gotch knew Carkeek was sincere in his description of Hackenschmidt, and he also knew the Russian Lion was, in all probability, as wonderful an athlete as Carkeek made him out to be. Yet, he knew he was human, and all humans, no matter how great, have weaknesses. He continued to listen closely.

"He defeated Jenkins, himself a very powerful wrestler, as you well know, Frank, in Greco-Roman wrestling in London. He threw him twice in under forty minutes, and Jenkins was unbelieving. He demanded a rematch, under catch-a-catch-can rules, and Hackenschmidt even agreed to come to America as he had a strong desire to see this country. The result was no different....he tossed Jenkins again in straight falls, in seven minutes less than an hour."

"But, Jenkins is the type of wrestler who would play straight into his hands," said Burns, a rough, calloused hand fingering his chiseled chin, then tugging slightly on the corners of his short, trim mustache. "It would be strength against strength, and Jenkins, strong as he is, would be no match for Hackenschmidt, it would seem. We won't use strength against strength; instead, we will pit speed, skill and conditioning against strength."

"Yes, a good strategy," said Carkeek, "at least in part. But don't underestimate Hackenschmidt's skill. He is very clever, and has learned his craft well. They say he has engaged in over three hundred bouts, and has not lost once, not even one fall. In fact, very seldom do his foes last near as long as did Jenkins. It is to Jenkins' credit that he was able to give the Russian Lion such a tough struggle."

It was the first time Carkeek had used the nickname of Russian Lion, and Gotch smiled at it. Yes, if ever a man was fit to wear the title of lion, it was this Russian, Frank thought to himself. He seemed to be a veritable Hercules, maybe even stronger than the fabled hero of ancient Greece. One thing Frank felt certain of, though, was that he would severely test this Russian Lion, test him deep into his soul and then he, as well as the entire world, would learn if Hackenschmidt was a lion or a man.

"But we know there is a problem in the lion's den, don't we?" asked Burns, arching an eyebrow as he studied the former European champion.

Carkeek shook his head slightly and stood, walking to a window. He stood for a moment peering out into the street below. There were still some horses and buggies in view, but mostly the street was filled with automobiles, the incredible machine that had been introduced just a mere twenty years earlier and was already threatening to engulf the world, at least the streets of America. He sighed, then turned and walked back to the two wrestlers staring after him.

"It pains me to speak ill of Hackenschmidt, for he is truly a great athlete and a great man," said Carkeek. "But you are my friends, as well, at least in heart and in thought. I am now an American, and I would like to see the world's title come to these shores and remain here. And just maybe, Frank, you are the man to do it, though I would not care to cast a heavy wager in that direction right now."

"Nor would I ask you to, Jack," said Frank, with a little smile.

"No, no, of course not," said Carkeek, not aware that the Iowan was joking with him, and didn't really care at all which way Carkeek would wager when the moment of truth arrived. He sat down again, and turned toward Burns.

"I saw this happen to him just once," Carkeek said, measuring his words slowly. "He seemed to lose heart the more the match wore on. He is used to winning quickly and easily, and the longer a match goes, the less enthusiasm he seems to show. I must admit that on this one occasion, I began to wonder about the depth of his fighting spirit. He is basically a kind man, maybe even a gentle man, and I believe he regards wrestling as a chess match of sorts, rather than a fight, if you know what I mean."

There was a long pause as all three men pondered Carkeek's words.

"The way to beat him, then, is to frustrate him and outlast him," said Burns, staring hard at Gotch.

"Yes, maybe so," said Carkeek. "But, that could also be a very dangerous game. It would be a disaster for most of the wrestlers in the world to exchange holds with him, and yet there is no other way to sap that marvelous strength. To make him use the strength is to make him spend it."

There was another moment of silence while Gotch studied the photos once again, and Burns sat lost in strategy planning. Gotch handed the photos to Burns, who turned them over to Carkeek without so much as a glance. Burns stood up, ran his thick hands over his trousers, and placed his derby on his head.

"Do I really look like Bat Masterson, that Old West gunfighter fella who is now writing sports for the New York papers?" he said. "I saw a picture of him the other day, and a couple of the wrestlers said we sure look alike."

Frank chuckled at his mentor's antics, and slapped his thighs hard. He stood and tossed an arm around Burns' shoulders. Frank was two inches taller than the Farmer, and now about forty pounds heavier, as well.

"Shoot, Farmer, you're about twice as ornery lookin' as Masterson. Probably could outdraw him, too, if it came down to a shootout."

Burns chuckled too, then pulled away, a serious expression overtaking his features.

"Tomorrow, gentlemen, we begin our work," he said. "We will plan our every move, our every workout, and within a year Frank Gotch will be the heavyweight champion of not only America, but the entire world. Or my name ain't Farmer Burns."

CHAPTER 11

T he year 1907 was a lean one for Frank in terms of wrestling as suitable opponents were tough to come by. His prowess as America's greatest wrestler was well earned and indisputable, after the grueling victories over Tom Jenkins in the previous years. In addition, his toe hold had replaced the strangle hold, officially illegal but still used to some degree, as the most dreaded hold in the sport. While the strangle hold could cause a wrestler to lapse into unconsciousness and, if not checked, could actually cause death, the toe hold was strictly a submission move. No wrestler ever passed out from its application, but the pain was almost unbearable.

Though other wrestlers sought to use the toe hold, after Gotch's success with it, they were never quite able to apply it with the same degree of authority Gotch managed. It was not simply in the way he positioned his legs between those of his foe, and then twisted the foe's leg around his by grabbing the toe and driving it in whatever direction he wished, but it was in the strength of his arms, and the special way he slapped it on. The toe hold of Gotch was enough to make most stout hearted matmen quake in fear when he began working for it, and was enough to keep those other than the stout hearted out of the ring.

After defeating tough and talented Fred Beell in Chicago in April, Gotch had to be content to grapple twice with Klank. It wasn't the best of arrangements, but Gotch needed action and the fans clamored to see him. He dispatched his manager with ease in front of nearly nine thousand fans in Denver in August, then threw Klank and the big Indian, War Eagle, on the same night, October 29, in Kansas City before another crowd of nine thousand fans.

He traveled to Montreal near the close of November to take on several men in exhibitions, and found the bitter cold almost too much to take. Sitting in a hotel room late at night, he wrote a brief note to Gladys on a postcard: "Hello Gladys: Beastly cold here, I'm going back to the states tomorrow." He signed it simply "Frank." He had made a point to visit her family during the last two years and they had become pen pals, writing each other on a regular basis. He looked forward to her letters when he was away from Iowa for extended periods of time. And on December 6, he closed out his competition for the year with another win over War Eagle.

After spending the Christmas holidays with his family in Humboldt and stopping by to see the Oestrich family twice, Frank opened 1908 with a trip to the east. He had no trouble dumping Hjalmar Lundin on January 21 in Lowell, Massachusetts, whipped Albert Solomon three days later, and moved west to Chicago for another bout with Beell. It was amazing how the crowds flocked to see Gotch perform against Beell, even though Gotch had now avenged the earlier defeat three successive times. Still, the upset by Beell in New Orleans in 1906 had caught the wrestling crowd's fancy, and they were captivated by the prospect of another startling upset.

But he handled Beell with ease in Chicago, before traveling back east to take on huge Yankee Joe Rogers. Promoters were reluctant to match Gotch with any wrestler under the normal conditions and the New York match with Rogers was contested under the conditions that Gotch had to throw the behemoth, who now weighed over two hundred and fifty pounds, five times in an hour. Gotch tossed Rogers twice, and the official result was "failed to throw"....not a loss, but not a win. Rogers, whom Gotch had defeated on several occasions, so impressed the Iowa grappler this time around, however, that Frank asked him to come to Humboldt while he finished training for the match of his life. Less than a month after wrestling Rogers, Gotch was scheduled to climb into the ring in Chicago at the Dexter Pavilion and meet the Russian Lion.

The Gotch-Hackenschmidt match had caught the fancy of America's sporting public, and the press, as well. Newspapers across the nation were full of information about the upcoming battle, labeling it the greatest athletic event since Gentleman James J. Corbett stunned fans everywhere by taking the world's heavyweight boxing title from the legendary Sullivan on September 7, 1892, at the Olympic Club in New Orleans with a knockout in the twenty-first round. That victory had made Corbett the toast of America, and there were plenty of folks who thought a victory by Gotch over Hackenschmidt - though highly unlikely - would do the same for the farm boy from Iowa.

Rogers, Burns, Klank and Gotch made the trip from New York in four days by train, and were dog-tired when they arrived in Humboldt after the auto ride from Fort Dodge, where they had departed the train. Though Humboldt had a train station of its own, it was smaller than Fort Dodge's and it was often much easier to book passage to Fort Dodge, then drive the fifteen miles to Humboldt. They were met at the station by Elmer Smith and several other Humboldt friends with autos. Riding in the front auto with Smith, Frank recalled the trip the two of them had made to Fort Dodge in December of 1899 to meet the Farmer. It had been just eight years earlier, yet it seemed to both of them like a century before.

"That was some night, Frank," said Smith, beaming with pride at being asked - he had received a telegram from Frank three days earlier - to meet his famous friend at the Fort Dodge station. "But just think of all that has happened to you since then. Why, you're more famous than Jeffries, Corbett, or any of them. Surely, you're ten times better known than that new guy....that fighter who's the supposed heavyweight champion of the world now. What's his name? Oh yeah, Burns. If he wasn't named the same as a famous wrestler, no one would even know who he is."

Gotch laughed heartily and looked over at Smith. The years had been kind to him, also. He wouldn't brag about it, but he had become very successful in his farming, and owned several hundred acres of prime Iowa farmland. Maybe not quite as much as Frank himself did - Gotch had invested most of his money in farmland, and was thinking about branching out into a number of other business ventures - but Elmer had certainly done well for himself. There was something to be said for just plain good old hard work on the farm, Frank thought to himself, and he admired the way Smith and others, like his pa and brothers, had made a good, clean and decent life for themselves.

But he couldn't have gone that route, he knew now, riding back to Humboldt with his friends surrounding him. He also knew he didn't wrestle just for himself. There was plenty of glory to be gained in the matted rings of America, as most of the country looked up to sporting heroes like himself and Cy Young, the great baseball pitcher, and Frank Baker, the man they called "Home Run Baker" because he smacked seven of them in just one season a couple of years previous.

Gotch knew he wrestled for Iowa, and for friends like Elmer Smith. Frank was a God-fearing and God-loving man, and knew he had certain God-given abilities and skills he was obligated to use, for the glorification of his creator, as well as for himself, his loved ones, and other Iowans. Yes, for Frank Gotch, wrestling on behalf of an entire state was gratifying and pleasurable.

"Why, old Tommy Burns isn't such a bad chap," said Gotch, bumping along. "I've met him on two occasions, and he always seems pleasant enough, even though half the newspapers I read these days sort of downgrade him, and say he's running from Jack Johnson."

"The other half say he's' running from you, Frank," returned Smith, keeping his eye on the road. He wasn't all that used to these automobiles, and still preferred horse and buggy in many circumstances. But he had wanted to make good time today, and no horse could match these new fangled contraptions for speed, he reasoned. It was hard for him to believe he could go twenty miles an hour, and maintain that speed for over an hour. He felt the automobile was around to stay, but he knew it would never go any faster than it was traveling right here today on this road. He doubted, in fact, it could ever be improved, so powerful was its performance.

"And don't forget, he's Jeffries own choice," said Gotch. "He wanted Burns and Marvin Hart to slug it out for the title, and was well pleased when Burns won. Jeff told me he thinks Tommy's a good one, and that he could beat Johnson, but just doesn't want to fight a black man."

They rumbled on in silence until before Smith worked up the courage to ask about Hackenschmidt.

"You worried about that Russian Lion fellow?" he asked, squinting into the sun. Gotch looked over at Smith quickly, and smiled. They had been friends for nearly twenty years, and Gotch knew how loyal Smith was. He would support Frank in any situation, any time. But, Gotch detected a note of concern in Smith's voice. Even Elmer had doubts when it came to George Hackenschmidt.

"What's to worry about," said Frank, flashing a big grin. He waited for Smith to look back at him, but soon realized the subject was too touchy, and Smith couldn't face him then. There was concern written on his face.

"Folks, even some good ones in Humboldt, are scared for you, Frank," he said stiffly.

"Not you, I hope," said Frank good naturedly, slapping his friend hard on the shoulder.

Smith grinned sheepishly, and finally turned to look at Gotch.

"Heck, no!" he said. "Why, I know you can whip that Russian Lion," he paused. "But, just how do you plan to do it, Frank? They say he's the strongest man who ever lived. And they say he knows more about wrestling than any man alive."

"Well, you can hold it right there," said Gotch, sounding half serious. "Do you really think any man alive, anywhere in the world, knows more than Farmer Burns about wrestling? And, sure, he's strong, but that's why I brought Yankee Joe Rogers back to camp to work out with me these last several weeks. Do you really think that Hack - that's what they call him overseas, you know - can be much stronger than Joe Rogers? Maybe a bit, but not much. And besides, I been studying with a man named Jack Carkeek for the past several weeks. Carkeek has wrestled Hack, and knows a lot about him. He sure doesn't think he's unbeatable." Gotch paused and chuckled again.

"But, he doesn't think I can do it."

Smith, puzzled, started laughing too. They roared for about two minutes, then stopped quickly, looking at one another. Frank's face had grown as serious as Smith recalled ever seeing it. His jaw was shut tight, his eyes blazing. Smith suddenly felt cold and alone under the menacing glare. He had heard stories of Frank's ability to turn his personality upside down at a moment's notice when he entered the ring, but he had always doubted it. To him, Frank Gotch was just a good old country boy....a friend and pal. He had never before seen the hardened side of the man. But, he saw it now, and it shook him.

"I mean to have that title, Elmer," he said, his voice low and controlled. It had a steel edge to it, and Smith felt a chill go down his back. Suddenly, he felt far better about Gotch's chances against the Russian Lion.

"The Farmer has mapped out a strategy, one that will carry us to the top. We're gonna win this one, Elmer. I want it for the Farmer, for ma and pa, for Humboldt and for Iowa."

Smith didn't know what to say next, but hoped that some topic of conversation would leap into mind, so he could feel comfortable once again. Finally, the idea came to him.

"Say, I saw that little Oestrich gal again - well, she's not so little, or young, I mean, anymore - and she asked about you right off. She and her mother, she asked about you too."

Gotch brightened, and his combative mood departed immediately. He turned to Smith with a new sparkle in his eye. Smith was delighted his friend's mood, no matter how short lived and directed elsewhere, had passed.

"I sent her a postcard card from Montreal not long ago. I'd sure like to see her when I get home," said Gotch. "What did they have to say, Mrs. Oestrich and her Gladys?"

"Seems they've been following your career quite close. They asked a lot of questions about your travels and your matches, then answered the questions before I could even open my mouth. They're real fans of yours, Frank, and that Gladys....why, I hardly recognized her. She's grown up a lot, and she's a real beauty, she is."

"Then, they don't look down upon my being a professional athlete, and a grappler, to boot?" asked Gotch. He had thought about Gladys a great deal during the past year, more than he had ever thought about any woman. He had met his share of attractive women; he found that men loved to introduce him to women when he was between matches, and even though it wasn't fashionable for women to attend boxing matches or wrestling bouts, a far greater number than ever before were starting to come, even though they continued to sit way in the back. He even met a young school teacher who he spent a great deal of time with, but they eventually went their own way. After all, each had a career to think of, and he was involved with heavy travel and various commitments.

But even when he was with her, Frank had found himself thinking of Gladys, wishing she would hurry and grow up, so he could keep the promise he made several years ago back in Humboldt when she sold him the tickets to a raffle. He was anxious to visit her when he arrived in Humboldt, but he knew he wouldn't be able to spend much time with her. After all, he would climb into the ring for the match of his life in just under thirty days.

As they came over the top of the last hill blocking Humboldt from view, Gotch felt a strange tingling in his back. He had been home for Christmas just three months earlier, but the land had been so different then, blanketed with snow, trees stripped naked. Now, in middle March, Iowa was experiencing an unusually early death of winter, and it was warm and comfortable. He had told Burns he had hoped the weather would be warm enough to permit long runs through the countryside, and luck had been on his side.

They thought about going south, to Arkansas or even Florida, to train, so important was running to their plan. But Frank had opted for Iowa because he felt he would be more inspired and would actually train harder among his hometown folks. Burns had agreed, and the southern trip was vetoed. Now, with the warm weather facing them,

Frank breathed a sigh of relief. He hated to run outside when it was cold, primarily because he had to bundle up so heavily in clothes just to keep warm that it hindered his motion and slowed him down.

They detoured to the south of town, and headed straight for the Gotch farm house. Chugging up the very last hill, Frank felt a sense of exhilaration he had not known since he had won the American title from Jenkins. He was coming home, and the next time he came home he would be heavyweight wrestling champion of the world....the first ever from America.

He saw his ma working in the garden, bent and dressed in black, and he was surprised when she didn't look up immediately. Then he remembered her hearing was fading, and she probably could not hear the approach of the automobile, despite its noise. They were almost to the driveway when she glanced up, and saw her son waving to her from the front seat. She straightened slowly, and let the hoe slide from her fingers. She lifted her dress a bit from her ankles, and began moving swiftly to the house, her eyes glued on the three automobiles pulling into her yard.

Before Smith had even come to a complete halt, Frank leapt out his side and raced toward his mother, grabbing her and lifting her off the ground, and swirling her around. He held on tight, then let her down slowly. Her face was wrinkled and hard, reflecting a rugged existence, but there was pride in her eyes. He kissed her tenderly on both cheeks, and they talked softly for several minutes.

"Hello, Mrs. Gotch," said a husky voice, and they turned to face the Farmer.

"Good day, Mr. Burns," Amelia returned in a stiff and formal voice. "I trust you've been taking good care of my Frank."

Burns smiled and tipped his black derby. He was as rugged as the day was long, yet he had a way with women, when he was of a mind to. And Mrs. Gotch was no different. She may have hated the Farmer without knowing him, but once she had come to know him well, and had been subjected to his impeccable manners and the great respect he held for women, her barriers had begun to crumble.

Frank introduced his mother to Yankee Joe, who left her speechless with his size, and to several other members of his entourage. They all tromped into the house, and sat around the living room chatting amiably while she busied herself fixing a huge meal. One by one, Frank's brothers filed in from the field, and his pa, and he introduced them all to his friends from the east, who would be his training partners for the next several weeks. Besides Yankee Joe, he had Jess

Westergard, who was smaller and quick as greased lightning, and Klank, who was the same size as Frank and tough and strong. It was all part of the Farmer's plan, wrestling in succession a big man, a small man and a man of ordinary size. The big man would test your strength, the small man improve your quickness and the man of ordinary size would help you to improve your endurance, if you wrestled them in that order, claimed the Farmer.

Though Frank was enjoying the reunion and talking to his brothers about the upcoming match, it wasn't long before Farmer insisted they move down to Frank's place and set up the training headquarters. Frank had offered his house to the men; he had two bedrooms upstairs besides his own, and the parlor, with thick bedding placed on the floor, would serve as another sleeping area.

Smith stayed around, as did the other Humboldt men who had driven to Fort Dodge to provide transportation up to Frank's farm, and it was nearly midnight by the time they departed. After the training partners turned in for the night, Frank led the Farmer upstairs to the bedroom he had reserved for him.

"Just one thing I got to do before we get real serious, Farmer," he said, looking his mentor straight in the eye.

"And what's that?" asked Burns, staring straight back and not giving any quarter.

"I have to call on a young lady, and her family." Seeing the Farmer was about to speak, Frank held up a hand, as if to warn him of the futility of argument. "Got to do it, Farmer, to get it off my mind. Then, I'll be all yours."

Burns stared hard at him, then nodded. He turned and walked toward the bed.

"I was going to agree with you right off, if'n you'd given me half a chance," he said. "It's about time you got to thinking really serious about some woman."

Frank stood in bewilderment in the doorway as he watched Burns strip to his long johns and climb into bed, pulling the covers up over his head. He dropped the blankets for just a second, looking up at Gotch.

"A good woman will only make you stronger, and more of a man. Just make sure she's a good one, like my Mary."

A rooster's crowing brought Frank upright in bed. It had been some time since he'd awakened to the sound, and he relished it. He figured

Burns would be up already, and he was right. He smelled coffee coming from the kitchen. But, he was just as correct when he surmised that the others, and especially Yankee Joe, who claimed he needed far more sleep than an ordinary man because of his size, would still be sleeping.

Frank came down the stairs and entered the kitchen where Burns was sitting at a table. The Farmer was already in his wrestling togs - a heavy cotton shirt and a heavy wool pair of pants. He looked bright and chipper, his short dark hair brushed straight forward in Roman style. Gotch figured he had even taken time to smooth down his mustache.

The Farmer glanced up from the table when he heard Gotch approach, and nodded at him.

"You look a sight," he said. Gotch remembered he had forgotten to smooth his hair, and put a burly hand on the back of his head, smashing the hair down. He also rubbed his chin, and realized he was in bad need of a shave. "Hope you ain't plannin' on seeing anyone special looking like that."

Frank smiled. "Nope, I guess I do have some tidying up to do."

When he came back down the stairs, his dark hair was neatly parted in the middle and he was clean shaven. He was also wearing his running outfit, heavy white woolen shirt and black work pants, and a pair of heavy black boots.

"Where you going now, dressed like that?" asked Burns.

"Figured I'd kill two birds with one stone," offered Frank. "As long as I'm going into town, I might as well run in. This way, I'll just run past the Oestrich home, and it'll look like I just happened by on my regular routine of running. Pretty cagey, huh?" he smiled, tapping his finger on his temple and winking at Burns.

The Farmer snorted in reply. But as Frank was heading out the door, he spoke up again, just loud enough so his pupil couldn't help but hear.

"Don't know if it's cagey or not, but if you're trying to win her sympathy you'll probably succeed. You look like you're in need of a little attention."

After limbering up briefly in the yard, Gotch jogged down the road, unmindful of Burns' parting comments. It was a beautiful morning, and a great day for just about anything, including running. It was a three-mile trip into town, and normally he would break it in half, running a hard mile and a half, then resting, then finishing up with a lazy mile and a half. But not today. He had two reasons for running hard: first, he couldn't afford to take it easy with the big match so close, and secondly, he was anxious to see Gladys.

He began having visions of what Gladys would look like as he put the miles behind himself and got caught up in the sheer joy of running. He recalled all the times he ran this route in his youth, fantasizing that wild Indians were on his trail, or Liver-eating Johnson, the feared mountain man of the west. Back then, those thoughts would provoke him to greater speed, but no longer. Now, he merely chuckled, recalling such terrors as nothing more than the fancy of youth.

He drank in the cool, refreshing morning air. He had been in the big cities, and enjoyed them for what they had to offer - excitement, big matches, huge and exciting crowds and big money. But he was an Iowa boy at heart. He had been prodded by a number of sports promoters and newspaper writers to move to the East for "business reasons", but he had too grand a stake in Iowa and Iowa's future now. He owned over five hundred acres. In addition, he was looking into several other business deals that would involve him more with Humboldt once he decided to retire from the ring.

The last thought made him angry; "here, I'm just about to enter the most important bout of my life, and I'm thinking of retirement," he thought. He chided himself, and pushed even harder, racing up a small hill that he normally would have coasted up. He was fighting for his breath at the top, but wouldn't allow himself to stop. "No, I've got to pay for the thoughts I've been allowing myself," he said firmly, and started down the back side of the hill at the same pace. But he was running too fast, not paying attention, and his momentum carried him even faster. Suddenly, he was tumbling head over heels down the gravely road. He rolled twice and came back to his feet the third time, and he kept running, though much slower. He looked around to see if there was anyone present to witness this ridiculous exhibition, but there were only a small herd of cows chewing nearby. Several of them glanced his way, but immediately returned to their meals.

He figured he left the farm by seven thirty, and it would be slightly after eight by the time he hit the outskirts of Humboldt. He trotted into the town with eyes straight ahead. There were a few scattered wooden homes on the outer limits, and then he moved silently through the residential area, heading for the downtown business area. Humboldt was a town of about one thousand citizens, and the downtown area was only about five blocks long, and three blocks wide. He ran past the country store, two saloons, a boarding house and several other businesses one couldn't recognize readily from the outside.

At the center of town, he turned northward. There was little activity, but two men standing on a corner looked up.....and stared hard after him as he padded past. They recognized him, shouted his name, and he half turned, waved and smiled, as he moved on down the street. He hadn't recognized them, but he had grown accustomed to people - even in big cities like Chicago - calling out his name. He was a celebrity, that he knew and understood. He surely wasn't held in the same esteem James Jeffries or George Hackenschmidt was. Not yet, anyway.

A group of school children trudged by, talking animatedly and pushing one another playfully. He ran past them, and nodded and winked without them knowing who he was. But one of the boys in the back shouted out his name - "Hey, that's Frank Gotch, the wrestler" - and Frank was almost out of earshot when he heard another voice from the pack say, "Aw, he ain't so hot." Frank chuckled as he turned west on Jacob Street. Leave it to the youth of Humboldt to keep him modest, he thought to himself.

He stopped running and walked a block. He was in a heavy residential area again, and was nearing the Oestrich home. Her father, Alfred, was a lawyer, and her brother, George, was employed by a bank, though he still lived at home. Gotch saw the two-story, white wood house and slowed to a walk as he approached it. Though he was hardly bashful with his friends or in a ring, Frank had always been shy in the company of women.

He figured it was shortly after eight, and he didn't know if the family would be up and about yet. He stopped short of the house, pondered the situation, and slowly turned and headed the opposite way. He walked down to the banks of the Des Moines River, and sat idly in the grass for a long spell, pulling out stubs of brown grass and chewing on the pieces, a hundred different thoughts parading through his mind. Suppose she really didn't want him to call on her. After all, he was almost thirty-one years old now, and she was but eighteen, just barely out of high school. She had said in her last letter she was planning on going away to college, probably at Ames, where Iowa State College was located, but she planned on remaining in Humboldt for one year to work and earn some money for the education she hoped to gain. Perhaps she had several suitors now. But she hadn't mentioned any in her letters, and she had seemed genuinely warm in her words, and had closed her last letter by saying that he must - absolutely must - stop by the house as soon as he arrived in town. She had followed up by saying her father and brother followed his wrestling exploits very carefully, and would be anxious to discuss them with him. They were, she wrote, very big fans of his. But, she hadn't written that she, too, was a fan. He wondered if she liked wrestling at all.

After what seemed an eternity, he pulled himself up from the grass and found the sweat had dried upon his body. That was a mortal sin, in the Farmer's book of training, and Frank felt stiff and uncomfortable. More than that, he reasoned, he stunk. Dried sweat. Hardly a proper fashion in which to meet a lady one hoped to impress.

He decided to scrap the entire affair. He would walk through town, and then run back to the farm. It was best to forget Gladys for now, anyway, he rationalized, and to consider approaching her again when he was the heavyweight wrestling champion of the world, not just America.

Humboldt was alive with people as he moved through it this time, and he was stopped a number of times. The editor of the paper discovered he was in town, and corralled him, dragging him by the elbow into the newspaper office for an interview. He told Gotch he was "hot news", one of the true sporting heroes of America, and Frank felt flattered, but uncomfortable, as other employees of the newspaper gathered around, smiling and shaking his hand. Soon, a crowd gathered outside the window of the office, with faces, young and old, pressed up against the glass, trying to peer in and catch a glimpse of the hometown hero.

When Frank finally broke away - insisting he had to get back or the Farmer would make him run one hundred miles the next day - he had spent over an hour in the office. He backed away, accepting best wishes from the staff and pushed his way gently through the door. He was amazed to discover nearly one hundred people had gathered outside. They reached to shake his hand and to pat him on the back, and though he felt desperately like sprinting away, he smiled and chatted back as best he could, nodding appreciatively at all the flattering comments.

When he had finally reached the street and was about to pull away, he saw a familiar face smiling, approaching with hand outstretched. Dressed in a three-piece suit with a derby sitting squarely on his head, he was the picture of affluence and respectability, and painted a strong contrast to Frank, who in his own mind looked the clown, attired in running suit and heavy black boots. But he knew there was no ducking Mr. Oestrich, no matter how ridiculous he felt.

"Frank, Frank, so good, so very good to see you," said Oestrich warmly, shaking his hand and throwing an arm around his shoulder.

Frank smiled but tried to pull away just a bit so Gladys' father would-n't have to go home that evening with a report of how Frank Gotch hit town, looking and smelling like a backwoodsman, or a garbage col-lector, or worse.

Oestrich would have none of it, however, and was oblivious to Frank's attire and discomfort. He talked a streak, telling him how proud all of Humboldt was of him. Frank merely nodded, and grinned sheepishly, searching for a way to extricate himself from what he saw as a very uncomfortable situation. But when Oestrich invited him to dinner that night, Frank felt a flutter in his stomach. He nodded agree-ment, heard Oestrich say how happy Gladys would be to see him again, and told him they would be expecting him at eight.

The run back to the farm was far easier than he had anticipated. He ran like he was thirty pounds lighter - at two hundred pounds, run-ning wasn't easy for Frank. He was spent by the time he reached the farm. He had run six miles, with just a two-hour break between two three-mile runs, and he was feeling the effects. He walked into the farmyard, and heard shouts coming from the back of the barn on the southwest corner. He headed in that direction, and turned the corner of the barn. There, some twenty yards beyond it, were Burns, Rogers, Westergard and Klank working at a brisk pace. They already had a heavy bag hanging from a tree, and wall pulleys set against the barn wall. In the ring, Rogers and Westergard were pummeling one anoth-er, with Burns and Klank watching from the sidelines.

Gotch grabbed hold of the lower rope and pulled himself up and slipped between the ropes into the ring. The two wrestlers stopped and looked over at him.

"All right," he said, a forced scowl on his features. "Which of you two buzzards is ready to go a few rounds with the next heavyweight champion of the world?"

CHAPTER 12

He arrived precisely at eight, and was greeted by Mr. Oestrich and Lawrence, who led him into the drawing room and leveled a barrage of questions. He had put on his best gray suit, and wore a derby for one of the few occasions in his entire life. He had wanted to erase the impression he feared he had left with Gladys' father earlier in the day.

The three men had been engaged in light-hearted conversation for nearly thirty minutes when Gladys entered the room with her mother. It was the first time he had seen the two of them together in some time, and the first time he had seen Gladys in little over a year. He was struck by the change in her. While she had been a cute little waif the first time he had met her selling raffle tickets six years earlier, she had grown into an attractive young lady. Still, he had not been prepared for the transition that had occurred the last year, or more. She was, in his estimation, completely grown up, a strikingly attractive woman of eighteen. She wore a floor length dress of light green, with lace at the hem and the wrists, as well as the neckline. Her raven hair was pulled back in a bun, accentuating her clean features. She smiled demurely at him, and he thought he caught the briefest blush, as well. He finally turned his gaze on Mrs. Oestrich, who seemed little more than an older version of Gladys, dainty herself, with her hair also pulled back in a bun.

"It's so nice to see you again, Mr. Gotch," said Mrs. Oestrich, with her hand outstretched. Frank touched it lightly, afraid to appear overly bold. Also, she was so frail appearing that he actually feared he might harm her. She seemed to detect his concern, and smiled quickly. "Don't worry," she said in her tiny voice, "you shan't harm me. We Oestrich women are much sturdier than we might seem."

The men in the background chuckled, and Frank felt the stiffness evaporate. He bowed slightly and kissed her on the hand, and felt somewhat foolish for doing so. But Mrs. Oestrich seemed pleased by the gesture. She turned slightly, extending a hand in the direction of her daughter.

"And you remember Gladys, I'm sure."

Frank stepped forward and reached for Gladys' hand, too. She hesitated a moment, then offered it, smiling slightly, and Frank bowed again and kissed her hand.

"Yes, I certainly do. We have exchanged letters from time to time."

Gladys smiled widely then.

"I was the envy of all the boys in school, and some of the girls, too, I might add, when I informed them I had received a letter from Frank Gotch, champion wrestler," she said. Frank listened intently to her words, trying to assess them. Was she proud of the fact he was a wrestler, or was she teasing with him? He couldn't tell.

"Dinner is ready, if you gentlemen are," said Mrs. Oestrich, and they paraded out to the dining room.

There was a smattering of polite conversation during the dinner hour, and then the men adjourned to the drawing room. The senior Oestrich was interested in hearing more tales of the big city, while his son asked a number of questions about the financial aspects of the athletic world. Frank's purses were well known, as they appeared in all the papers. The two men expressed amazement at the size of Gotch's earnings, and Frank spent a considerable amount of time trying to explain all the costs which must be subtracted. There were travel and hotel expenses, plus he had a manager in Klank and a trainer in Burns to pay, as well as sparring partners. Even now, he said, he was paying for Rogers, Klank and Westergard, and that was no small matter, the way they ate.

When it was ten o'clock, Frank stood to excuse himself. He had searched for Gladys, and was keenly disappointed she had not come into the room at all. He had enjoyed talking with the men, but he had come for the purpose of sharing some time with Gladys. The elder Mr. Oestrich saw him to the door, and bid him good night, wishing him well in the big match in Chicago. He issued a standing invitation for Frank to visit at any time. "Just drop by the office any day," and "we'd love to have you again for dinner."

Gotch donned his derby and stepped down off the porch and returned to his automobile. He stepped to the front and cranked it up, and turned around....only to let out a short gasp, one which was met by a series of giggles.

Standing directly behind him was Gladys. She had approached so silently that she would have given pride to any Indian who walked these very spots less than a century before.

Frank was speechless. There was only the light of a full moon overhead, and a gas streetlight half a block away.

"I didn't mean to frighten you, Mr. Gotch," she said, smiling at her joke. "But I guess I should have let you know I was right behind you, or else I might have gotten trampled when you turned around and started for your auto."

Frank was glad it was so dark, and she couldn't see the red which was rushing to his cheeks. He stammered for a moment, trying to tell her he was not at all frightened, but merely surprised, and delighted, to find her there. He cleared his throat, and started over.

"Hardly frightened, Miss Oestrich," he said in a light voice, trying to show his tenderness. He was frightened, though; frightened she would think he was a brute of a man who was nothing more than a professional wrestler who went through life slapping toe holds on people and making them beg for mercy. He wanted to let her know he was far more than just a wrestler....that he merely wrestled for a living.

"I am, however, surprised to find you out at this late hour." He immediately felt he had said the wrong thing, and she would scamper back into the house. He hoped to add something to keep her from doing just that, but he was tongue-tied.

"It's not that late," she offered back. "And besides, I didn't get to talk with you at all. My father and brother so dominated the evening that we weren't allowed a minute to talk. After all," she said with a smile, "they have never written to you, have they?"

Frank laughed gently, and suddenly felt warm and comfortable again. She was taking pains to make him feel at ease, and they both sensed she was succeeding.

"Can you go for a short drive, or would you like to take a walk?" he asked. She turned her glance back at the house, and then looked up at Frank. She was standing very close, and he realized how small she really was. About five-foot tall, and less than one hundred pounds, he guessed. She slipped her hand between his chest and arm, and placed it on his arm.

"I can think of nothing I would like better than to stroll with you down to the park," she said. He caught scent of her perfume, and felt intoxicated, with her hand resting on his arm and the sweet aroma drifting upwards, surrounding him. "And, I might add, there is no one in the world, even that Mr. Hackenschmidt, that I would feel safer with as an escort."

Her mention of the Russian Lion startled him, and he looked down at her.

"You know who George Hackenschmidt is?" he asked, incredulously.

"Certainly I do," she said, starting to walk and tugging lightly at him, as he stood rooted in place. "Don't you think I read the papers, and listen to people talk?"

They walked some distance in silence, his mind still reeling by the sudden and unexpected turn of events. Just moments ago, he had written the night off as a total disappointment, and now it had turned abruptly into exactly the opposite. Here he was walking down the street toward a park with the woman he most wished to be with in the entire world and talking about the wrestler he most wanted to talk about. It was a dream come true.

They reached the little park, and moved through it slowly until they came to the swings. Gladys withdrew her arm and sat in the swing, glancing back over her shoulder at Frank. He moved behind her, placed his hands on her back gently, and pushed. He pushed harder each time she returned until she was swinging so far into the dark he could hardly see her. But he could hear her laughter, and smiled widely, sharing her merriment. At last, she asked him to stop, and when the swing had grown still once again, she lifted herself out. She grabbed Frank's hand and led him twenty yards away to the merry-go-round. She sat down and looked up at him, and he started to push it.

"No," she said softly. "Just sit here with me, and we'll talk."

Frank deposited his husky body next to hers, and turned his gaze on her. It was dark, but he could see her well. He thought she was, at that moment, the most beautiful woman he had ever seen. Other men might not, he knew, but that was of small consequence. In his mind, she was, and that was all that mattered.

"Tell me," she said, her voice soft and almost as if she were singing, "what is this Hackenschmidt man really like?"

Frank sighed, and then looked down at his feet.

"Well, Gladys, they say he is the strongest man in the world, as well as the most perfectly developed man. They say he can do amazing things with lifting of weights, and that he is also a marvelous wrestler."

"Has he ever been beaten?"

"Jack Carkeek says once, very early in his career, when he was still just learning the craft. But not even once in the last seven, eight years."

"And how many times has he wrestled?"

"I'm not sure, but Farmer Burns - that's my trainer - says he has probably wrestled well over three hundred matches in all."

They were silent for a moment.

"How many times have you wrestled?"

"I'm not sure of that, either," he replied with a laugh. "I guess I've been in the ring about one hundred times officially, where there are announcers and other bouts on the card, and things like that. But including pick-up bouts at fairs and the like, I would guess around two hundred times."

"And how many times have you lost?"

"I'd have to count them," he said. "Let's see, I'll name then, and you can count, okay?

"There was Dan McLeod, who tricked me back in 1899, saying he was someone else when really he was the American champion. Then, I lost to the Farmer in Fort Dodge back in 1899. I lost three times to Tom Jenkins, the man I defeated for the American title, and let's see....there was that one to Fred Beell, when I was knocked dizzy by running my head into the ring post."

Gladys broke out laughing, covering her mouth with both hands, and then stopped.

"I'm sorry to laugh. That must have been very painful. But it sounds like such an awful, and silly, way to lose."

"Yes, that's what I thought, even at the time. But, crazy things can happen sometimes in sports. I dove for his legs to take him down, he sidestepped, and my head slammed into the rock-hard ring post. I didn't even know my name for about an hour."

"Then, that's just six times," she said. "You've only lost six times in nearly two hundred matches?"

"Well, yes, I guess that's about it," he said shyly. He didn't like talking about his ring accomplishments, it was too much like bragging.

"I think you'll beat this Russian Lion," she said firmly.

Frank glanced at her, turning his big neck just a bit, and casting his gaze downward. He reached out and put a hand on her dainty hands, folded neatly in her lap, and then quickly withdrew it.

"Thanks," he said huskily. "That's very nice of you. Only Farmer Burns feels that way right now. Not even my good friends or my sparring partners think I have much of a chance."

She reached out and grabbed his hand, and held it. He felt warm all over, warmer than he had ever felt in his life.

"What do you think, Frank?" she asked. It was the first time she had ever called him by his first name.

"I think he is probably stronger than me, and maybe more experienced in the ring," he said, his voice tight. She was making him speak about things he had never thought even to himself before, much less spoken aloud.

"But, I think I can wear him down. I think I can tire him out. And," he said solemnly, "I think I want to win more than he does. He's been champ a long time, and he's been on top a long time. He's brought great pride to his homeland. Everywhere he goes, they call him the Russian Lion, and men know where his home is. Well, I want to bring the title to Iowa, and to Humboldt. I want men and women the world over to know the kind of people we grow here in Iowa. Strong, because of the land, and strong as the land. That's what I want, Gladys."

They sat for just a moment more in the silence. And then he rose to his feet, his hand still in hers, and pulled her up.

"And, I think I know a beautiful young lady who I had best be returning home before her mother and father come out looking for her."

He walked her back to the house, relishing the small talk and the feel of her being so close. They stood by his auto talking for another ten minutes, and then he told her he had to leave.

"I know," she said. "It's very important that an athlete gets the proper amount of sleep. My brother talks about that all the time."

Frank nodded. And then, impulsively, he leaned down and kissed her lightly on the cheek. She smiled up at him, and he withdrew slightly.

"Good night, Gladys," he said. He climbed into his auto, then glanced over at her, suddenly brimming with confidence. "I plan to be seeing a lot of you in the future, Miss Oestrich..... if that's okay."

She smiled.

"I think that would be wonderful, Mr. Gotch," she said, standing by the street as his auto slowly pulled away.

As sweet as was the memory of the previous night, Frank made himself a vow to remove it from his mind, at least until he turned in each night. Now, there could only be one thought in his mind.... preparation.

The day after the walk to the park with Gladys, he rose early and ran hard, returning to work the pulleys, the heavy bag and to spar. He seemed to have a new fire and a new enthusiasm in his training, a fire even Burns could detect. He became obsessed with the battle plan of perfect conditioning. The plan was simple, as devised by the Farmer. Hang onto Hackenschmidt's neck and shoulders and tire him. Burns had sat up all night when Gotch visited the Oestrichs, and figured out mathematically just how much weight they could bring to bear on Hackenschmidt over an hour's time. Frank concentrated on the tie-up he would use, an old variation of the "elbow and collar" fashion of wrestling devised during the Civil War, when men wrestled with one another for entertainment, for betting purposes and to prepare mentally for the strain of combat. It was the system of catch-as-catch-can wrestling which took roots in Vermont, and spread west, even catching the fancy of young Abe Lincoln, who was considered one of the finest rough and tumble wrestlers in New Salem, Illinois, as a long and gangling youth.

Burns loved to spin yarns about the famous men of the past who had carried a love for wrestling. Lincoln was one of his favorite topics of discussion, and he often told of the time young Lincoln and the town bully of New Salem, Jack Armstrong, squared off, with people coming from miles around to watch the encounter. Lincoln, almost six foot four and long and wiry, was difficult to wrestle because of his leverage and balance. He was also undoubtedly very strong from splitting logs, and when he defeated the bully, he became a local celebrity. Burns also liked to quote the part from Genesis in the Bible where Jacob wrestled the angel of the Lord. He said, with a smile, that he was simply going about the Lord's business when he engaged in wrestling matches.

The elbow and collar style of wrestling had been popular in America back as far as Revolutionary War days, but had been largely confined to the East Coast. While Europeans originally preferred the Greco-Roman style of holds above the waist only, the free-spirited Americans were more inclined to the wide open style known as catch-as-catch-can; yet to this day no American had ever been able to win acclaim as the world's heavyweight champion.

Jenkins had claimed the world title for a few years, but when

Hackenschmidt came to America in 1905, he silenced that claim. There were many sports fans who called Burns the world champion in his heyday. Burns was never a legitimate world champion. Now, he saw he was going to have his chance to share in the world title, if only he could guide this Humboldt farmer who had become his close friend past the awesome, imposing figure of the Russian Lion. And the key was in the styles both men would employ: Hack would use basically Greco-Roman moves, slow and ponderous in execution. Gotch would use the catch style, striking quickly, like a jungle cat.

The month of March flew by for both Gotch and Burns, though it undoubtedly was a much longer period of time for Rogers, Westergard and Klank. Serving as Gotch's sparring partners, they saw, and felt, the transformation that was overtaking him. No longer was he mild mannered and easy going, as had always been his style. During the first eight years of his wrestling career, Frank had always been known as one of the most friendly, courteous and available of champions. Here, in his Humboldt environs, however, he attacked the chore at hand - which was preparing himself for the greatest ordeal of his life - with a grim determination that would have given credit to a Spartan of ancient Greece. He pushed himself relentlessly, and even Burns surveyed the transformation with a feeling akin to awe. The Farmer retreated as he saw that Frank didn't need him to push or cajole him; Gotch was assuming that responsibility himself. If anything, Burns became concerned that Gotch was pushing too hard, would reach his peak too soon and then, possibly, burn himself out.

Every morning Gotch rose at six, ran six miles, then returned for a light breakfast of eggs, bacon, toast and milk. He would take a short nap of thirty minutes, and then play handball with Westergard on the side of the barn, perhaps for as long as an hour. Burns and Gotch would then go into a planning session, where they would detail once again the strategy they had devised of tiring Hackenschmidt out, physically and emotionally. The hard part of the workout followed, with two hours of non-stop wrestling. Gotch would spar with Rogers until the big man was nearly blue in the face with exhaustion. Without pause, Gotch would then grapple with Westergard, and then Klank, those two men entering fresh, while Gotch grew steadily more tired. But, Gotch's endurance, already honed to a fine point over the previous eight years, was remarkable. After two weeks of this program, he was nearly as fresh at the end of wrestling all three men non-stop as was Klank, the last man he faced.

A light meal would follow the wrestling part of the schedule, and another short nap. Then, Gotch would return to work on the pulleys attached to the barn's outside wall, straining to build greater strength and endurance. Gotch knew he was stronger than ninety-nine percent of the men he had ever climbed in the ring with - in fact, he would concede that only Jenkins was his superior in strength, and even there the margin was miniscule - but the stories he continued to hear of Hackenschmidt's power convinced him he needed to improve his strength as much as possible in the short time remaining. After fifty minutes with the pulleys, Gotch would take a ten-minute rest, then begin a ten-minute limbering up period. Then, it was off on his last run of the day, a four-mile trek. An invigorating shower, a rubdown from the Farmer and a good meal were the last items of the day, before turning in by nine o'clock.

He was invited to town on a number of occasions, but declined all of the invitations, even when Oestrich rode out to the farm once to extend a personal invitation. He was polite to all of them, and especially to Gladys' father, but there could be no compromising now. The stakes were too high. He heard over a hundred citizens of Humboldt and the surrounding area had already purchased tickets to the match, and would be leaving for Chicago at approximately the same time his group would. While it pleased him to think Humboldt would be well represented, he didn't allow himself the luxury of dwelling upon it. He was, for the time being, possessed by a dream he had carried inside him since his youth.

March 28 was the day Burns selected for departure. They rose early in the morning, and Frank went over to the old homestead for brief goodbyes to his parents, and his brothers and sisters. There was little emotion, just good-natured ribbing and assorted "good lucks". Frank hugged Amelia, and shook his father's hand, aware that his father could no longer really grasp what was happening.

Elmer Smith, who was making the trip to Chicago, and several other men drove autos to Fort Dodge, transporting Gotch, Burns, Klank, Rogers and Westergard to the train station. Both Westergard and Rogers were wrestling in the preliminary matches, and both claimed they were in the best shape of their entire careers, thanks to the grueling workouts with Gotch on the farm. There was a band and a small group gathered at the train station to see the wrestlers off, and Frank figured he must have shook hands with at least one hundred folks. But he had enjoyed it all immensely, the occasion being the first time in three weeks he had allowed himself to forget about the Russian Lion, if only for a moment, and drink in the hospitality and affection being shown him by his Iowa neighbors. He wasn't much for idle promises, but he did tell the crowd just before boarding the train that he would do his best, his very best, to bring the world's heavyweight championship back to Iowa. The words brought a great cheer from those assembled, and Frank's last sight as the train pulled away was of nearly three hundred people, men, women and children, waving wildly.

CHAPTER 13

Chicago was ready for the wrestling match of the decade. Gotch's train was met by over twenty reporters when it pulled into Chicago's Main Station, and the wrestling party was surrounded as it stepped down off the big wooden car. Even Burns, who was used to traveling to the larger cities of America and therefore accustomed to large turnouts, was shocked by the number on hand. But Chicago had been, along with Kansas City, one of the cities that had taken Gotch to its heart. He first wrestled there in September of 1906, defeating Jim Parr. A month later, he returned to do in Leo Pordelo, and over eight thousand fans showed up April 26, 1907, to watch him defeat Fred Beell for the second time since Beell had stripped him of his American title with the fluke, head-banging victory. At the end of the year, he decisioned War Eagle in Chicago, and he whipped Beell for the third time, just February 7. And here he was again, set for the biggest match of his career.

But Gotch wasn't the only reason the press of the city was so taken with this match. It marked the first appearance of Hackenschmidt, who was already a legend in this part of the country. He had arrived a week ago from New York, where he had trained for two weeks after the long Atlantic crossing by ship, and the sporting public was infatuated with his presence. When he strolled down Michigan Avenue by the lake, fans flocked around him, asking for autographs, the braver ones reaching out to feel the mighty arms of the undefeated world champion. A gentle man out of the ring, Hackenschmidt took it all in good nature, and was patient with all but the most boorish of fans. He was a dapper dresser, with cane and top hat, rather than derby, and was charming in speech, his rustic English sharply punctuated with a heavy Russian accent.

Burns had arranged for two associates with automobiles to meet him at the station, and searched the crowd for them while Gotch was busy answering questions. Yankee Joe Rogers attracted a good deal of curiosity, as well, due to his size. It wasn't often one could see a man who weighed well over two hundred and fifty pounds in this day and age.

Burns was about to give up on his associates when he saw them fighting their way toward him. They shook hands, and the three men broke away to retrieve their bags, Burns imploring the assistance of Klank and Westergard, Rogers being a lost cause due to his sudden celebrity. After loading the baggage, Burns returned to extricate Gotch and Rogers, pleading with the journalists and fans to allow them to leave and depart for their headquarters at the Morrison Hotel. After assuring the reporters Gotch would be available for interviews later in the day, the three men made their way to the waiting automobiles, and left for the hotel.

The Morrison was one of the grand hotels in America in 1908, and the Gotch party had seven rooms reserved on the third floor. Burns did the checking in, while the others retired to their rooms.

"Where's Carkeek?" Gotch inquired of Burns when he at last joined him in their room. "Shouldn't he be here by now?"

"He's somewhere in Chicago," said Burns. "He's been here for several days taking care of the arrangements, like transportation to and from the hotel to the Chicago Athletic Club, to the arena, these rooms, and things of that nature."

"He's also been meeting with the Hackenschmidt people, hasn't he?" asked Gotch.

Burns nodded, busying himself with hanging up his clothes in the closet.

"I'd like to talk to him," said Frank quietly.

"Why's that?" asked the Farmer, not paying much attention.

"Just like to hear what he has to say now about this amazing fellow," said Gotch. Burns couldn't help but catch the tone of irritability in Gotch's voice. Apparently, the members of the press had managed to upset him, leaving the impression they thought he was little more than a sacrificial lamb on the altar of the unbeaten - and unbeatable - Russian Lion.

"We already know all we need to know to beat him," said Burns matter-of-factly. "All we have to do is stick to our game plan. His power will be largely nullified in the early going if you can keep him at arm's length. He is strongest when given an opportunity to pull an opponent inside, where he can use the power of his arms and shoulders at close range. All you need to do is keep circling in the early going, and wear him down. There isn't any way he can be in as good shape as you are, Frank. You've run like no man your size has ever run before. Your conditioning is beyond doubt. The Russian Lion will not be able to keep your pace."

Burns sounded firm and convincing, and Gotch knew he was correct. For a moment, he had allowed the newsmen at the train station to cast doubts on the outcome of the match, but no longer. Just having the Farmer around was worth his weight in gold, he reasoned. Immediately, Gotch felt his mood begin to change.

"You're absolutely right, Farmer," Frank said, slamming a fist down hard on the small table in front of him. "Why, I know what I've gone through - what we've all gone through, and those reporters sure don't. Oh, they were polite enough, but you could just tell they think I'm a goner already, before we even put foot in the ring.

"I guess it'll just be up to me to show these fellows in Chicago what an Iowa farm boy is made of, right?"

Burns nodded his agreement.

"Tell you what, Farmer, I'm going to search out the Humboldt boys. They told me they were staying here at the Morrison, and would be on the fifth floor. Think I'll go up and chat with them a bit, then we can go over to the Chicago Athletic Club for a quick workout. Then I'll do some running along the lake tonight."

"A workout today and tonight is fine," said Burns, glancing up from a newspaper he had picked up. "But, then I think you should lay off until the bout. Maybe a little jog the night before, but that's all, Frank. You're ready, wound tight; there's no need in overdoing it."

Gotch nodded and slipped out the door. Burns sat for several minutes, reflecting on the days ahead. Even though he himself wasn't climbing into the ring to do combat, it would be the pinnacle of his career. Frank was like a son to him, and, Gotch looked up to him as a son would to a father. They had worked hard together for nearly eight years, and had been apart only during Frank's sojourn to Alaska and assorted wrestling trips when Burns couldn't free himself to travel alongside. This was the moment they had both been waiting for, and neither man was about to let it pass without fulfillment.

The long-awaited day, April 3, dawned with a drizzle, but the sky cleared by noon. It was only about a thirty-minute drive to Dexter Park Pavilion, but Burns was already nervous by five p.m. The match of the decade was to get under way at 10:30 that evening, and there was Frank, sitting in the drawing room with several reporters and his friends from Humboldt, talking idly just hours before the match was to start.

C. J. Murray, a sports writer from the Buffalo, New York, newspaper assigned to the fight, was relating his meeting that very morning with Hackenschmidt, and the Humboldt contingent was hanging on every word.

"Despite his wonderful physique, his great strength and the fact that he is regarded by just about everyone as the logical winner, George seemed worried and ill at ease when I encountered him walking on Michigan Avenue," said Murray.

"Can you recall what he had to say?" asked Elmer Smith, leaning forward on the edge of his seat, anxious to hear more.

"Well, I can remember he kept tapping his cane on the sidewalk, like he was quite nervous. And he asked me how big Gotch is. 'He is a great fellow, yes?' he asked, and then said, 'I shall wrestle well. I shall do my best. I hope Mr. Gotch will wrestle fair.'"

"He's afraid of that old toe hold, Frank," shouted a member of the party, and they all joined in, declaring that, yes, indeed, Hackenschmidt should be quite fearful of the dreadful hold. Gotch, laughing all the time, acted as though he actually had a foot in his grip and was trying to twist it off. He went through a series of motions, his tongue sticking out, and he grunted heavily, as if exerting himself. Everyone laughed at the scene.

"Then, Mr. Hackenschmidt changed the subject abruptly, and wanted to know how his friends in Buffalo were," continued Murray. "When he walked away, I thought to myself, there goes a worried man."

That brought a round of cheers from the Humboldt group, and also brought Burns in from the next room. He surveyed the room filled with about thirty people, most of whom he recognized.

"Well, how are all the boys back in Buffalo?" asked Gotch merrily. "I don't suppose they think I've got much of a chance, do they?"

Murray shook his head. "No, not many folks do, Frank. I heard even old Muldoon is saying no one can beat Hackenschmidt. But all of us here in this room sure do, don't we boys?"

Again, a cheer went up. And Burns stepped into the middle of the room.

"Thanks for all of your support, men," he said, with no trace of a smile. He was dead serious now. The time for merriment had ceased, to his way of thinking. "But, Frank has to get ready now. I'm asking you all to leave. We'll see you at the pavilion."

"Yeah, we want to get there early and make some wagers," said Smith, leaping to his feet and motioning the others to follow. "This is a chance for us to really clean up."

"I doubt you'll have any trouble finding any takers," said Gotch, watching as his friends stood and filed toward the door. "I'll see you all at the arena."

Dexter Park Pavilion was a large amphitheater in the middle of downtown Chicago, just five blocks west of Lake Michigan, and near the great stockyards. It could house over ten thousand fans, and by the time Gotch and Burns arrived the streets were packed with autos, most parked but some still full of fans trying to make their way to the match. Posters with pictures of the Russian Lion were on every street corner, tacked to the light poles, and to the storefronts. Hackenschmidt's name was much larger than Gotch's, and there wasn't a picture of Frank on the poster, either. But his name did carry the words, "American champion."

A policeman halted them when they drew close to the pavilion, and stared inside the auto. Burns told him who they were, and showed a pass signed by Klank, who had an official position as one of the promoters of the card. The policeman took a good look at Gotch, and waved them inside the parking area, but not without first wishing the American champion well.

Burns parked the auto and they moved to a large door at the back of the pavilion, each carrying a black bag. Two knocks brought an elderly man, who asked to see the same pass once again. He nodded and moved aside to let them through, staring Gotch up and down.

"Don't look very big to me," he muttered as Frank moved inside.

"Big enough," said Frank without stopping.

"Hope so," came the reply.

"Bet on it," said Frank almost yelling it out as they were already ten steps past the doorman.

They walked down a long passageway and turned to the right.

"You seem to know your way around here pretty well," said Frank to Burns.

"Got a tour from Emil yesterday," said Burns.

"Say, where's he been anyway?" asked Gotch. "Only seen him once the whole time we been here."

"Lotta details to be taken care of in this business, and especially a match of this size," said Burns. "He's been busy making sure everything is on the up and up, and that there aren't any last-minute surprises."

"Well, that's good," said Gotch. "But, for some strange reason, even though I've never met the man, I trust Hack. I don't think he'd pull anything funny on us, Farmer."

"Neither do I," said Burns. "But you can't be too sure in this business. There's a lot of money at stake here. This is gonna be the biggest purse in the history of wrestling. Why, they're expecting over ten thousand fans here tonight."

They stopped before a wooden door. So far, they had encountered no one other than the doorman at the outside entrance. There was a white tape on the door, with the name "Gotch" printed on it in neat, big letters. Burns banged hard on the door twice, and it swung open.

Klank was inside, along with Yankee Joe Rogers, Westergard and several other men. Yankee Joe was in his wrestling togs, sitting on a large table at the back of the room. He was in the second preliminary match, and was due out soon. Westergard was working on him, limbering him up and pounding on his enormous back. His eyes were shut, and he was gently swaying to and fro, like an elephant in the zoo, contentedly munching on a trunkful of hay.

Klank and two nattily dressed men stepped forward with hands outstretched.

"Frank, Farmer," said Klank with a big grin. "Glad to see you. Been wondering when you'd show up."

"Still plenty of time," said Burns. "Just a bit after nine and match don't start till ten fifteen."

Klank introduced Gotch and Burns to the two men with him, explaining one was from the promoter's office, representing Jake Smith, the man responsible for bringing off the match. He was there to oversee the operations and to answer any questions that might arise, said Klank. The other man was from the camp of Hackenschmidt. He was a surly looking gent who smiled little and watched everything. He was very interested in meeting Gotch, and quickly sized him up. He looked a bit concerned, like maybe he had been expecting less. Klank said that sending a man from the other camp was something boxers did before all the big matches, and added Burns should select someone to go over to the dressing room of Hackenschmidt on the opposite side of the pavilion. Burns immediately agreed, and dispatched Wester-gard, who was off in a minute, obviously excited about being picked to go into the dressing room of the Russian Lion. Before he left, Hack's man signed a small piece of paper that would allow him to be recognized as an official from Gotch's party.

"What should I look for?" asked Westergard. The Farmer merely shrugged. "Just make sure he shows up," he said, loud enough so Hack's man couldn't help hearing.

While Klank and Burns discussed some last minute details, Gotch stripped down in a far corner of the room. He noticed he had begun to sweat under his arms, unusual for him. He admitted to him-self that he was more nervous than he had been for any engagement since the first match with Tom Jenkins, when he felt at the last minute he wasn't ready, experience wise, to be facing a champion of Jenkins' quality. He had gone into the match with the intention of not winning, but just staying close. That was a fatal error, because a champion like Jenkins - or Hackenschmidt - can sense that in a man, just like a dog can sense when a human is afraid of it. In the past several years, Gotch had been on the opposite end of that feeling on numerous occasions.

Frank lifted his black bag to the table and deposited it, sifting through it for his equipment. He pulled out the black tights, and the big thick cup he would wear to protect his groin area, slipping the cup on and then the tights, which had a strap at the bottom that went under-neath his feet, like a stirrup. He pulled the tights up snug against his waist, tying the string in the front tight. He squatted twice to make sure they were on right, and that they felt good. Then, he pulled on a pair of black trunks over the tights. He sat down on a bench and pulled on his black shoes, tying the laces tight, ending with a double bow. He hated it when he had to stop a match to tie his laces, and he didn't want that to happen tonight, of all nights.

He stood and walked to the full-length mirror hanging on a wall and gazed into it. He wasn't a vain man, and very seldom looked into a mirror to assess his appearance. But, this was a special day. He gazed at the figure in the reflection, critically. He wasn't displeased. His chest was lightly covered with dark hair, but the muscles were thick and bulgy around the shoulders and the upper arms. He put his hands on his hips, and turned slightly, to see how the tights fit in the rear. It was the first time he had ever worn this pair. His dark hair was parted squarely in the middle, and was neatly trimmed. He scowled into the mirror, and shook his head slowly. Then, he smiled faintly.

Burns called him over to the scales, and all gathered around, especially Hack's man, who was anxious to see what Gotch weighed. Frank stepped up, and the man representing the promoter took out a pen and wrote down the weight: one hundred and ninety-six pounds. Hack's man seemed a little concerned, and whispered over to Klank, who merely nodded with a smile. Gotch couldn't hear what was said.

Gotch walked back over to the bag Burns had carried in for him and pulled out a long, green robe, and quickly put it on, pulling the robe together and securing it at the waist. Then, he sat down on the bench, content to wait for Burns' next move. The other men continued to talk for several more minutes, and then Burns cleared his throat. Klank looked over at him, then spoke.

"Oh, yes, Mr. Winegaard," he said, addressing Hack's man. "Mr. Gotch will need some privacy now while he and Mr. Burns discuss strategy and while Mr. Gotch readies himself for the match."

Winegaard stood his ground, a frown growing. "I was told I was to remain right up until the contestants left for the ring."

"That will be impossible," said Burns. "We will not tolerate it."

Winegaard turned to the promoters' man, who merely shrugged. Then, Winegaard stepped to the door, opened it and slammed it behind him.

"Haughty," muttered Klank. Rogers nodded.

There was a sudden pounding on the door, and Klank moved over to open it, expecting to see Winegaard. Instead, there was a young man with eyes as big as saucers.

"It's time for Mr. Rogers' match," he said in a squeaky voice, peering behind Klank and trying to steal a glance into the room, hoping to catch a glimpse of Gotch. Klank thanked him, and shut the door.

Yankee Joe moved off the table where he had sat unmoving for nearly thirty minutes. He did a series of quick knee bends, the knees cracking, and swung his arms to and fro several times. He nodded quickly, as if telling himself he was ready.

"That's quite a limbering up process you got there, Joe," said Gotch good-naturedly. Yankee nodded in his direction, and smiled. "Good luck," said Gotch.

"Same to you, Frank," said Rogers, heading for the door with Klank at his side. Rogers stopped at the door, and turned back. "I'll be there at ringside when it's time." Frank and Burns nodded, and Rogers headed out, shutting the door behind him and Klank, who was to serve as his second during the bout.

"About an hour," said Burns. "You ready to start?"

"Yeah," said Frank. He moved over to the wall, placing his hands on it solidly, and then moved his feet back, so he was leaning at a considerable angle. He lowered himself to the wall, and then pushed off, repeating the exercise twenty times. Then, he stood square and did some squats, as had Rogers. But Gotch repeated the motion thirty times, the blood flowing freely when he had stopped. He swung his arms together across his chest a number of times, and breathed deeply while doing so. Then, he nodded to Burns, who moved behind him and slipped his arms underneath Gotch, and clasped his hands together on his chest. Burns pulled in tight, and then leaned back, lifting Gotch off his feet. Burns bounced him up and down several times off his own chest, and then, suddenly, pulled in with all his might. There was a cracking sound, and Burns set him back down. Gotch turned and smiled.

"No one can crack a back quite like you, Farmer," he said.

The two men tied up several times in a collar and elbow grip, pushing one another around the room. They began to get rough, shooting takedowns at one another at about three-quarters speed. Several times they slammed into the wall. After they had been engaged in their limbering up process for about twenty minutes, Westergard came barging in, his face red.

"Boy oh boy, they are angry over in Hack's dressing room," he said. "The fellow who was in here came hustling in all hot and bothered because you wouldn't let him stay. They got angry - there's about twenty fellows over there, I reckon - and started yelling in German or Russian, I don't know which. Everyone seemed real upset, except Hack. He didn't say nothing, or change his expression in the least. They even forgot I was in the room for about ten minutes, until that Winegaard fellow spotted me. Then, I thought they was going to lynch me. They ran at me, grabbed me, and shoved me out into the hallway." He started laughing, and so did the others.

Burns grabbed him by the elbow.

"How did Hackenschmidt look?"

Westergard let out a low whistle.

"What a body," he said. "That man has muscles where most people don't even have places. He's huge. Muscle-wise, I mean. Big bulgy things, with veins running all over them. But, he's not as tall as I figured he would be."

"Just how tall is he?" asked Burns, raising an eyebrow in concern.

"Not as tall as Frank," said Westergard. "About an inch shorter, maybe even more."

"That's what Carkeek said," Burns said. "That's good, Frank. You can overhook the way we planned." Gotch nodded. He had planned to overhook - drape his body over the top of Hackenschmidt's - in the early going one way or another, and this made it all the easier. Much easier, in fact, if he was more than an inch shorter.

"How much did he weigh?" asked Gotch.

"I couldn't actually see on the scales, they were all pushing around. But I think someone said two fifteen."

"That's good," said Burns. "The heavier, the better. Just that much more he will have to carry around."

"I don't think he's planning on a very long match," said Westergard, looking squarely at Gotch, who had started warming up again. He was pushing his hands together, palms flattened, in front on his chest, then took both hands up to his head and gave it a little twist, the neck muscles creaking.

"I think he plans to win early, both falls within an hour, or even less," said Westergard.

"Well," said Burns firmly, "he's in for a little disappointment, then."

Rogers and Klank returned to the dressing room. Rogers had won easily and was far more interested in talking about the upcoming title bout than his own match. Ten minutes later, the small group was summoned by four Chicago policemen. Gotch strode down the narrow, dimly-lit corridor, with Burns and Klank at each side, and Rogers and Westergard trailing, carrying several bags and a water pail. Klank wore a dark suit and even kept his derby in place, while Burns removed his coat, revealing white shirt and suspenders. He had replaced his tie with a towel around his neck. When the fans caught sight of the group, a huge howl went up, and Frank could hear his name being shouted by several strong-throated fans.

It was dark in the back recesses of the pavilion, but it lightened considerably as they moved toward the ring. Cigar smoke filled the air, and after just twenty yards, the crowd pushed in on them from all sides. Frank looked up, and smiled. It seemed like the biggest crowd he had ever seen. The Dexter Park Pavilion seated over ten thousand, and it was packed to the rafters. The noise was deafening as they approached the ring, with Burns and the policemen shoving fans out of the way, trying to open a clearing for Gotch. He reached up and grabbed the bottom rope and pulled himself up to the ring apron, then slid between two ropes and into the ring. He looked quickly over at the other corner, but it was empty. That was as it should be, he thought;

the heavyweight champion of the world should not have to wait for his challenger. It was prearranged Gotch would enter first, and he was scheduled to arrive at ten p.m. It was now, Burns had told him as they reached the ring, exactly ten. Gotch didn't want to be late, to show any disrespect for the champion of the world.

He turned and gripped the ring ropes at his corner, looking out over the sea of faces. It was unbelievable. He had wrestled before large crowds before, and often drew over ten thousand whenever he appeared. But this crowd was louder and more boisterous than any he had ever seen. Men were standing on their chairs, waving at him and shouting his name, and he grinned and waved back to various fans. He was searching for the Humboldt contingent, but couldn't find it before Burns pulled him away, and began massaging his thick shoulder muscles and the trapesius, which lead to the neck. Gotch rolled his head slightly from side to side as Burns' thick fingers dug hard into his muscles.

"Quite a sight, huh, Farmer?" Gotch asked.

"Yeah, it sure is," said Burns. Gotch smiled. He knew the Farmer liked to take everything in stride, and never show his feelings. But even he was impressed. It promised to be quite a night.

Two men entered the ring from the other side, dressed impeccably. They came over and introduced themselves to Gotch and Burns.

The referee had been agreed upon two days earlier by Burns, Klank and the Hackenschmidt group. He was Ed Smith, the sporting editor of the Chicago Daily Newspaper. He was known as an honest man, one who would call the match the way he saw it, and would not be intimidated by either corner. The Hackenschmidt people were concerned Gotch would be able to wrestle "rough" - or mix it up more than they wanted - while the Gotch corner was concerned that a referee keep the pace moving, and not allow either competitor to hang back and not exchange moves. That would bore the crowd, and would work against the Gotch game plan, which was to make both wrestlers expend a great deal of energy early, so endurance and conditioning would play a large role in the outcome.

Klank introduced Gotch and Burns to Smith and to Jack Edwards who would serve as the ring announcer. They all shook hands. Burns asked when Hack would arrive.

"Any minute now, Mr. Burns," said Edwards in his strong voice. He sounded as though he were already announcing. "I just left their dressing room, and the Russian Lion was just about done with his preparations."

Frank smiled. "The Russian Lion." He wondered what they would be calling him two hours from now.

Gotch heard his name called, and looked down at ringside. The first row of seats were given to members of the sporting press, and they were seated all around the ring, with a narrow platform in front of them to allow writing. He searched the faces until he saw Murray, from Buffalo. He had called up to him, and he now winked at the American champion, as if to wish him good luck. Gotch winked back, and smiled. He looked over the press row for other familiar faces, and spotted Sol Plex of the Chicago Examiner, who had reported on his match with Leo Pardello some months earlier in Chicago. The match was held at Brooke's Casino, and ended abruptly when Gotch had caught Pardello, a real rough customer who liked to mix it up, in a toe hold. Applying the pressure, Gotch had snapped a ligament in Pardello's leg, rendering him helpless. Plex had written in an article that "Gotch, tall, perfectly built, handsome, took the crowd immediately" and later called him an Adonis. He wrote that "Gotch put up a clean argument throughout that won him many friends."

Frank appreciated the kind words and winked at Plex, too, who smiled broadly.

There were many others who Gotch recognized, but couldn't attach a name to. But his game was cut short by a tremendous roar, and he turned slowly to try and catch a glimpse, for the first time in his life, of the Russian Lion.

Hackenschmidt was moving up the aisle, but he was obscured by his large entourage and the fans who were standing and cheering wildly. Though Gotch was wrestling in a state which neighbored his own homeland and he was representing the United States of America, it was clear he was not the crowd favorite. The cheering bestowed upon Hackenschmidt was far greater than that which greeted him. But it didn't make Frank envious; instead, it served to inspire him and to get his emotions involved. It's a great champion, and a great man, who can elicit this kind of support from a foreign crowd, he thought. He greatly admired what Hackenschmidt had accomplished as an athlete. He was well known and respected around the world, and certainly no less so here in America, where wrestling rivaled boxing as the most popular of all sports. Gotch shook his head as if to wipe such thoughts from his mind. It was time to begin hating the Russian Lion, to instill the desire to defeat him by punishing him physically.

The entourage was at ringside, and still Burns hadn't been able to get a clear view of the great Hackenschmidt. He saw the top of his head twice, but hadn't seen his face.

Several husky men climbed into the ring, and stood on the lower rope, pushing the middle strand up with their arms, creating a wide space. Then Hackenschmidt, wearing a long, gray robe, burst into view, stepping between the ropes and into the ring. He turned his back to Gotch immediately, without even glancing in his direction, and faced the crowd. Slowly, he turned first to the right and then to the left, amid a deafening ovation, and bowed slightly. The crowd continued to roar, almost out of control, and Hack repeated the bowing gesture. Then, he turned abruptly and stared across the ring at his opponent.

Their eyes met squarely, and for a moment it seemed there was no one else in the entire pavilion. "Just you and me," Hack seemed to be saying to Gotch. He was a ruggedly handsome man, with a thick, powerful neck. His hair was short cropped and brown, neatly parted on the left side. Gotch smiled, and turned away, facing Burns.

"The Russian Lion has arrived," he said.

Burns just nodded, grimly. What little he had seen of the Russian Lion had impressed him.

Gotch continued to stand with his back to Hack's corner, resting with his hands on the ropes. He searched the crowd in front of him, and noticed not a single face was turned his direction. All eyes were on Hackenschmidt. He felt a hot flush of anger welling up inside him. He knew he was ready for the match of his life.

The announcer was in the center of the ring, and was blaring out the news of the next matches in Chicago, though few were listening. The crowd had quieted to a constant buzz. Several prizefighters were introduced, and the crowd responded with polite clapping. But it was clearly a wrestling group, here to witness the most important wrestling match to be held in America since Hackenschmidt's last trip, when he humiliated Tom Jenkins in New York's Madison Square Garden. Though only one in ten felt Gotch could win, most thought him plucky enough to put up a game struggle and to thereby show off Hack's ability to the utmost. That was all most hoped for....a strong showing by their American champion.

Burns and Klank were introduced, and took short bows. Burns received the biggest hand of the night up to that point. Still, Gotch had not turned his back away from the opposite corner.

".....and in this corner, weighing in at one hundred ninety six pounds...."

The voice droned on, but Gotch was oblivious to it. He heard, yet didn't hear. He was preparing himself for the most important moment of his entire life. He had dreamed since his youth of being a champion, not just of America, but the world.

".....the farmer from Humboldt, Iowa...."

Gotch breathed in deeply a series of quick, explosive motions.

"....the man who took the American title from the great Tom Jenkins....."

Gotch felt his hands tighten on the ropes; he wanted to rip the ropes from the ring post, so anxious was he to wrestle. The intensity inside him was building almost out of control.

"....the popular champion of America....Frank Gotch!"

Frank turned and acknowledged the ovation. It lasted for almost a minute and was loud and clear. He held one hand above his head, and smiled, turning in a small circle. He stood facing the opposite corner, hands on hips.

"And now, ladies and gentlemen, may I present the legendary Russian Lion...."

A massive overwhelming cheer broke out in the pavilion, sounding like thunder across the plains. Gotch smirked as Hackenschmidt stepped forward, acknowledging the ovation with a slight nod of his head. His eyes were on Gotch, and they were now just ten feet apart.

Edwards had to wait for the cheering to subside, then continued.

"....born in Estonia, trained in Russia, considered to be one of the strongest men ever to live...."

Putting it on pretty thick, thought Gotch, smiling across at Hacken-schmidt. I wonder, are you really that strong?

"....second trip to the United States, and first ever here to the heartland of America...."

Hack looked nervous, Gotch thought suddenly. Is it because I'm smiling? He's undoubtedly accustomed to his foes quaking in terror at this point. Or, maybe, he's thinking about the toe hold. That made Gotch smile all the more.

"....the undefeated heavyweight wrestling champion of the world, the Russian Lion, George Hackenschmidt...."

The last name was obliterated by the cheering. Hack raised both arms slowly above his head, and turned from Gotch, bowing shortly and quickly in all directions. When he had completed full circle, Smith beckoned the two men to approach, and a man with camera popped into view.

"Gentlemen," said Smith, "a photograph for posterity's sake."

No one had mentioned there would be photos taken at this point, and Burns began to object. But Gotch held up a hand, and Burns capitulated.

"Would the two of you shake hands, please," said Smith, moving between them.

Gotch reached across at Hackenschmidt, offering his right hand. Hack hesitated briefly, then reached out, too. It wasn't a genuine shake, as neither man made an effort to pump the other's hand. The photo-grapher took his shot, smiled nervously, and hastily departed.

Gotch was surprised at how soft Hack's hand had seemed, and again at how soft his voice was.

"Now, Mr. Gotch," Hackenschmidt said softly and with a heavy accent, "you know this is to be a wrestling match, and not a fight."

"Don't tell me about the rules," replied Frank with a broad grin. "Here's the referee. He'll take care of that."

Hack made no reply. Smith placed a hand on the shoulders of each man and issued orders they were both well acquainted with. Nothing new - just ceremony, and routine. Smith waved to the time-keeper, asked each man to return to his corner. Gotch shed his robe, and handed it to Burns, who grabbed it and stepped between the ropes, out of the ring, and squatted on the apron. Gotch heard the crowd roar again, and turned.

Hackenschmidt had taken off his robe, and for the first time the wrestling fans of Chicago saw the body that was considered to be as close to perfection as man could mold it. Gotch saw Hack from behind as he tossed his robe to his attendants ... the thick back, with powerful slabs of muscle clearly defined at the base of the neck and down the sides. Hack turned suddenly and rotated his massive arms across his chest, then dropped them to his side, exposing his upper body. It was so thick with muscle that it looked almost armor plated, and Gotch was suddenly aware of why Hackenschmidt did not anticipate a long match. He had wrestled hundreds of times without a loss, and knew, through experience, that his mere presence won him many a battle before the gladiators had even looked up. He was the most amazing physical specimen Gotch had ever seen, far more muscular, even, than the powerful Jenkins.

The referee nodded at the timekeeper, then toward the keeper of the bell. There was the sharp ring from the bell. The match was on.

The first tie-up came quickly. Gotch had envisioned it a thousand times before, in his mind's eye. Running down country roads, and even in his sleep, he had reached out his right arm and grabbed Hack's thick neck with his right hand, his left hand catching Hack's right arm at the elbow as Hack reached for him. It was the tried-and-true style of elbow and collar wrestling. It was from this position the wrestlers would set up their moves, and jockey for position against one another, pushing and pulling. It was also here, in this position, Gotch knew, that many wrestlers lost their heart against Hack, becoming truly aware, for the first time, of his incredible strength.

And now it was happening to Frank for the first time. This was no dream, no moment of fantasy. With over ten thousand spectators at the edge of their seats, straining for the first tell-tale sign in the struggle, Gotch was about to find out once and for all about the legendary power of the Russian Lion.

Frank waited to be thrown easily away. Hack's hand was on his neck, pulling him forward, but Gotch was able to hang back. He squeezed tight at Hack's elbow. Hack suddenly changed his tactics of pulling, and pushed mightily, sending Gotch flying from him. The two men stood several feet from each other. Hack scowled menacingly, and stepped forward. Gotch showed no expression and they tied up elbow to collar once again, testing each other's strength. Hack tried to muscle Gotch down to a knee, but was totally unsuccessful, and Frank heard him grunt once.

"So early," Gotch thought to himself. "He shouldn't gasp, not even once, at this point, not if he's truly in shape for a long, tough match." He began to wonder about Hack's conditioning.

The crowd was roaring, and there was a steady stream of babble from Hack's corner, all in Russian. Meanwhile, Burns was yelling at Frank to follow the plan, to come over on top of the Russian. He decided to try. As Hack reached for him in the familiar tie-up, Gotch went over the top with his left arm, laying it along the back of Hack's head, pulling down. Hack tried to pull up, but Gotch kept his foe's head tucked down and began to move backwards, jerking Hack after him. Hack went along willingly at first, to see if he might be able to initiate a move of his own. But, after thirty seconds of this, he decided to break free. It took him several seconds to do so, but at last he pushed Gotch away, heavily. He scowled again, and moved in....only to find himself in the same predicament. Again they repeated the pattern, Gotch moving backwards and Hack trailing along, his head bent low, only to push himself off. Four times the process was repeated, and at last Hack turned to Smith, the referee.

"He must wrestle me, and stop this," he said in a heavy voice. He sounded upset.

Smith motioned them together impatiently.

"There is nothing illegal being done. Just wrestle," Smith said sternly.

Hackenschmidt came in quickly and tried for a headlock, hoping to trap Gotch's head in a painful grip between his right arm and side. But Gotch evaded it, moving quickly away. It was apparent to the trained wrestling eye that Gotch was much quicker than Hackenschmidt. And there was another matter becoming apparent to Gotch and Burns: Hackenschmidt was not nearly so strong as they had feared. In fact, it was Burns, sitting at ringside and watching the first few minutes of action very, very intently, who recognized the real truth of the matter: If Hack was any bit stronger than Gotch, the margin was hardly worth noticing, and would make very little difference in the outcome of this engagement. The strength of the Russian Lion lay to a large degree in his appearance, which intimidated most wrestlers, and in his ability to lift heavy, unmoving objects. Against a wrestler like Gotch, who refused to be intimidated and who was anything but unmoving, the strength of George Hackenschmidt could be effectively nullified. Burns could not restrain a smile as that fact became increasingly clear to him.

Both men were dripping with sweat. It was a warm night, and the exertion was extreme. They continued to push into one another, searching for openings. Hack had been the aggressor for the first twenty minutes, but was growing frustrated in his ability to trip up Gotch and take him to the mat, where he hoped to begin serious wrestling and work for a fall or submission hold. Time and again Hack would work in close to Gotch, then shoot for a leg, or try to maneuver his way behind Gotch, all to no avail. Gotch would spin away, and face Hack with a big grin, his confidence growing by the minute.

The crowd had settled down, aware this contest was going to take a while before a winner was determined. Realizing they were witnessing a bout between two very evenly-matched adversaries, those who had bet on Hack were beginning to worry just a bit. Surely, their man would prevail, but they were concerned about his inability to corner Gotch, and the fact that the Iowa farmer was so much quicker. Now, even the untrained eye was able to discern that fact. As the match neared the hour mark, the contestants paused to stare hard at one another, taking a brief respite from their efforts. The crowd came to its feet and cheered them on lustily, stamping its feet and clapping its hands. Many shouts ripped the night air, encouraging both wrestlers to greater efforts as they pushed and shoved, each trying to find an opening.

Finally, at the eighty-minute mark, Hack got solidly behind

Gotch and secured a waist lock. Gotch bent forward, trying to make it more difficult for Hackenschmidt to lift him. Twice, Hack leaned back and strained mightily, the muscles standing out in attention in his thick back, but he couldn't quite lift Gotch all the way off the floor and slam him to the mat, because the Iowan had his body bent so far forward, a tactic he and Burns had perfected back in Humboldt.

Hack then initiated a trip, wrapping his left leg around Gotch's left leg, and driving forward heavily. Any other foe would have been slammed to the mat at that point, but Gotch, sensing the move was about to come, wrapped both hands tightly around Hack's left wrist. The moment they started for the mat, Gotch tore Hack's grip away and spun out to the right. When they hit the floor, Gotch was off to the side, free from Hack's grip, and back up in a second, flashing a big grin. Hack arose more slowly, and began to back away when he got to his feet, with Gotch moving in toward him. It was obvious to everyone in the place that the great effort had tired the world champion considerably.

"Where's this Russian Lion I've heard so much about?" asked Frank as he approached. Hack's chest was heaving from the exertion, the heavy muscles fairly rippling across his front. He looked unmistakably tired. "Why, I think old Farmer Burns could give you a going over," said Frank, smiling widely.

Hack stood his ground, and the two tied up once again. Hack tried to push Gotch backward, but the challenger was unmovable. He pushed back fiercely, and Hack had to give way. They moved into the ropes, with Gotch leaning heavily into the Russian champ, until the referee separated them and brought them back to the center. They had been wrestling for nearly ninety minutes. Sweat poured down both bodies in rivers, and they both began to breathe with their mouths wide open, not able to get enough air through their nostrils to satisfy their heaving lungs. But Gotch had prepared for such an epic struggle with miles and miles of lonely, torturous running, and had caught his second wind. He moved forward and began pushing Hack around the ring, shooting for the legs time and again. Three times he secured a leg with his iron grip and started to lift it, but Hack fought him off with desperation. Gotch shifted for a waist lock, but Hack was able to thwart him once again. And then the Russian Lion shocked the Iowa farmer.

Standing just two feet from one another, Hack held up his hands in front of his chest, signifying a break in the action. Gotch stopped.

"Mr. Gotch, we shall call this match a draw, yes?" he asked.

Frank could hardly believe his ears.

"No, not at all," he said, shaking his head. "We will have to wrestle on, Mr. Hackenschmidt."

The referee heard the proposition, and shook his head too.

"Go on and wrestle, you two. I'll stay here til morning if need be," Smith said.

"But, Mr. Gotch, you can't throw me down," said Hackenschmidt, staring at Gotch with dark eyes under furrowed brows.

"Well, you can't throw me down either," replied Frank.

"That's why I say call this a draw," replied Hackenschmidt. "The people don't like this kind of wrestling."

"Oh, come on and wrestle a couple of more hours," said Gotch, reaching out and taking hold of Hack's thick wrist. "You wrestle, and I'll do the same, and they'll be all too happy to watch us."

From that moment on, Frank knew the contest was his. He was uplifted tremendously by the stunning proposal to quit from Hackenschmidt, and he felt as fresh as when they started. In addition, he knew now he was stronger than Hack was at this point of the match. He had been amazed as the first hour of the match wore on to realize he was on a nearly equal footing with Hack with regard to strength. There were times the Russian Lion felt very strong, but Gotch felt during the course of the match he would rate Hackenschmidt's strength only second among the men he had faced. Jenkins was tops in that area, Gotch felt.

Gotch bulled Hack into the rope and then pulled him from it. He caught the Russian Lion in a crotch hold and lifted him high, then slammed him heavily to the canvas. It was the first such move in the match, and the crowd reacted with cheers and stomping, half of the huge congregation leaping to their feet. They sensed the first fall was near, and it looked to be an ending far different than they would have dreamed possible upon entering the pavilion.

Hack tried to push himself off the mat, but Gotch reached out and hooked his arms, and pulled them away. Without arms for support, Hack crashed face first back to the mat. Twice Hack tried to rise, and both times Gotch thwarted him. With Hack lying stretched out, Gotch dropped back in a flash and grabbed hold of a leg. Terrified of the toe hold, Hack broke Gotch's grip by kicking his leg out straight. Gotch secured another leg seconds later, only to have his grip broken once again. But on the third time, Hack couldn't break Gotch's grip. He was about to experience the most dreaded hold in all of wrestling.

Hackenschmidt turned on his side so that he was facing Gotch.

"Get up, if you will, Mr. Gotch," said Hack in a voice that was heavy, and sounded ready to break. "I yield the match, and give you the championship."

Frank could hardly believe his ears, but he stopped just short of applying the toe hold in full measure. He looked over at Smith, who was on one knee watching the action, to see if the referee had heard. Smith nodded solemnly.

"There will have to be a fall of some sort," said Smith, looking at Hackenschmidt with puzzlement. Hackenschmidt nodded, then looked back at Gotch.

"I surrender the title, Mr. Gotch," he said firmly.

Gotch released the toe hold, and stood up, staring down at Hackenschmidt, who had come to a sitting position. Hack's eyes were downcast, he couldn't look up.

Smith rose and came over to Gotch and grabbed his right hand, raising it aloft.

At that very instance, bedlam ensued. The ring filled with men pouring into it. Burns, Westergard and Klank flew to Gotch's side, hoisting him in the air. Newsmen scrambled into the ring as fast as they could, trying to snap pictures of Gotch and Hackenschmidt. Gotch was jostled about on the shoulders of a number of men. He felt far less elated than he would have thought before the match, and he tried to peer down through the mass of writhing bodies to catch a glimpse of Hackenschmidt. There was still another fall to wrestle, and he wanted to see if Hackenschmidt was up to it.

Frank finally managed to reach the mat again, but there was chaos all about him. Police were trying to remove the spectators, but were having an impossible time doing so. Someone had brought an American flag into the ring, and draped it around Gotch's corner post. Burns was talking to the announcer trying to find out what the status was for the second fall of the two-out-of three falls match, but the announcer kept shaking his head and pointing toward Hackenschmidt's corner.

Gotch felt an urgent tugging at his arm, and turned to face Elmer Smith and several other Humboldt men who were being dragged away by policemen. Smith yelled at Frank, grinning from ear to ear, and Frank smiled back, but didn't try to intervene. Instead, he pushed his way over to his corner. Burns had left the announcer who was now calling for the crowd's attention, and pulled Frank toward him.

"Hackenschmidt has forfeited the second fall," shouted Burns into Gotch's ear. "He says he is too exhausted to go on, and that you are the greatest wrestler he has ever seen. He congratulates you, and surrenders the title."

Then, Burns held up a thick, black leather belt, with a huge gold buckle on the center, with red lettering. The words "World Heavyweight Wrestling Champion" were printed neatly on it. Gotch had never seen the belt before, and hadn't even thought about it. But now he suddenly recalled seeing it around the waist of Hackenschmidt in the pictures he had seen of him back in New York, with Carkeek. The belt belonged to him now.

Gotch took it, and held it in his powerful hands, turning it over and over. The announcer's voice cut through the air.

"Mr. Hackenschmidt has declared himself unable to continue," he said in a booming voice, and then paused for the great ovation which followed, resuming when the noise had leveled off, "and he surrenders the world championship to Mr. Frank Gotch of Humboldt, Iowa."

It was bedlam once again. Gotch gave the belt to Burns and tried to make his way across the ring to Hackenschmidt, but it was useless. The police were trying desperately to keep the ring from becoming a battleground for fans gone half mad with the ecstasy of the moment, and Gotch turned back. Men were hanging on him, and twice he was almost pulled to the mat. He fought and shoved his way back to the corner, where Burns and the others were trying to leave the ring.

"Let's get out of here while we're in one piece," he shouted to Burns, who nodded and moved quickly down the steps to the main floor of the pavilion. There were ten more policemen waiting for the Gotch party, and slowly they pushed their way up the packed aisle.

After twenty minutes, the party reached Gotch's dressing room, and barged inside, slamming the door shut behind them. The twenty or so reporters in the room offered their congratulations, then began firing questions one after another. Gotch smiled and nodded hello to those he recognized and found his way to the large rubbing table, sitting down heavily. He had not felt at all tired in the ring, but he was suddenly on the verge of collapse. In fact, he had never felt so weary in his entire life.

His mouth was like a cotton ball, puffy and dry. He tried to swallow, and found that he couldn't as he had no saliva in his mouth. He coughed heavily and asked weakly for a cup of water. Westergard brought one, and he drank with relish, tipping the cup and draining it to the very last drop, then asking for more.

He tried to answer the questions as best he could.

Yes, he was surprised Hack had quit. No, he wasn't surprised he had won. He had followed the plan devised by the Farmer....please be sure and give plenty of credit to the Farmer, he stated, and to his training partners. Yes, Hack was very powerful. The strongest he had ever faced? He wasn't prepared to say so - though he was not - as he did not want to injure Hackenschmidt's feelings. He was sure the Russian Lion felt poorly enough, without reading in the papers that Gotch had insulted him.

Yes, he was tired, too, but no, of course not, he had never considered asking for a draw, or settling for it when Hack asked for one.

Gotch sensed acute fatigue overtaking him, but felt obliged to stay and discuss the match with the newsmen. They had been very generous to him leading up to the bout, and their stories had helped create the tremendous crowd, which Frank admitted had stunned him at first. Yes, he would tell them his share of the gate....he was to realize ten thousand dollars from the actual match, and then a share of the profits from the movie, which was being taken at ringside. It was the first championship wrestling match ever filmed.

After nearly thirty minutes of interviewing, Burns asked the newsmen to leave the room so Gotch could get showered and rest. After all, said Burns, it was one of the most grueling wrestling matches ever held in America, or anywhere in the world, for that matter.

Frank slid off the table. The sweat had long since dried on his body, and he was wrapped in his heavy green robe. His hair was tousled and his eyes were deep set and distant. He had trouble talking, but he wanted to make a final point for the writers.

"George Hackenschmidt is a great champion and a great man to travel this far to give me a crack at his title, and I am indebted to him," said Frank, the words coming slowly. "And I will gladly give him a rematch, if and when he desires. He deserves that.

"But it is very likely I may never be as good a man because of this match. The strain of such a contest is not appreciated by those who look on."

The reporters chuckled at the last statement, and cries of "you're the tops, Frank," and "no one could ever possibly beat you," echoed around the room. Only Burns, of those present, could possibly understand the sincerity of Gotch's words, and he showed no expression as he listened with considerable pride to his friend and pupil. Burns would respond to these statements at another time, another place.

The rest of the night was a blur to Frank. It took an hour to leave the arena. The same guard who had questioned his size a few hours earlier was delighted to see him, shaking his hand vigorously.

"I took your advice," he said. "I picked up a couple hundred in side bets."

Gotch nodded at him with a faint smile and slipped out into the crisp air. It felt very, very good. Elmer Smith and Klank had conspired to take their newly-crowned world champion to a swinging nightclub, the Ivanhoe, and Frank agreed. But his heart wasn't into it. After an hour of toasting and boasting from the entire Humboldt contingent and various other Iowans who had discovered who was in their midst, he found Burns about to depart, and they snuck away when the group's attention was diverted elsewhere.

"With women like that around," said Burns, nodding to a stage where three women were dancing with very little to conceal their lovely bodies, "they won't even notice we've left."

It seemed like he had just barely fallen asleep, yet there was Klank at his bedside, talking so fast and so excitedly that Frank couldn't keep up. He ducked his head under the blanket and pulled a pillow up over his ears.

"Hey, Frank, cut that out," said Klank, pulling off the covers and yanking the pillow away. "Your adoring public awaits you. People want to hear what you have to say. You're the biggest hero in America right now. Come on out here and read some of these telegrams."

Gotch pulled himself from the bed, slipped on a robe and followed Klank into the adjoining room. Burns was there, but no one else.

"The newsmen have been hounding at the door for hours," said Klank. "I keep telling them you're sleeping, but they're starting to think you're hurt, or something. You need to talk to them."

"What time is it?" asked Gotch, rubbing his eyes, and blinking heavily. He felt groggy, unsure of himself.

"Why, it's almost noon," said Klank. "Heck, you've had far more sleep than I have. Shoot, we stayed at the Ivanhoe for hours after you and the Farmer ditched us."

Gotch moaned. "Heck, Emil, we didn't get back til two a.m., and I had a heck of a time falling asleep."

Klank paid him no heed and grabbed a handful of telegrams, waving them in Gotch's face.

"Read these, if you want to wake up," he said. He filed through the pile, and pulled out one in particular. "Here, read this one first."

He sounded so authoritative that Frank reached out for the telegram, fearing Klank would shoot him if he didn't. Klank's eyes were bulging and he was nearly drooling with anticipation.

"Congratulations on your tremendous victory. It has brought great pride to all Americans. Please come visit us." It was signed by Theodore Roosevelt, President of United States.

Frank sank down heavily in the big chair by the window, shaking his head slowly. He read the telegram over several times, stunned by the name at the bottom.

"I knew Roosevelt was a devoted sports fan, and that he follows boxing and wrestling closely," said Frank, looking up at Klank. "But this still surprises me. A telegram from the President of the United States, within twelve hours of my winning the title."

Klank threw a dozen other telegrams in Frank's lap, all of which expressed admiration for his accomplishment.

"Humboldt went crazy when it received word," said Klank. "We got a report today that they had huge bonfires all over town, and that they danced in the streets until morning. They're planning a huge celebration, and they're expecting a thousand people. Going to call it Frank Gotch Day."

Gotch glanced over at Burns, who nodded as if in verification of all Klank had been saying.

"You're the talk of the country, Frank," Burns said. "Already been half a dozen businessmen from Chicago up here wanting to see you about business deals. They all claim they can make you a couple thousand dollars. Even been one fellow who wants you to star in some kind of play. And, of course, there are a couple of men who want you to take up boxing right away."

"Not that again," said Klank, slapping a hand off his forehead. "Now Frank, you ain't getting involved in no boxing ventures, right?"

"Naw, Emil," said Gotch, "I'm not. Got enough things on my mind right now without taking on that kind of a project."

He turned back to Burns.

"When we leaving?" he asked. "I'm anxious to get back to Humboldt. Want to see ma, pa, the family, and some other folks right away."

Burns pulled out his pocket watch and glanced at it.

"Just been waiting for you to come around and get moving. We can take off as soon as you're packed."

CHAPTER 14

Humboldt was agog. It had been three days since Gotch had become the world's heavyweight wrestling champion. He had spent just one half a day in Chicago after the victory, and had taken the train to Fort Dodge, where he was met by over five hundred people at the station. Ten autos - several of them the brand new, shiny black Model T Fords now being mass produced by the new assembly line system up in Detroit - were waiting for his party, and they chauffeured them into Humboldt. Heading onto Main Street, the caravan passed under a large banner tied from tree to light post, proclaiming Gotch's victory. Another, a short way down the street, stated "Humboldt is proud of its most famous son, Frank Gotch."

The caravan stopped in front of the bank, where nearly one thousand people were assembled. They began cheering wildly when the caravan broke into sight. Frank had been told by his driver, George Miller, that his family had already been brought to town for the festivities, and he was most anxious to see them. He remembered the promise he had made to his mom years ago, and he felt a warm glow deep inside.

The high school band was playing as the autos stopped. Mayor Joe Chaney stepped forward to greet Frank, Burns, Klank and the others as they stepped from the automobiles. They had even gone to the trouble of erecting a small platform, and had several chairs on hand for the ceremonies. There were more pennants flying, and a dozen or so American flags hanging from the various businesses around the bank, in recognition of the fact that one of the world's two most prestigious sports titles - heavyweight wrestling champion of the world - now rested in Humboldt, Iowa.

Frank spotted his mother and father on the platform and rushed to them, hugging first his mother and shaking his father's hand. Amelia had tears streaking down her face, and dabbed at them with a hanky. She was unabashedly proud of her son's accomplishments, and Frank felt like he had, at last, won his biggest victory of all - his mother was no longer ashamed of his activities in the athletic world. His father was beaming with pride, but said nothing. He continued to shake Frank's hand, and after they stopped, continued nodding his head in approval, his eyes watching his son's every movement.

The town's fire bell began ringing, and for just a moment Frank felt a terrible churning in his stomach, fearful that a fire had broken out somewhere at the most unfortunate of moments. But when he saw the loud clanging went unheeded, he realized the bells were in honor of the occasion, and he breathed a sigh of relief.

The mayor addressed the crowd, speaking of the great civic pride fostered by Gotch's accomplishments. He said the efforts of one man had done more to spread the fame of Humboldt than the combined activities of all the men and women who had ever lived in the town. He held up a wad of telegrams. They came, he said, from the governor, various senators and representatives, and from dignitaries in the world of sport, including James J. Jeffries, who had retired as undefeated heavyweight boxing champion of the world in 1905, but was still considered the champion by most sporting folks.

Then, the mayor paused. Turning to Klank, he asked him to read the telegram from Roosevelt. After Klank obliged, the clapping and cheering went on for what seemed like an eternity, causing Frank to fret and stare down at his feet. He appreciated the affection his hometown was showering on him, but he was beginning to feel uncomfortable. He looked up through the crowd, and recognized almost every face there. Right off the bat, he had seen Marshall Green, the chicken picker, his very first professional victim; and many friends from his school days. He smiled at all of them, and nodded at a few; but he was searching for someone else. He was hoping to catch a glimpse of the Oestrich family, and Gladys in particular, but he was unsuccessful. ·

He realized he was being introduced. The mayor was telling the crowd in detail just how tremendous an athlete he was, and Frank began to ponder what he should do and say once he was introduced. Speaking was not his forte, but he wasn't fearful of addressing a crowd.

A thunderous ovation followed the mayor's speech, and all eyes turned toward Gotch. He rose from his chair, walked to the podium, and stood in silence as the crowd continued to cheer and clap. He finally held up his hand, a grin growing on his lips, and the crowd quieted.

"Well, I hardly know what to say to all of this," he began, scratching his head as if perplexed. "I think it was a lot easier on my nerves going up against the Russian Lion than to come here and try to speak before all of you, my friends who know me so well and know all of my shortcomings and faults."

"You ain't got no faults today, Frankie," yelled a man from the audience. "You're the world champion, and we love you."

Frank laughed, and the crowd cheered wildly again.

Frank continued: "It almost seems like a miracle that all of this has happened, and I know God is certainly with us today, just like he's been with me all along these past few years."

He paused, not knowing what to say next, then decided he'd talk a little about Hackenschmidt.

"You know, George Hackenschmidt is the most perfectly built man I ever laid eyes on. Picture to yourself what you think a perfect physical specimen should be and you have Hack to a dot. He does not have one superfluous ounce of meat on his bones; he's all muscle and sinew. He is certainly a magnificent specimen of manhood, a sight to look upon.

"I think that the main reason that foreign wrestlers always show so poorly against our athletes in recent years is that across the water they stick to the same old methods year in and year out. They do not seek to improve, to build on what they had, to let go of worn out things. They go at it too leisurely and do not seem to like the exertion of throwing themselves into a sport so thoroughly as to make it evolve to higher and higher efficiency under experimenting and hard work. Over here, our fighters and wrestlers make the game a study, work at it, think over it, figure out improvements and seek for some way to get results. They do not do this across the water.

"Wrestling is a grand sport and so long as it is on the square it appeals to the public as few sports do. I have never wrestled before a poor audience.

"For nine years I have been wrestling, meeting all comers and wrestling under all conditions, and have never mixed up in a queer match or failed to give the public my best. And it is gratifying to me, of course, to hold the undisputed world's title. I am glad that it is held in America, glad that I brought it here.

"But I mean my life to be more than a mere wrestling exhibition. I expect to wrestle for only a short time, but I will be an Iowa farmer all my life. I hope that every year may find me a little better man in some way than I was the year before. I want to be a good citizen, and a useful, helpful man.

"And most of all, I want to be those things right here in Humboldt, Iowa, the town where I was born and raised, and the town in which I will live and die."

Frank returned to his seat as the crowd cheered wildly once again, and then returned to the podium. Holding up his hands, he finally quieted the crowd.

"I forgot to pay my due respects to some fellows who did just as much as I did to bring this title to Humboldt." He introduced Klank, Rogers and Westergard, purposely saving Burns for last.

"And who can ever properly figure the thanks that goes to this last fellow," he said. "I first met him in 1899, when he gave me a whipping in Fort Dodge. But he told me later that night he could make a world champion out of me if I would listen to him. We've been side by side ever since and, folks, I want you to know that I think Farmer Burns is the greatest wrestler, pound for pound, the world has ever known.... including me and George Hackenschmidt."

Gotch went over and shook Burns' hand, pulling him to his feet. The Farmer acknowledged the ovation and tipped his hat. Gotch gave him a bear hug, and the two laughed heartily. It had been a long time coming, this moment, and both were savoring it to the utmost.

The ceremony was over, but the celebration continued long into the night. Men who drank took to the bars, while others milled about in the streets. Gotch and Burns, who never touched liquor, spent a great deal of time at the establishments, however, laughing and talking with old friends, but refraining from drink. Several times Gotch asked after the Oestrichs, and was told the family was in attendance at the ceremony, but had remained far to the rear, and had apparently left after Gotch's speech. He was saddened to think he had missed an opportunity to talk with them, and was plagued by the thought they may have felt he would not make special time to talk with them. He decided to call upon them as soon as he could gracefully break away.

It was almost six p.m., five hours after his arrival in town, when Frank walked up the steps to the porch at the Oestrich home. It was growing dark, and he could see an oil lamp burning in the living room. He knocked at the door, and waited. He knocked again, a bit harder.

Just when he was preparing to depart, he heard a slight noise, and the door opened.

He had seen Gladys just two months ago, but he was amazed at how much older she now appeared. Her dark hair was not in a bun, like he was accustomed to seeing, but fell freely about her shoulders. She had on a light blue dress, with white lace and strings up the front. She also was wearing reading glasses, and had a book clutched in one hand. It was the glasses, Frank thought, which made her seem so much older.

She was surprised to see him, but immediately broke into a shy grin.

"Hello, Mr. Gotch," she said sweetly. "Or, should I now address you as Mr. World Champion?"

"No, please don't," said Frank quickly, putting up a hand in protest. He suddenly felt very uncomfortable. He hadn't mapped out in advance what he was going to say or do, if she should happen to answer the door. But before he could say anything, she was talking again.

"My parents are not at home at the moment," she said. "They're down the street, visiting friends. But won't you come in and wait for them? My father will never forgive me if I let you get away. He's so anxious to chat with you about the match with the Russian Lion."

Frank laughed. Somehow, the words Russian Lion hardly seemed as dramatic when she spoke them as when one read it in the papers, or heard other wrestlers saying them. In fact, she made the words sound almost as though she were talking about a character from a story book, and not the world's most feared wrestler.

"Well, yes, if you're sure it's okay," he said. She moved aside, and he brushed past her into the hallway. She shut the door softly, and walked past him, leading him into the sitting room. She returned to the chair by the lamp and sat down. She motioned to the couch and he sat also.

"I must have dozed off while reading," she said. "After all, this has been quite a week in Humboldt, thanks to you. The night of the match, my father and my brother were up town until word came in that you had won. There was.....quite a commotion. Bonfires and bells clanging, and lots of shouting. It was a wonderful night for Humboldt."

Frank shrugged, smiling. He was beginning to wish he hadn't come. Sure, he wanted to see her, and to spend some time with her, but he didn't know what to say next. He certainly didn't want to talk about the wrestling part of his life, that would only sound like he was bragging.

"Are you reading something for school?" he asked.

"Oh, this," she said, holding up the book for him to see. It had a black cover, with yellow words on it, but he couldn't read the words. "No, it's just something that I'm reading for pleasure. Have you read it? It's entitled A Tale of Two Cities, by Charles Dickens."

"No, no I haven't read it," he said.

There was a moment's pause.

"Farmer is thinking about writing a book about wrestling," he volunteered. There. He had done it. They were back on the subject of wrestling. He felt hopeless.

"Really? That's so exciting, to know someone who has actually written a book."

"Well, he hasn't yet. But, he says he's going to, and Farmer Burns does everything he says he's going to."

"Like make a world champion out of you?"

Frank nodded, but said nothing.

"Frank Gotch," Gladys said suddenly, and with a tone which made Frank look sharply at her. He was sure she was angry at him, but he couldn't guess at what, unless it was for talking about wrestling too much. Had he really said all that much?

"You just aren't going to tell me about that wonderful match in Chicago unless I plead with you, are you?"

He was nearly speechless. Here, he had been trying to avoid talking about wrestling, and it's what she wanted most to hear.

"I mean, here you've just done the most amazing thing that anyone in Humboldt has ever done, and you won't even talk to me about it." She looked as though she was going to pout....or worse yet, cry.

"Wait a minute," said Frank, leaning forward on the couch, his eyes drinking her in. "Please, don't get upset. I just didn't want you to....well....I didn't think that you'd want to....I mean....hear about wrestling, and all that sort of thing."

"Of course I do," she said. "After all, it's the most important part of your life, and you're a very special...." Her voice trailed off, and Frank felt his face grow hot. He stared at her and for the first time since he had known her, she looked away from his eyes.

Frank leaned back on the couch, suddenly very much at ease. It was as if a huge wall between them had collapsed. Just as Gideon had blown a horn and the walls of Jericho had come tumbling down, so had Gladys turned a phrase, and the barrier that had existed between them crumpled.

"I would love to tell you all about it, Gladys. I'm pleased that you are interested. Where should I start?"

She asked him a series of questions then. She wanted to know what Chicago was like, and how tall the buildings were. When he mentioned several were over forty stories, she couldn't hide her amazement. Though her father was wealthy, they hadn't traveled much, and had never been to a city larger than Omaha in Nebraska. She asked him about the style of clothing, and what the stage shows were like. They talked about the size of the crowd at the match, and Gladys told him the telegraph office in Humboldt had stayed open all night long to receive reports of the match, with over one hundred people hanging around the office most of the night.

"I couldn't go to sleep until I'd heard, no matter how late," she said, without modesty. Frank felt sure her interest was magnified by the attention the win could bring her hometown, but he also allowed himself to suppose she cared for his sake, as well.

She said the fire bells had sounded about one in the morning when the final results were received, and she could hear shouting and singing for the next hour. She hadn't left the house, but she and her mother had seen a huge bonfire glowing a long way off through their window.

Then Frank told her more about Hackenschmidt, and how perfectly developed the man was.

"But wrestling is more than just strength, Gladys," he said softly. "It takes four parts strength, three parts knowledge and three parts nerve to make a complete wrestler. Hack was very strong and had a lot of knowledge, but he lacked the nerve it took to win, at least this time."

"Will you wrestle him again?" she asked.

"I don't know yet," he said. "That will be more or less up to Emil Klank, my manager. You see, Farmer handles my training, and Emil my matches. He lines up the opponents. Right now, there are a dozen or more Americans who want a shot at the world title. This is the first time it's been on these shores, and there are a lot of wrestlers who deserve a chance to say they wrestled for the championship of the world.

"Then, there are a lot of cities that would like to host a bout for the championship of the world. Kansas City and St. Louis have already been after us to come there. And then there's a doctor in Seattle who's telling everyone he can beat me. I just might go out there soon. I love that part of the country, and when I wrestled Tom Jenkins out there in 1904 in Bellingham, we had the largest crowd ever to see an athletic event. Something like six thousand people, I think, with several thousand more turned away 'cause there wasn't enough room. And the writers were very kind to me."

"A doctor who wrestles?" asked Gladys with a giggle.

"Yes, and a very good doctor, wrestling wise. His name is Roller, goes by the initials of B. F., I guess. We've already wrestled once, for an hour, and neither of us gained a fall. But, in all truth, he did run from me, and refused to mix it up. He knew there was an hour limit, and he just wanted to last, not win. This time will be different. I doubt Emil will agree to any time limit, certainly not one of less than two hours."

"Is that certain, then, that you'll be going out west?"

Frank laughed.

"Well, there is something else. You will not believe this when I tell you, no indeed. I laughed when I first heard of the plan, and haven't stopped since. But it seems these fellows are serious enough."

"What's that," she asked, leaning forward. She was enjoying sitting and talking with this rugged and world famous man very much. He was warm and considerate, affectionate, she felt, and caring. He was, she thought, a great man, and very handsome, as well.

"Two men approached me the day we were leaving Chicago. One was named Irving Lee, who had authored this play called Yankee Regent. I had never heard of it, but apparently it was doing well. Anyway, he said he has written a play, called All About a Bout, and wants me to play the lead role. I couldn't help laughing outright in his face, and spent a good deal of time apologizing to him, because he acted like I had hurt his feelings. I hadn't meant to, of course, but he insisted I take his card and keep it in mind. I had forgotten it, but there was a telegram waiting for me at the Fort Dodge train station, saying he wanted me to read the script. Well, that's pretty funny, don't you think? Me, on stage, acting." He leaned back on the couch, slapping his hands on his knees and chuckling.

Gladys sat still, unsmiling, stopping Frank short when he saw her reaction.

"No, I don't think that's funny at all, Frank," she said. "I think you would be marvelous on stage. I think you can do anything you've a mind to do. But, would you want to do that?"

"Well, I don't know," he said, puzzled by her vote of confidence. He had thought the proposition too preposterous for words. But now, he took a different viewpoint toward it. If Gladys didn't think it was so odd, then maybe it wasn't. He trusted her instincts. Besides, he wanted to please her, and maybe this would go further toward that end than anything else he could do.

"Will you promise me something?" she asked.

"Why, yes, of course," he responded.

"That you will at least look into this matter, that you won't just laugh it away without thorough investigation?"

He nodded.

They carried on a polite conversation for what only seemed like several more minutes, but when the clock on the wall struck eight times, Frank was surprised to find he had been there nearly two hours. He had promised Burns he would return to "rescue him" in an hour, and he was already late. He rose and made apologies for staying so long, but Gladys seemed not a bit concerned with the hour.

"We've talked so much of my plans, but I would be very interested to know what you are going to be doing in the coming months," said Frank.

"I'm going to attend college in Ames," she said. "I've been working and saving some money, and I want to continue my education."

She walked him to the door, but didn't open it. They stood in the entranceway for a minute, neither knowing what to say next.

"I would like to write you, if I go out west," he said stiffly.

"That would be most delightful," she said. "I would love to receive letters from you, Frank, and to hear about your fascinating travels and the results of all your matches, though I am sure you will win them all with ease."

Frank stuck out his big hand, offering it for a handshake.

"We have a deal then," he said. "We will correspond, and keep in touch, right?"

She reached out and stuck her tiny hand in his, watching it disappear. His hand was massive and exuded strength, yet she was surprised his touch was so gentle, and his hand was softer - much softer - than she would have thought. She wondered how a man so powerful and fierce in the ring, so fierce that he was now the heavyweight champion of the entire world, could possibly be so gentle.

He started to withdraw his hand, but she tightened her grip, stopping him. She laid her other hand over the top of his.

"We are all very proud of you, Frank," she said softly. "Please don't forget Humboldt."

"I would never do that," he said, just as softly. "This town, these people, they mean more to me than any title ever could."

"You'll have so many people wanting to have you for themselves, though," she said. Her voice was breaking a bit, as though she were about to cry.

He put a hand on her shoulder, lightly.

"I'll never leave Humboldt," he said firmly. Then, he leaned down quickly and kissed her lightly on the cheek. He pulled back, and started to withdraw his hand a second time. But again she held firm. She looked up at him, her soft, brown eyes starting to fill with tears. He leaned down again and kissed her on the cheek again, quickly and lightly. Then, he withdrew his hand.

"Goodnight, Gladys," he said. He turned and opened the door. "I won't forget."

He walked away into the night, and she stood watching him go until he disappeared in the darkness.

CHAPTER 15

As the new heavyweight champion of the world, Gotch was in huge demand. Offers poured in from dozens of cities. He traveled first to Kansas City and then to St. Louis, dispatching his two opponents with ease before huge crowds. The fans cheered for him as never before, on his way to the ring, in the ring and as he left.

He faced Roller on July 1, 1908, in Seattle; Klank had succeeded in removing all time limits, and it was regarded as a finish match....to be contested until one of them could go no further. Gotch demolished the game doctor in straight falls and received rave reviews from reporter Ed. R. Hughes in the Seattle Times:

"Frank Gotch of Humboldt, Iowa, is still the wrestling king. The match last night demonstrated that Dr. B. F. Roller of Seattle is one of the gamest men in the world and that Frank Gotch is his master.

"Seattle has now seen the toe hold made famous by Gotch, in all its thumbscrew cruelty, and Dr. Roller has felt it. No torture ever practiced in the Inquisition could be keener than what Gotch inflicts with the bone-breaking hold when he gets it right. It is a perfectly fair hold, but it is devilish in its cruelty.

"Gotch put it on Roller just once last night, with nearly the proper leverage, and those at ringside imagined they could hear the bones of the foot and ankle crush and snap. Eddie Gafney, the referee, on hands and knees near the wrestlers, could not stand it.

"'Let up a little, Gotch, you will break his leg,' he said.

"Roller, fast as a flash and tricky as a fox, was blocked in his every move by the greatest wrestler this country has ever produced, and he lost the match in two straight falls in the greatest wrestling bout ever seen in the west. Gotch took the first fall in 15:25, and the second in 21:54.

"The match for the championship of the world attracted the finest crowd that ever turned out for an athletic event in the northwest. Bankers and lawyers rubbed elbows with doctors and racetrack men. Salaried men whose sporting blood ran faster than their better judgement filled the cheaper seats, the price of any one which meant a new pair of shoes. And the big crowd saw a wrestling match that will live in the history of the northwest as a tremendous struggle between two real giants."

Two weeks later, Gotch threw three men in a total time of nineteen minutes in Dallas, Texas, his first visit ever to the Longhorn State. But after that trip, he decided to hang up the wrestling tights for nearly half a year. He had not been unmindful of Gladys' plea on behalf of the stage show, and when he was approached again, he said he was interested. The telegram from Lee caught him in Texas, and he journeyed to Chicago to work out the details, and to begin rehearsals. Within just one month of arriving in Chicago, he opened as the star of the three-act comedy in Kalamazoo, Michigan. He had six other members in the cast and the three scenes took a total of just twenty-six minutes to perform. The tour was scheduled to cover a number of cities and last for thirty-eight weeks.

Before the first production in Kalamazoo, he stood in front of the mirror, chastising himself severely.

"You an actor," he said. "You ignorant, gawky country lout. You on Broadway? What would George M. Cohan think." And he broke out laughing at the mere thought. He was stunned when he read the review in the Kalamazoo paper after the first showing.

"The season of 'Greater Vaudeville' at the Majestic Theatre in this city was ushered in under brilliant auspices last night and was made notable by the appearance of Frank A. Gotch, the champion wrestler of the world, as the head of his own company of seven people, in a dramatic playlet in three scenes by Irving Lee, entitled 'All About a Bout'.

"It was the first public presentation of the sketch on any stage, and also marked the debut of the famous mat king in vaudeville, and the ovation he received at the hands of the admiring throng attested to the success of his bold plunge into the realms of the near-drama.

"The theatre opener was a corker, every seat in the big, beautiful playhouse being occupied at each performance; the playlet made a pleasing hit, and as for Gotch - he scored one of the greatest personal triumphs of his career, being called to the front of the stage at the conclusion of each act and showered with applause."

Frank dropped the paper and sat in silence. Sure, he had received big and long ovations, but he had thought they were merely being polite. He refused to believe he was a good actor.

Klank was the only member of his entourage he could talk into a part, and he played the role of Atlas Stetzel, the champion wrestler of Australia. The two wrestled for nearly ten minutes in the play, flip-flopping all over the stage. Gotch played the role of a college athlete named Frank Contry, and loved every minute of it.

The play moved on to New York, opening at Hammerstein's and the review was, once again, extremely kind:

"No one expected to find the champion wrestler of the world an actor, nor did anyone probably imagine that important athletic personage, Frank A. Gotch, would invade New York City with a real, genuine, comedy sketch to present his prowess on the mat. Mr. Gotch sprang the surprises, however. In this New York Vaudeville debut Mr. Gotch is the center of a very well and brightly written comedy sketch, containing several laughable situations and employing a competent cast.

"When it is considered that other than the fame and drawing power attached to the champion wrestler of the world, Mr. Gotch has surrounded himself with a most capable piece and company, it follows that Frank A. Gotch is a valuable act for vaudeville."

Frank was little less than amazed by the acceptance of his acting, and was equally surprised to learn that President Roosevelt had requested that he stop by the White House during the tour. The invitation came after the closing night in New York, and was delivered personally back stage by an under secretary of the army, who had come to see the play.

He drove to Washington the next day with Klank. They were impressed by the beauty of the great city, and the huge monuments that had been constructed as tributes to presidents George Washington, Thomas Jefferson and Abraham Lincoln. When he spotted the Lincoln Monument, Gotch ordered Klank to park the auto and they climbed the steps and walked between the massive pillars into the huge area where the nation's sixteenth President sat regally on a chair. They stared up in awe at the huge statue of the Great Emancipator.

"He was a wrestler; did you know that, Emil?" asked Frank as he regarded the statue.

"Go on," said Klank, glancing at Gotch with skepticism.

"No, really," said Gotch. "A fan came up to me once in Kansas City and gave me a story about Lincoln. And Farmer told me he was, as well. He did a lot of wrestling in his days as a log splitter. He had a great build for wrestling....long limbs and a lean body. Great leverage."

They drove up to the front gate of the White House, and were actually surprised to find their names on the list. The guard directed them to the back gate, and they drove in past another security check, where they were greeted by several men in very stiff looking suits. They were escorted into the grand house, and led to a very large reception room, and asked to wait for the President.

"I feel out of place here, Frank," said Klank, looking around the elegant room they were in. "This is the same place Abraham Lincoln lived in, for crying out loud. And all the other great men who served as leaders of our country. So what are we, just a couple of thick-eared wrestlers, doing here?"

"I don't know either," said Frank, his hands folded in his lap. "But apparently Teddy is a man who likes wrestlers. Let's see what he has to say and then get the heck out of here."

Ten minutes later, Teddy Roosevelt strode into the room, dressed in a three-piece suit and wearing his eyeglasses halfway down his nose. Two official appearing men in blue suits trailed along behind him. Frank and Klank stood immediately.

"Men.....I'm Teddy Roosevelt," he boomed in a thick voice, grinning from ear to ear. He glanced at them quickly, then zeroed in on Frank, sticking out his right hand. He was a thick, powerful looking man who exuded energy.

"By gad, you're Frank Gotch, aren't you? The man who defeated The Russian Lion, that mountain of muscle from overseas. I met him, you know. Very impressive fellow. Didn't think the man could be beaten. But you did it, by jove. What a glorious accomplishment, for both you and the nation. Yes sir!" he beamed.

Frank took his hand, and shook it forcefully. The President continued beaming, staring directly into Frank's eyes with unstinted admiration. Frank remembered an article he had read about Roosevelt as a youth, when he had been taunted by two older boys at a camp. He had been devastated by his inability to stand up to the boys, and upon returning to his home in New York had pleaded with his father to buy him boxing equipment. His father had responded by equipping a small gym in their home, and Roosevelt had reportedly become a fitness fanatic. This inner drive had changed his life, and he was well known for being a rugged outdoorsman. And then, of course, he had become a national figure by leading the Rough Riders in the famous charge up San Juan Hill near Santiago, Cuba, during the Spanish-American War of 1898.

Gotch introduced the President to Klank, and Roosevelt engaged them in small talk for several minutes. Then he leaned toward Frank, glancing back over his shoulder as though he was about to share a secret which he didn't want anyone else to hear.

"Frank, what do you know about this jiu-jitsu craze that's got everyone talking?" he asked, lowering his voice considerably. His expression told Frank that it was a serious question.

"A little bit," said Frank. "I know some of the special moves they use. That's about all."

"Do you think you could whip a jiu-jitsu expert?" he asked.

Frank paused for a moment, then glanced over at Klank.

"Sure," he said.

The president leaned back, beaming, and clapped him hard on the shoulder.

"Good!" He nearly shouted. "The ambassador from Japan has been staying here for two days. We're doing some.....negotiating with him. And he's got this big, hulking fellow with him who he says can handle any American athlete, boxer or wrestler. Of course, that offends those of us who take pride in the American fighting sprit. I thought of you immediately as the perfect man to defend us, and when I heard you were appearing in New York, I knew I had to invite you here."

He turned to the two men behind him.

"Tell the ambassador to bring his champion with him to the East Room. We will see him there in half an hour."

Within thirty minutes, Gotch was escorted into the huge East Room of the White House, still somewhat numb from the rapid developments. The president had wrestling gear brought to Frank in a much smaller nearby room, and Frank changed quickly, exchanging glances with a bemused Klank the entire time. When Frank returned to the East Room, it was filled to near capacity, with at least one hundred men seated in the large ornate chairs. In the center of the room was a small mat which the President kept handy for such occasions, Klank was later told. And across the room stood three Japanese men, regarding Gotch and Klank stiffly.

The President himself took over. He moved to the center of the room, and introduced the Japanese ambassador and his jiu-jitsu expert, then swiveled and introduced Gotch and Klank. It was to be nothing more than a friendly contest between two great champions from two great nations, said Roosevelt, but Gotch knew instinctively that it meant far more than that to the President

The contestants circled one another warily, a dead hush in the room. Then Gotch exploded. He shot in with a powerful leg tackle and drove the Japanese warrior hard to the floor. Fighting to catch his breath, the Japanese fighting expert tried to wrap his legs around Gotch's waist, and to gain a position from the floor where he could work to slap on a deadly submission hold. Frank knew from working with Burns that jui-jitsu experts could launch a powerful attack while on their backs, if they could catch a foe in a scissors hold with their legs.

But Gotch was too fast and too strong. He caught his foe's left leg at the knee, slipping his right arm under it, then tightened sharply, and spun his body to the right. The Japanese wrestler groaned and arched off the floor as Gotch stepped over his torso. He was employing one of Farmer Burns' favorite hooking moves, a tortuous knee lock submission hold, and Frank was turning on the pressure. Gasps filled the room as Frank leaned back onto his foe's buttocks, cranking hard on the leg he held tight. The Japanese wrestler jerked and writhed for several long seconds, trying desperately to free himself. Then, he tapped the floor hard with his palm, surrendering.

The bout had lasted less than two minutes. Frank released his hold and stood, staring down at the vanquished foe. Then, he extended his hand and helped him to his feet. Roosevelt was already at Frank's side, pounding him on the back.

"Magnificent, simply magnificent, Frank," he exclaimed, his eyes wide. He glanced over the Japanese ambassador, who looked crushed. Roosevelt smiled hugely, then turned back to Gotch.

"Stay the evening, Frank. We have a great banquet planned, and you and Mr. Klank are to be my guests of honor. Yes sir, never doubt the great American fighting spirit," he exclaimed, and turned and walked back to the group of men who were talking excitedly, glancing back at Gotch and the Japanese trio.

The night lasted long, with Roosevelt toasting Gotch's victory at the banquet, and then singling him out several times at the reception afterwards to congratulate him on his great career. Everyone else in the banquet hall, including many of the women, seemed determined to chat with him too, and several times he had to explain how a man who seemed so friendly on the outside could be such a fierce competitor on the mat.

He and Klank were exhausted when they finally turned into their beds at a hotel two blocks from the White House. But it had been a day neither of them would ever forget. They returned to New York to discover that Lee had made plans to take the play abroad. At first, Frank was hesitant. Not only had he never been on an ocean liner, he wasn't wild about being away from Humboldt for such a long time. His father was in poor health, and he knew he would not be able to get home quickly if something terrible was to happen. Nor did he relish not seeing Gladys for such a long time. They had been corresponding regularly, and he couldn't hide his delight at the warm tone of her letters to him.

But Lee was insistent, saying he had received very favorable responses from all the theatre agents he had contacted in Europe. Frank finally gave in, and they sailed from New York on November 17 on the ship Campania, heading for London.

Besides the play itself, Frank had another reason for going to Europe. After Hackenschmidt had reached his native shores, he had changed his tune about the Chicago loss. He was suddenly accusing Gotch of being a dirty wrestler. He accused Frank of greasing his body so as to make it impossible for Hackenschmidt to gain a hold, and even went so far as to claim Gotch had soaked his body in oil for days to make himself slippery.

"Doesn't he realize that you'd have destroyed your health with such a stupid move," shouted Klank, hurling a newspaper across the hotel room after reading the article. "What a stupid thing to say. Besides, you'd be spreading the oil and grease on him, too, and he'd be just as hard to grasp hold of. How could those ignorant reporters believe such a thing?"

Hackenschmidt accused Gotch of other foul tactics, like thumbing his eyes. Frank was outraged at first, but began to cool down after he made the plans to go to England. Once there, he reasoned, he could meet with the press of Europe and tell his side of the story. Klank was just as eager to have Frank do so, saying it would only create greater interest in a return match, though Hack had shown little interest in another bout with Gotch.

When the Campania docked at Liverpool, several hundred sports fans were there to greet the new world champion. A representative of the famous Sporting Life Journal publication, James McIntyre, came aboard to interview him. McIntyre, was straightforward when introduced to Gotch. The two walked down the rail of the ship, and stood apart from the crowds that had wanted to be near them and listen. Gotch spoke in a steady voice as the smaller man jotted away in his note pad.

"You have no doubt heard Hackenschmidt's version of the contest with you. How does it reconcile itself with the facts?" asked McIntrye.

"First of all, let me say that I have not come here to hound him," said Gotch, tapping his finger on the rail for emphasis. "It would be undignified, but all he has said is false. The pictures prove it, and when they are shown no more need be said. The public of England will not convict me until I have been tried. I only plead for a fair trial. I beat him fair and square. After the match, he shook my hand and said he could never defeat me. Why has he now changed his tune?"

"Was the referee your choice?" asked McIntyre.

"Certainly not. I had no more to do with selecting him than you."

"Were you greased in the ring?"

Gotch laughed heartily.

"Greased? Hack is perverting the truth. Where would be the advantage? I had long tights on, but my upper body perspired heavily, as did Hack's. Whoever hatched the story about the grease told a good one. I think I moved so fast that it surprised and dismayed Hack. He's used to wrestlers who stand in one spot and wait for him to crunch them. Well, that's not my style. I will forfeit one thousand dollars gladly - and the title - if anyone can prove I used grease."

"He said also you used profane language."

Gotch became miffed now.

"I never swear, and certainly wouldn't at a time like that. I teased him a bit, but certainly did not use profanity."

"And what of the request for a draw?" asked McIntyre, writing furiously all this time.

"That was Hack's idea, and I rejected it. I knew at that point he was a beaten man."

"He has also claimed you gouged him; what do you say to that?"

"False, every line of it. With the exception of a scab, which was removed in the struggle, and bled, he did not have a mark upon his face. No man could have had fairer treatment extended to him by the people of Chicago. Ed Smith was the referee. Our contract stated that in the event of not agreeing, Rob Edgren was to select him. He declined and I left the referee to Hackenschmidt and the press. Siler was nominated, but his health prevented him, and so Smith took over."

"What is your opinion of Hackenschmidt as a man and as a wrestler?"

Frank drew a deep breath. He had mixed emotions now about the man. Once, he had respected him as much as one possibly could an opponent without giving in to fear and awe. But during the match, he had lost a bit of the respect he had previously held for him. He did not want to appear arrogant or unkind, but in truth his opinion of the famed Russian Lion had begun deteriorating in Chicago, and was now at an all-time low.

"As a wrestler, he is handicapped because he tells you what he is going to do before he does it," said Frank, measuring his words. "He is not clever, but is very strong. His conditioning was not what it should have been for such an important match. Maybe he didn't think it was that important, and didn't take me seriously as a challenger."

"Did he have a chance with you?"

"A champion always has a chance, of course," said Frank, rubbing his chin as he reflected. "But he was never in a position to win the match. Even after he forfeited the match to me, the referee followed him to his corner and said that forfeit constituted just one fall, and he could return for the second. Smith asked him to return, but he said no.

"I waited for him for two years, aching to wrestle. He would not come to America for less than twelve thousand dollars, and wound up making a good deal more because of the fantastic crowd. But he was guaranteed twelve thousand dollars - win, lose or draw. He was treated like a prince in Chicago, I have heard. The town was wild with excitement and wanted to see him. Did you know Teddy Roosevelt even said he would like to be like Hackenschmidt, if he were not President?

"But, I must tell you this. Hackenschmidt's abilities are over-exaggerated. He is not a terror nor a wonder. I am ready to wrestle him again, or to meet anyone else in any style. I have never refused a man a match. I bear no man any ill will.

"I have made a great study of wrestling, and have benefited greatly from having Farmer Burns as my confidant. Wrestling Hackenschmidt, I soon found out his plan of attack. When he pulled me forward, I went with him, and did not retreat as most men do. His favorite head hold I trifled with, put my chest against his head, and got close, with head downward, like a boxer."

After the interview with McIntyre, Frank was accosted by several dozen more reporters upon leaving the ship, and during his first week. He and the play appeared in a number of theatres, drawing more overflow crowds. Though he continued to hear stories of Hackenschmidt's people accusing him of dirty wrestling in Chicago, he did not see Hackenschmidt during the entire trip. His only wrestling match came about as a misunderstanding, when he refused a challenge from a Sheffield wrestler named George Dinnie. At first, Frank thought it was a joke, and laughed it off. But the next day a headline in the paper declared he was unwilling to meet the man and hinted Gotch was ducking him. Frank was hurt when a group of small school children spotted him, and one cried out he was afraid of Dinnie.

Gotch made Klank arrange the bout on a day when the play wasn't scheduled, and pinned the Sheffield wrestler in one minute and six seconds in the first fall, and fifty-five seconds in the second. The last fall was questioned, though, because Dinnie said he was not pinned. Frank relented to the crowd's demand for another fall. He scowled at Dinnie and grabbed him hard, hurling him to the mat and pinning him in little less than ten seconds. This time the crowd roared its approval, and Dinnie limped off, rubbing his back and shaking his head. The next day in the paper, he told everyone what he thought of the world champion.

"Gotch is the most wonderful of all the great wrestlers I have met," Dinnie declared. "Hackenschmidt altogether takes a back seat. Gotch worked with his brains as well as his body, in a way Hackenschmidt never did and never could do. He is strong and moves like lightning. A man stands no chance against him. He is a master of ring craft. I have never met or read of a man like him. There is not an ounce of science in the ring he does not know about."

Reading the story, Frank appreciated most of all the fact Dinnie approved of his fairness in the ring, taking the sting from some of the charges leveled by Hackenschmidt.

"Gotch is a straight gentlemanly fellow and I don't think he would do anything outside the rules," said the Englishman. "If he were beaten, he would not shake hands and then go away saying bad things. If all Hackenschmidt says is true, why then did he shake hands with Gotch in a friendly way after the contest? Why did he not leave the ring disgusted? Gotch is not only a straight man, but also a gentleman.

"But when he goes into the ring, he means to win and he follows you like a lion. I have never experienced anything like the bouts with him. There was something about every touch he gave you. He wears you down. His brain works with a wonderful rapidity."

The Gotch company played four weeks in London, then moved

about England, with stops at Leeds, Nottingham, Sheffield, Liverpool, Birmingham, Glasgow, Edinburgh and Newcastle-upon Tyne. At every city, from five thousand to ten thousand people crowded about the party as it journeyed to and from the hotels.

But the heavy schedule was beginning to have an effect on Frank. Though he was pleased by the turnouts, it was making him restless. He wanted to return to the United States, to resume wrestling, and to visit Gladys. She had been on his mind constantly, and he waited impatiently for the letters to arrive. Though he had never been a letter writer himself, he now sat down faithfully several times a week and wrote short notes. Hers were just as regular, and always much longer. She talked at great length about Humboldt and the various goings on, and he realized that she, too, harbored a great, deep-seated love for the town, its people and Iowa. It caused him to miss both her and Iowa all the more.

He remembered the vow he had made to Elmer Smith the day he had bought the raffle tickets from her. Yes, he wanted to marry Gladys, he knew now. And he was worried about her going away to college, in Ames. He knew from her letters that he had moved his way into her heart, and she was very fond of him, and perhaps did even love him. But if he was gone long enough, he thought, she just may find her interest waning, and there would be plenty of young eligible men there in college to move into a privileged spot.

When Frank arrived in New York, Klank went ahead of him to Chicago trying to arrange some more matches, and Gotch visited some friends in New York, including Carkeek. He also ran into James J. Corbett, the legendary former heavyweight boxing champion, who gave him some disturbing news: Corbett said Jeffries had decided on coming out of retirement to fight Jack Johnson, the black man who had demolished champion Tommy Burns just two months before Gotch's arrival in New York. Johnson was a devastating fighter of incredible skills - lightning fast, elusive and with a murderous punch in either hand. He had played with game little Tommy Burns in their title bout in Sidney, Australia, before stopping him in the fourteenth round.

"He sneered at the crowd, and laughed at all the white folks," said Corbett, gritting his teeth. "Someone has to set the white man back on the throne, Frank, and Jim has agreed to do it. It would help if you would say a word or two to him, as he greatly admires you."

Gotch was caught in between. He wanted to see Jeffries back on top, not because of the fact Johnson was colored - that didn't bother him a whit - but because he was so cocky and boastful, and because he liked Jeffries. But he had heard reports Jeffries was woefully out of shape, and he doubted his ability to regain his old form. Four years had passed since he had last fought, and time has a way of eroding a man's skills, Frank knew.

Corbett was waiting with anticipation, scanning Gotch's features in that scrutinizing style of his. Gentleman Jim had been one of Gotch's early heroes. Most sporting fans admired this man after he dispatched the old bully, John L. Sullivan, with relative ease. But after he had gotten to know Corbett, he preferred to keep his distance. Not that he didn't like or admire him, but he was doubtful of his motives on many occasions.

"But, I heard Jeff is up to around three hundred pounds," said Frank, frowning at Corbett. "Can he get ready again to fight, and especially the likes of Jack Johnson?"

"Nothing to it," said Corbett, with a flip of the hand. "With me and Fitz training him, why it'll just take a little dedication, that's all."

"Bob Fitzsimmons is involved in this, too?" asked Frank, surprised. Fitzsimmons, the skinny blacksmith with a punch like a mule, had taken the title from Corbett with a vicious solar plexus punch that left the ex-bank teller kneeling on the deck, trying desperately to regain his wind. Fitz had always refused to fight Corbett again, and they were rumored to be bitter enemies.

"Certainly," said Corbett. "This is a crusade, to get that title back in the hands of the white race. We're all in this together, Frank."

Gotch pondered the situation considerably on the train ride to Chicago, and intended to talk it over with Burns. The Farmer would know best whether or not the old Boilermaker could make it back to top form after so long a layoff. Personally, Gotch doubted he could, and he didn't want to see Jeffries, who had retired undefeated, go out on his back. That was almost unthinkable.

When he arrived in Chicago, Klank met Gotch at the train station, full of excitement.

"Gotcha a great match, Mr. Gotch," he said. "You've heard of Yussif Mahmout, the Bulgarian?" Gotch nodded.

"Well, we take him on April 14 in the Chicago Coliseum, a brand new facility. How's that?"

"Great," said Frank. "But I'd better start getting ready immediately. Hasn't he already beaten Beell?"

"And some others, like Cutler and Americus, old Gus Schoenlin. They say Mahmout's a great one, faster than Beell, and much bigger.

I've got you two other matches lined up, as well, in Kansas City and Omaha. They'll help get you ready for Mahmout."

"Then we'd better make tracks for Humboldt, so that I can get started with the serious training," said Frank.

CHAPTER 16

His return to Humboldt after the tour of Europe brought Frank one of the biggest surprises of his life. In his absence, the town had taken up a collection to build him a training camp in Bicknell Park, down by the river, near the center of town. The mayor admitted to the incredulous Gotch that they had ulterior motives: not only did they want to do something special for their world champion, but they wanted to insure he would continue to live in Humboldt, and they felt the establishment of a training camp would encourage him to do so. Indeed, he said, the attraction of having Frank Gotch training in Humboldt would help stimulate business for the entire town, as fans would surely come from miles around to watch the world's greatest wrestler in any kind of sporting activity.

The camp area was an entire acre, and included an elevated ring with iron posts at all four corners, a handball platform, and a small building for dressing and showering, as well as a set of bleachers for fans to sit on while watching their champ train. Frank accepted the camp with sincere humility, and began immediate training for his two bouts.

He stopped by to see Gladys, and was crestfallen to discover she was in Ames and not expected home for some time. He had missed out on several letters from her after his arrival in New York, and, in fact, had not received one for nearly three weeks. In addition, his latest letter to her sat unopened on her vanity, said her mother. She asked if Frank would like it back, but he declined.

He threw himself into his training with a fervor, and at first found himself sidetracked by the number of persons who showed up to watch him. Each day saw almost one hundred people in the stands or milling about the campsite, and Burns became a little annoyed, shooing the youngsters away when they approached and asked to feel the champion's muscles. Still, Frank would slip away after a vigorous session and sit down by the river, knowing the young boys would discover his pattern sooner or later, and join him. He even fell into the habit of taking a number of them up the street to Karson's general store and buying them all ice cream cones. Frank always ate right along with them. He didn't have many weaknesses when it came to training, but ice cream was certainly one. He could eat it all day long, especially in the summer, if the Farmer didn't find out.

He journeyed to Kansas City to dispatch a French wrestler named Raoul De Reduen in straight falls, and appeared in Omaha the next evening after an all-night train ride, doing away with John Perrelli just as quickly. Then, it was back to Humboldt for the last round of training before departing for Chicago to take on Mahmout, a truly formidable foe by all accounts.

Before he departed from Humboldt, there was an unexpected visitor at camp. Frank had just finished a long, winding run through the countryside and had returned for a quick game of handball with Westergard when he heard his name called. He turned to see Robert Oestrich approaching, sporting a big grin and offering a handshake. Gladys' father apologized for missing Frank the night he had come calling, but added, with a wink, that perhaps it was just as well he and his wife had been absent, because Gladys had confided to them she had very much enjoyed having Frank "all to herself for a delightful evening of conversation."

Frank and Oestrich made small talk for some time, and then the older man stammered about, as if searching for words that weren't going to come easy. Gotch suspected Gladys would be the subject, and he began to wonder if it was going to be bad news.

"This sort of thing isn't easy for a father to talk about," said Oestrich, sending the worst fears flying through Gotch's mind.

"What is it?" asked Frank anxiously, reaching out a hand and grasping Oestrich's arm gently. "Has something happened to Gladys?"

"No, nothing like that. It's just....well, her mother and I have the feeling you two are quite interested in one another." He stopped to search Frank's face, and was reassured by the show of concern he saw.

"We just want you to know we are very much in favor of you calling on her, if that's your intent. Maybe I shouldn't even bring the subject up, but I did run into Mr. Smith, a friend of yours, I believe, who suggested you might be, uh, sort of....worried about what appears to be a large difference in ages. But I would like to assure you Mrs. Oestrich and I - and most importantly, of course, Gladys - have no difficulties with any of that at all."

There was an awkward silence, broken when Oestrich reached out his hand. Gotch took it, and the two men shook.

"I appreciate your coming here and saying these things," said Frank. "Gladys is a very special person to me, and I hope some day to begin a proper courtship. It's just that I'm so busy now, with all of the matches I have lined up. Of course, I have Mahmout in just a couple of days in Chicago, and Klank is already lining up many more, including one with the giant Polish wrestler, Zbyszko. But I hope to be able to settle down in the not too distant future, and I hope to see a lot more of Gladys. And the age thing had been on my mind, but I feel much better about it now."

The two men chatted for a brief spell, and then parted company. For Oestrich, the meeting had cleared his mind considerably. He would have been doubly proud to have a man like Frank Gotch in his family. But the talk only made Frank's thinking more muddled. At age 30, he yearned to begin building a family life, and if Gladys had been on his mind prior, she was to occupy his thoughts twice as much in the months to come.

But not in the immediate future. First, there was the Terrible Turk, as Mahmout was known in some circles. Over eight thousand fans were on hand at the Chicago Coliseum to cheer their champion against the latest foreign challenger. Mahmout came into the match with a tremendous reputation, having demolished Beell, the last man to have defeated Gotch - though Frank had avenged that rather curious loss four straight times - and was exceptionally powerful and quick. Mahmout had one peculiarity, in that he demanded to wrestle barefoot, a practice he had come by in his native Bulgaria. Klank objected at first, but finally gave in at the insistence of Mahmout's manager, Anton Pierri, who said they would forfeit five hundred dollars for the infraction of the rules.

Mahmout was considered the best contender on the horizon, and was given a sizeable buildup by the Chicago newspapers. But Frank was far too fast for the slightly smaller Bulgarian, wrapping up the first fall in exactly eight minutes, and the second, and final, in just another nine minutes and ten seconds. Ed Smith, who refereed the Hackenschmidt match, also officiated this time, and informed the reading public - he was sporting editor of the Chicago American newspaper - that no man in the world could come close to matching Gotch now.

Mahmout, wrote Smith in his paper, "was simply outclassed every inch of the way by a wonderful athlete of high mental as well as physical force. It wasn't the same Frank Gotch that worked and pulled and tugged and hauled through two awful hours with George Hackenschmidt in the same ring just one year and ten days before. The victor this time was a splendidly trained athlete, conditioned like a racehorse and fit to do battle for the whole state of Iowa."

Frank felt like he was on a roller coaster for the rest of the year. He crushed Hjalmar Lundin just three days later in Chicago, then defeated Dan McLeod, the former American champion, April 20 in Waterloo, Iowa. He hadn't really wanted to wrestle McLeod again as he had already defeated him five straight times over the years, but he knew Dan was down on his luck and needed a big payday with the world champion. For the first time in his life, Frank held back considerably during the match, trying to let his old adversary make a presentable showing. It hadn't been easy to make McLeod look good, so great was the disparity between their skills now, and Frank had struggled internally with his decision to carry the ex-champ. But the Waterloo crowd didn't seem to notice and cheered wildly for Frank as he left the ring.

Off the mat, he and McLeod enjoyed a friendly relationship that only real professional athletes could truly understand. After gaining his revenge on McLeod in their first real professional match several years ago, he had come to sincerely like the former champion, and enjoyed talking with him whenever their paths crossed. But he also felt sorry for him in that for all his great skills, McLeod had never been able to make much money as a wrestler. And now, well past his prime, he was still traveling the nation in search of matches, as it was the only way he knew to earn a living, however meager.

"You're the king, Frank," McLeod had told him after the Waterloo match. "You have taken wrestling to a new level in the United States. You've made it very popular, and have even helped create interest in colleges taking up the sport. I hear Yale and Princeton are now fielding teams, and you are the main reason why. You've made the sport respectable enough for the college boys to take a whirl at it. Why, any young boy who reads wants to be like Frank Gotch."

Coming from the man who had given him his first real lesson in the art of professional wrestling, the words meant a great deal to

Frank.

Two days later, he was in Boone, Iowa, to pin Ben Reeves, then whipped Dr. Roller for the second time, in Kansas City. He traveled to Memphis, Tennessee, to defeat a wrestler by the name of Charles Hackenschmidt, who was no relation to the famous Russian Lion, though it was rumored they were cousins - probably to help draw crowds.

He wrestled twenty-five times in 1909, and easily eliminated all respectable contenders. Jenkins, now far less than he was when Frank first took the American title from him, fell in straight falls June 14 in Des Moines, the Iowa capitol, and Roller went down to defeat for the third time in Kansas City on November 15. But it was Gotch's twenty-fourth match of the year that caused the biggest surprise in the athletic world, and set the stage for the second most monumental match of his career - second only to the victory over Hackenschmidt for the world title.

Stanislaus Zbyszko was without question one of the strongest men to ever appear in a wrestling ring. At five feet eight inches and two hundred and sixty pounds, he was very difficult to work with. Zbyszko, whose real name was Cyganiewicz, was an extreme rarity among wrestling, because of his education. He was a graduate of the University of Vienna and spoke twelve languages, with varying degrees of success. He first arrived in America in 1909, and reportedly had over 900 bouts behind him - without a single loss. Those who first saw him upon his arrival in New York City felt he was a threat to Gotch of the most serious nature, and there were many who were ready to place a wager on him when the two met.

Klank arranged the first match between the two on November 25 in Buffalo, just ten days after Gotch had thrown Roller in Kansas City. Though he was in the best physical shape of his life, Frank was exhausted by the long train ride to the city in upstate New York, and found the Pole to be an unyielding foe. The two battled for an hour without either gaining a fall, and the match was declared a draw. It was the first time in over forty matches - and in three years - that Frank hadn't prevailed with ease, and it made front page headlines all across the sporting pages of America.

It also began talk of a fake match. Many fans simply refused to believe anyone could hold Gotch to a draw, and they speculated that Gotch held back in order to build excitement for a rematch, which would make lots of money for everyone involved. The talk infuriated Frank.

"Can't someone have an off day?" he mumbled to Klank in the hotel room two days later. "Heck, the best baseball team in the world loses once in a while. So does everyone. I'll take this guy apart the next time we meet."

Frank closed out 1909 with an easy victory over Con O'Kelly in St. Louis, and scored two easy wins in early 1910, setting the stage for a rematch with Zbyszko in Chicago on June 10.

Once again, the Chicago Coliseum was packed to overflowing, and the betting was the heaviest on a Gotch match since the battle with Hackenschmidt two years earlier. This time, the outcome was one hundred percent different than in Buffalo, providing the fans with one of the most amazing wrestling performances ever seen anywhere in the world.

Frank and Burns had planned their strategy to perfection. The big Pole was a notorious slow starter, preferring to take his time to feel his foe out, and picking up the tempo of the match after the first thirty minutes or so. He had been successful in that style in Buffalo, slowing Gotch down with his near sixty-pound weight advantage and effectively neutralizing the great speed advantage the Iowan possessed. Gotch found it increasingly difficult to pick up the tempo, with the result a sixty-minute contest of mostly pushing and shoving. Burns knew the surest way to confuse Zbyszko, a slow thinker on the mat for all his academic standing, was to wrestle like a whirlwind. Also, any move Gotch could make to confuse the giant would be to his advantage.

Frank entered the Chicago ring in his familiar long green robe, and waved to the cheering crowd, signing autographs in his corner. He was cheerful and outgoing, as was his nature before a match, but the Pole came to the ring amidst a small smattering of applause, mixed with a few jeers. Zbyszko showed no expression, even during the introductions, and when he pulled off his black robe, a chorus of "ooohs" swept through the audience as the fans got their first glimpse of the massively muscled body. He wasn't of the same type of physique as was Hackenschmidt, with each muscle standing out in rigid attention, but he was huge and impressive, nonetheless. His waist was thick and heavy, but without much excess and his arms were as big as the thighs of a normal man. He gazed expressionlessly over at Gotch's corner, waiting for the bell to ring, signifying the start of the match.

He didn't seem concerned by the fact Gotch had turned his back on him, and kept it turned throughout the introductions. When the bell rang, Gotch backed from his corner, still facing away from Zbyszko, then wheeled suddenly and shook his hand in the customary greeting between contestants. Then, without pausing, he grabbed the giant and caught him in a half nelson and bar arm, pulling him to the mat. They hit the mat in a shattering collision, and Frank, moving like a panther, shifted to a pinning position, with the giant's shoulders firmly embedded in the canvas. Even the referee, Dick Fleming, was shocked by the explosion of action, but he recovered his senses in time to check the pin, and call the first fall. It had all transpired in barely seven seconds.

The crowd was stunned, and then broke out into a riotous applause, mixed with laughter at the Pole's predicament. Frank was already back to his corner smiling at Burns, while Zbyszko's attendants rushed to him to help him back to his corner. It was reportedly the first pin he had suffered in all his years of wrestling.

The reporters at ringside were caught unaware, as well, and hardly knew what to write. In the next day's paper, the Chicago Tribune said Gotch could probably remain champion for time indefinite. "Perhaps no more sensational match has been seen in Chicago in years, and the sudden termination of the first fall, which took the heart out of Zbyszko, will go down in wrestling history as a feat which may never again be accomplished in a world's championship contest."

After a five-minute rest, the two-out-of-three fall match resumed. The Polish giant exercised extreme caution, scowling angrily at Gotch but saying nothing. He was determined the debacle of the first round wasn't going to repeat itself, and he wrestled with great reservation. The crowd, mistaking his caution for fear, turned against him all the more and roared at each offensive maneuver Gotch made. Twice, Gotch threw him to the mat and worked for the toe hold, bringing the crowd to its feet in eager anticipation. But Zbyszko managed to break the hold both times by kicking his powerful leg free and scurrying away. The match finally ended when Frank slapped on a bar arm and wristlock, forcing the Pole onto his back, and his huge shoulders to the mat. Weighing just two hundred and two pounds, Frank had humiliated the two hundred and sixty pound giant, pinning him twice in less than thirty minutes....and handing him his first defeat in over nine hundred matches.

When Fleming signaled the last fall, Burns, Klank and a number of spectators swarmed the ring, hoisting Gotch to their shoulders. Two fans were carrying a huge American flag, and draped it over his shoulders. The victory was worth nearly thirty thousand dollars for Gotch, and stamped him as the highest paid athlete in the world. It was an amazing sum, considering the average working man in America in 1909 was earning three thousand for an entire year's work. Gotch earned twenty three thousand from the purse and an additional six thousand from movie picture rights. But the win was more rewarding than from the mere financial aspect as it left Frank unchallenged around the world as the greatest heavyweight wrestling champion of all time.

Two weeks later, Emil Klank walked down the aisle of the train nodding hellos to those who happened to glance up and see him. He was nattily attired in a three-piece suit of gray, and sported a big cigar. It wasn't easy to smoke anything in the presence of the Farmer, but if one wanted to smoke, then a cigar was the only recourse. Burns would simply not tolerate anyone smoking a cigarette in his presence.

Klank sat down next to Burns, who looked over at him and scowled upon seeing the cigar. Klank looked back at him, then shrugged: "Heck, Farmer, I haven't even lit it yet."

"See that you don't," said Farmer curtly. "It will be far better for both of us."

Burns turned his attention back to his lap, where he had a big stack of paper spread out. He thought for a moment, then continued writing in a very slow manner.

"How's the book coming?" asked Klank. Burns muttered that it was progressing very slowly.

Gotch was staring out the window, sitting across from them, and was paying little, if any, heed. Klank turned his attentions on him.

"Look's like something's eating at you, Frank," he said.

Gotch sighed, his heavy shoulders moving with the deep breath. He glanced over at Burns, then his eyes settled on Klank.

"Been thinking about the future," he said.

"And...."

"Well, I'm getting a little tired of wrestling, Emil."

Klank continued to stare, so Frank continued.

"Thinking a little more about getting settled in."

"You're certainly in a position to do that now, Frank. Figure you pulled in about thirty thousand against Zbyszko. That's not a bad day's work."

"Excepting it ain't just a day's work, Emil. It takes weeks, months, to get in good enough shape to take on men like Zbyszko and Mahmout. And, heck, I'm thirty-one years old. I need to be planting some roots."

"You own half of Humboldt County," said Klank, raising his eyebrows, and taking the cigar from his mouth. "How much more roots you need, lad?" Even though he was just two years older than Gotch, he enjoyed calling him "lad", as though he had accumulated a great amount of wisdom, and maturity, in the extra two years.

"And didn't you buy into that car dealership with that Saul fellow in Humboldt?"

"Yeah, sure did," said Gotch. "We're gonna make the Mitchell the most popular car in the world, or at least in northern Iowa." He laughed at the thought, but was well pleased with the deal that he had struck up with Fred Saul, a Humboldt businessman and longtime friend. The Mitchell was a classy car, and the one Frank liked the most, except for the rare Sterling he had purchased the year previous. The Sterling was a gorgeous, smooth-running machine, but there was such a limited number of them that they were hard to get serviced. He had sold his Sterling after a year, and replaced it with a Mitchell.

He had been interested in investing his money and making it work for him, and it hadn't taken much talking from Saul to get him involved. They agreed to use the Gotch name, and some of the Gotch money, as his share of the investment, while Saul also put up some money, and contributed the labor of actually running the dealership.

"And then there's that land in Minneapolis, right?"

"Yeah," said Gotch. "There's some real estate in Minneapolis and in South Dakota. But, I mean different kind of roots, Emil."

There was a pause.

"Emil, he's trying to tell you that he's in love," injected Burns not even looking up from his writing.

"Oh ho, so that's it," said Klank, slapping his thigh in delight and moving closer to his charge. He peered into Gotch's eyes with such intensity that Gotch finally reached out a fist and flicked at him in a joking fashion. Frank felt his face grow slightly red.

"So, you're going to break up this wonderful gang, and this wonderful organization, for a dame, huh?" said Klank, leaning back in his seat next to Burns.

"First of all, she's not a dame," said Frank, somewhat testily. He knew Klank was merely joshing, but he didn't like the choice of word. He would never call his mother that, nor his wife, when he married. "Her name's Gladys, Gladys Oestrich."

Klank looked surprised.

"Then it's not that actress - what was her name, Emerson, I think

- that was sweet on you back in Kalamazoo?"

"Nope."

"Or that gorgeous babe in Chicago who kept trying to sneak into your hotel room?"

Gotch looked at his long-time manager with a confused look.

"What woman was that?" he asked.

"Didn't you tell him, Farmer?" asked Klank, looking at Burns. The latter glanced up, first at Klank then over at Gotch, and shrugged.

"What for?" he asked. "He wouldn't have been interested."

"That's probably right," said Klank.

"Anyway, I just brought all this up to let you two guys know I'm thinking about retiring," said Frank. He waited for a reaction, but there wasn't one, so he continued.

"You know, I felt after the Hack battle that I may never be as good a man again. The strain of such a contest really isn't appreciated by people who look on. Why, you know after the first hour I couldn't even sweat.... we had lost all the moisture from our system. I lost nine pounds in just that one match."

Burns was interested now in the conversation, and laid his manuscript aside. It was a book about wrestling, including his ideas on training, diet and techniques. It was to be published by A. J. Kulhman out of Omaha, and was to be called Life Work of Farmer Burns.

"Frank, you know it's not something to worry about, you losing weight like that. You're in excellent shape, the best, maybe, I've ever seen. It's remarkable a man your size can run like you do, sometimes up to fifteen miles a day when you're in top training. You have all the ingredients to wrestle for years. You're strong as a bull moose, and getting even stronger. That happens with some people as they age naturally. Hack isn't getting stronger, and is maybe even regressing, because his strength was artificial. By that, I mean it wasn't natural, from the good hard work of youth, like on a farm. Instead, it was gained in gymnasiums with barbells and other lifting devices. Not that that's bad, mind you, but it's just not as good as plain old hard work and good, clean, outdoor living. That's a point I'm trying to make in this here book."

"You're the most famous sportsman in America," said Klank, worried he might lose his champion, and meal ticket. "I got a stack of telegrams from promoters all over the country, Frank. They want to see you in action. There's never been a wrestler as popular as you, ever. Why, you can almost name your price in the coming years. This one reporter, in some Chicago paper - I think the Inner Ocean - says he can't imagine you being beat for the next ten years, if ever. Says you're so far above everybody else that you can just wrestle half-speed and win easily."

"Yeah, I know all that, Emil," said Frank, starting to fidget in his seat. "I mean, I know the writers are saying that sort of thing, and I appreciate it. I've worked hard for the success I've had, and it means a lot to me that folks care about me and my future. It feels good being the man who brought the championship home to America. But, I just don't know how much longer I want to wrestle. And, I do think I want to get married in the near future."

The train click-clacked on, working its way toward Fort Dodge. The three men sat in silence for some time before Frank turned to Burns.

"Are you going on out to Reno, to work with Jeff?"

Burns nodded.

"He sent me a cable just before the Mahmout match," said Burns. "Said he didn't want to interfere with your training, but wanted to know if I'd come out as soon as my obligation to you was ended. Also said he'd sure appreciate it if you'd tag along."

"Sounds like he needs encouragement," said Frank.

Burns nodded solemnly. "Yep, it sure does."

"What do you think his chances are, Farmer?" asked Klank.

"Ought to ask Frank; he knows more about boxing than I do," said the Farmer. "At least he's had himself some matches, which is more than I ever did."

"But no one knows more about training and preparing for a match - boxing or wrestling - than you," countered Frank. Both he and Klank leaned forward, eager to hear Burns' assessment of the upcoming fight between Jeffries and Johnson.

The bout had caught the fancy of the sporting public in a fashion that matched the excitement of the Gotch-Hackenschmidt battle. Here was Jeffries, who had retired unbeaten as heavyweight boxing champion of the world, attempting to put the white man back on the boxing throne. The crown was in the extremely capable hands of Jack Johnson, who delighted in tormenting the white establishment by flashing his golden smile - his front teeth were capped in gold - running with white women, and knocking the white boxers senseless.

After his conversation on the streets of New York with Corbett upon returning from Europe, Frank had telegramed Jeffries, asking him his intent. Jeffries had replied that he was undecided, but was leaning on coming back. Though he hadn't fought in five years, he was confident he could whip Johnson. Gotch wasn't so sure; he knew he won many of his own wrestling matches with speed and cunning, and that's how he had beaten Hack. Gotch felt Johnson was of the same mold, and would be able to use his speed and cunning to offset the brutal power of Jeffries. He had hoped he was wrong, but felt he wasn't.

They had corresponded several times, and when Jeffries at last made up his mind to take on Johnson, he asked for Gotch's support, at least verbally. He invited Frank to his camp in Indiana, and Frank had gone, only to be dismayed at the site that greeted him. The famed Boilermaker looked like a boiler stove, and was in the vicinity of three hundred pounds, nearly seventy-five over his best fighting weight. As the two talked, Frank detected a decided lack of commitment on Jeffries' part. In fact, Jim had dropped an arm around Gotch's shoulder and confided he was being pressured into the fight by public opinion, and by Corbett, who pounded away at him relentlessly, day after day.

"That old Gentleman Jim, why he's hard to turn your back on," said Jeffries soberly. "He sure wants that Johnson out of the way. And, he thinks I'm - and, by the way, perhaps, you, Frank - the best bet to do it."

"Not me, Jim," Frank had countered. "I'm having trouble enough just taking care of my wrestling title. Don't need to worry about fighting any hot shot boxers."

"And, hell, did you see what Jack London went and wrote a year ago?" asked Jeffries, referring to the famous author of Call of the Wild and White Fang. He ambled off and returned with a dog-eared newspaper, and plopped down beside Gotch.

"Just listen to this, Frank. It was written right after Johnson knocked out Tommy Burns to take the title in Australia.

"'Johnson play-acted all the time, he played with Burns from the opening gong to the finish of the fight. One thing now remains, Jim Jeffries must emerge from his alfalfa farm and remove that golden smile from Jack Johnson's face. Jeff, it's up to you. The white man must be rescued.'"

Jeffries put down the paper and stared at his friend.

"Sounds like a real feud a brewin' here, Jim," said Frank. Jeffries nodded, his features solemn.

"How good is Johnson, in your estimation?" asked Gotch.

"Why, little Stanley Ketchel had him in real trouble," said the Boilermaker, referring to Johnson's bout with the fierce middleweight champion of the world, regarded as one of the toughest men ever to set foot in the ring. "Ketch had him down in the twelfth round of their fight in Colma, California, this year, but was just too small to keep him there. Stanley only weighed one seventy, while Johnson was around two twenty. And that weight finally made the difference. He put Stanley away in the same round."

"They say he took five of Stanley's teeth with him back to the dressing room," said Frank, "all stuck in Johnson's glove. Hit him so hard they just stayed there, instead of inside Stanley's mouth."

Jeffries chuckled, but looked serious.

"Just rumors, you know, Frank. He don't hit that hard. He grabs and holds a lot, cause he ain't got real knockout power. But," he added after a pause, "he is an awful hard man to hit. He just doesn't stay in one spot very long. He's a defensive master."

The two parted with a promise to keep in touch, but Gotch's travels had destroyed that promise. He followed Jeffries through the newspaper accounts as much as possible, and was amazed at the excitement generated by the bout. He had never seen anything like it. It was as though the nation was dividing itself between black and white, each putting the prestige of their race on the line. Gotch was saddened by it all, but had promised Jim he would be there the day of the fight. It was set July 10 in Reno.

Now, Burns was echoing what Frank suspected.......that Johnson was indeed going to be a very difficult opponent for the Rocky Mountain Grizzly Bear. But Burns saw the fight from a different angle than Frank. He wasn't as concerned with Johnson's ability to float around the ring and defend himself as he was with Jeffries's state of well being, both physically and mentally.

"I think a man like Jeffries loses a lot with that long a layoff," said Burns. "He was grossly overweight just one year ago, and I hear tell he has worked extremely hard to melt most of it off. Last I heard, about three weeks ago, he was around two thirty, which ain't bad. But it's the quality of the weight that concerns me. Two thirty now ain't near as good as was two twenty about five years ago. And, I suspect Jeff is a lot slower than he thinks he is....not necessarily of foot, though he's bound to be off his mark there, too - but with the reflexes. I must confess, I have a bad feeling about this fight."

"So do I," said Frank. "I guess maybe I'll go out to Reno, too. Jeff's going to need moral support, as well as training advice." He paused. "When you going out, Farmer?"

"I told Jeff I'd be there a whole two weeks before the fight, so I'm leaving as soon as possible."

"I can't go that soon," said Frank. "I'll probably show up the day before is all. Can you pick me up at the station when I get there?"

Burns nodded. And they were both lost in thought, contemplating the ordeal facing their friend.

CHAPTER 17

Reno was half-crazy with excitement. Everyone who was anyone in the world of sport was on their way to the town on the edge of the wild frontier. Positioned on the border of Nevada and California, it separated the sprawling, wild west from the more civilized California, fast becoming the land of dreams and opportunity.

The great fight had been the subject of unprecedented ballyhoo from the day Jeffries agreed to terms. It was being billed as the "battle of the century" - the first of many, no doubt, since this was just 1910 - and had unmatchable drama: a former white champion who was considered invincible, and a hated black man, whose talents were awesome. At first, the fight was to be held in San Francisco, but the governor of California, James J. Gillett, came under such fire from protesting groups, who didn't want to see the races pitted against each other in what they considered a barbaric contest, that he turned down the affair. Even though the promoter, Tex Rickard, had a thirty-thousand seat arena half completed in Frisco, he had to withdraw, though not before he threatened to sue the governor.

Governor Denver S. Dickerson of Nevada then offered Rickard his choice of three sites, and the promoter opted for Reno, largely because of the heavy network of train traffic. Requests for tickets poured in from all over the world, and a twenty-thousand seat arena was in the works when Burns arrived in town. The builder had promised it would be completed in just two weeks, and with less than one week until fight time, he was right on schedule, amazingly enough.

Members of the press flocked to Reno like never before to an athletic event. The legendary John L. Sullivan was on hand, now a strict abstainer from all forms of liquor, and officially working for a New York paper as a reporter of the fight. In addition, the old gunfighter-marshal from the tough cow towns of Kansas - Bat Masterson, but now an established and respected New York sportswriter - was due in. Author Jack London, who had implored Jeffries to return to the ring, was on hand, as were a wide variety of cowhands, Indians, toughs and hoodlums. The city was a paradise for hustlers, thieves and pickpockets, preying on the innocent and unsuspecting. Men slept everywhere, as the town had run out of proper accommodations long ago.

The train station was packed with people milling around, waiting for who knows what. Gotch had telegramed Burns of his arrival, and the Farmer was waiting for him at the train station. They drove through the heart of Reno, and Frank was amazed by the crush of people, seemingly everywhere. They filled the streets and, presumably, the bars. Every hotel was booked solid, with men camping in the lobbies. Trolleys, filled to capacity, clanged and ran along the main thoroughfares, and automobiles were reduced to a mere crawl, as the crush of humanity poured out off the sidewalks and into the streets.

Jeffries' camp was on the west side of town, and was guarded heavily by security guards who took a close look at the auto bearing Gotch and Burns, and then waved them on in. Burns explained that Corbett was keeping security as strict as possible, not wanting any "spies" in camp. Gentleman Jim, who was acting as Jeffries' main trainer, was taking this fight as seriously as any of his own. He wanted the title back on the head of a white man, said Burns.

Walking to the outer rim of a huge crowd, Frank could see a sparring session was already in progress, and they pushed their way to the front. Frank was disappointed, and saddened, by the sight that met his eyes. His old friend Jeffries, was the center of attention, and was sparring loosely with Joe Choynski, a tough and rugged slugger who had held Jeffries to a twenty-round draw in 1897. It was a typical day for Reno in the summer - boiling hot, and both men were perspiring heavily even though they were obviously just going through the motions.

Frank could tell at a glance it was hardly the feared Boilermaker of days gone past. His mouth was set in a grim posture, and he moved much slower than Gotch had ever seen him move. His face was gaunt, as happens when a man loses a lot of weight much too quickly. He looked fit to the untrained eye, perhaps, but to Gotch he appeared drawn too tightly. Jeffries had lost about eighty pounds since he had last seen him, but Frank knew the weight had come off too fast, and he would not have much endurance.

Burns and Gotch watched silently as five rounds went by. The crowd cheered wildly at every move the former champion made. The open area where they sparred - with no ropes - was ringed by men and women on makeshift bleachers. Some sat on the ground, but all watched intently. It was clear they were here by special invitation of Corbett for the purpose of bolstering the confidence of Jeffries. When the session ended, Jeffries and Choynski shook hands, patted each other on the back, and departed, working their way through the crowd.

Burns nudged Gotch and nodded his head in the direction Jeffries had taken. The two trudged off after the former undefeated heavy-weight boxing champion of the world. They caught up with Jeffries just as he was preparing to strip and take a shower. Corbett, lean and aging very gracefully, saw them first and shouted their names. Jeffries turned, a big grin on his face.

"Frank," he said, walking toward them briskly. He threw a brawny, sweaty arm around both of them, standing in between them, and playfully pulled them into him.

"How about a little wrestling, Frank?" he said jovially. "I prom-ise not to get too rough with ya."

"Waddaya say, Farmer, shall we rough him up now, or wait til later?" said Frank as he ducked away from Jeffries grasp and grabbed the arm, quickly pushing it into a hammerlock and forcing it behind Jeff's back. The champ let out a mock scream, and Frank released his grip.

Jeffries stepped back and sized Frank up, nodding his head in approval.

"Don't look in too bad 'a shape for a wrestler, does he Jim?" Jeffries said, turning to Corbett. The fact Corbett and Jeffries were in the same camp, working together, underscored the desire the men had in restoring the crown to white America. Jeffries had begun his box-ing career many years earlier as a sparring partner for Corbett, and had been nearly laughed out of camp for his crude fighting techniques. Later, the two had fought for the title on two occasions. Jeffries won the first fight, in 1900, by surviving a boxing lesson for over twenty rounds and kayoing Corbett in the twenty-third when he was far behind in the scoring. The rematch, in 1903, had been much different, with the bullish champ simply over-powering the aging Corbett and knocking him out in the tenth round.

Corbett stepped forward and offered a hand to Gotch, grinning and agreeing he looked in tip-top shape.

"Glad to have you aboard, Frank," he said, "though you're a bit late. Most of the serious training's been done, as you can tell from his appearance. The Farmer and I been working him pretty hard. He cuts a dashing figure, doesn't he? Why, that black fella won't stand a chance this time, now that he's not fighting a boy."

The reference was to Johnson's easy win over Burns for the title in 1908. It had been a mismatch from the opening gong.

After several minutes of light conversation, Jeffries begged off for a shower, and Gotch and Burns sat down on a long wooden bench with Corbett. Despite the heat, Corbett was wearing a tie. He unfastened it, and pulled it from his neck, laying it neatly over one leg. He unsnapped his collar, allowing some air to enter his shirt at the neck. He stuck a finger in the collar, and pulled it out.

"Hot, what?" he said.

"Quite," said Frank, with a grin. He saw sweat spots under Corbett's arm, and knew "the gentleman" would be disturbed by that. He was an impeccable dresser and a ladies man, and liked to look sharp as possible at all times. Weather like this, with the temperatures hovering around the one hundred degree mark, was rough on a man like Corbett, and Gotch inwardly enjoyed the discomfort he felt certain Corbett was going through.

"Well, what do you think of Jeff, there?" asked Corbett.

"Don't know," volunteered Frank, shaking his head slowly. He removed his derby, and placed it on his knee. He took a handkerchief out, and wiped his forehead, looking at it and marveling at how wet it had become after just one pass across his head.

"Looks kind of peaked, Jim."

"What, exactly, do you mean, peaked?"

Gotch sighed. "You know, like he pulled too much weight too soon. It might hurt him in the latter rounds, when he needs to call up some reservoir of strength."

"Hell's bells, Frank, he didn't have time to worry about taking off weight slowly," said Corbett. "He was over three hundred twenty pounds just a year ago. We had to get it off. And, besides, he ain't going to need to worry about latter rounds, cause it'll be over in ten, or less."

"Maybe so," Burns interjected, "but like I been telling you guys, you can't train for that. Frank threw that giant Pole Zbyszko in seven seconds the first fall, but you can't count on that sort of thing. You gotta train for a long, hard battle, of twenty rounds at least. And I don't think Jeff can hold on that long, at least from what I been seeing lately. He was puffing hard today from minimal exertion, and that don't look good. Choynski ain't a mover, and Jeff can plod along after him. He needs to be working out with guys who have speed, like Johnson has. He shoulda been working out with little guys, some middleweights, that can flit all over the place."

"Someone said Ketchel is here. Has he been training with Jeff?" asked Gotch.

"Naw," said Corbett, dismissing the thought with a wave of the hand. "He's such a pompous little ass. Can't stand him; never could. Jeff doesn't much like him, either. We had Papke here....but that didn't work out so well. Ask the Farmer why not."

Burns spit on the ground and leaned against the back of the bench. Gotch glanced at him, and suspected he was about to hear a good story, judging from the expression on his old friend's face.

"He had it coming," said Burns matter-of-factly.

Frank knew Papke was the former middleweight boxing champion of the world, who had engaged in three ferocious battles with Ketchel, winning one and losing two. He was reported to have a hot temper. Frank was staring at Burns, who had suddenly grown silent. Frank turned to Corbett, and shrugged.

"So what happened?"

Corbett smiled, delighted at the opportunity to tell the story.

"Farmer was doing some wrestling with Jeffries, to try and get him in better shape, and to get used to brawling along the ropes, in the event Johnson turned it into an alley fight. Papke disagreed with Farmer's training methods, and made a point of saying so, over and over and over. I think Farmer didn't take kindly to the criticism. Hot words flowed, and suddenly Papke climbed into the ring and took his shirt off."

"He challenged me," Burns cut in. "Can you imagine that? He thought he was going to punch me out, the no-account."

Corbett continued: "Papke threw a couple of punches, and that was it. Farmer blocked them with his shoulder, took Papke down to the mat and...what was that you said, Farmer? You hooked him?"

Gotch smiled. He knew what was coming next.

"Had him begging for mercy," said Burns without a trace of emotion. "Hooked his ankle. Shoulda broke the darned thing. But instead, I just let him up - and he decided to keep his comments to himself from then on."

"It was something to see," said Corbett, the admiration in his voice obvious. "I'll tell you this about you wrestlers....boxers better take you out with the first punch, or they're in for a hell of a lot of pain and anguish."

Gotch broke out laughing, leaning back against the bench. He could easily picture the scene, the boxer sprawled out and banging his hands on the mat in pain, trying to figure out what the heck was happening. And Burns turning up the pressure, ready to break the ankle if need be.

"Papke ain't been back to camp since," said Corbett.

Shortly after, Jeffries joined the trio and they sat and talked for an hour, after moving over to the camp's headquarters. He asked Gotch all about his recent matches with Mahmout and Zbyszko, but he seemed preoccupied. His hair was much thinner on top than Frank remembered, and the features in his face were ragged and drawn. He had aged quite a bit since they had last been together, Frank realized, and wondered if it was the pressure of the fight.

"Folks are making a lot more of this than just a boxing match, you know, Frank," said Jeffries after supper. "London's still writing that stuff about the great white hope, and how I have to put this fellow in his place. Some writers are acting like this is bigger than the Civil War, for crying out loud. Heck, Frank, it's just a boxing match, ain't it?"

"You bet," said Gotch, wanting to reassure his old friend. He knew Jeffries needed some good, old fashioned encouragement and that he hadn't yet put his heart into the match. Sure, he had trimmed way down, and looked pretty good by comparison with a year ago. But he sure didn't resemble the awesome fighting machine that had retired undefeated five years earlier after demolishing all the competition with his bruising, never-say-die style of fighting.

"Have you studied Johnson much?" asked Frank.

"Naw, I've left that up to Corbett. But that Choynski fellow I was sparring with today? Well, he and I went twenty rounds to a draw in 1897, when I was still a babe, so to speak. Only my seventh pro fight. And he knocked this black fella out in three rounds in 1901. Pounded him pretty good, from all reports. Then I been talking to Tommy Burns - he's here too you know - and he's given me some pointers. Says I won't have much trouble with this guy, cause he ain't very strong. Likes to move around a lot, though."

"Well, you'll have to be doing some chasing, then. How's the roadwork been coming along?" asked Frank.

"Been doing a lot," Jeffries said, then his voice trailed off. "Not as much as I should, maybe. Been doing a little too much fishing, maybe. And Corbett says I ain't throwing enough punches in training, that I'm taking too many. But I'm trying to get this body of mine used to absorbing some punishment. Got to be able to absorb, you know, Frank."

Gotch nodded, and the two men talked until Corbett told Jeffries it was time to turn in. Sleep was precious for a fighter or a wrestler. Jeffries stood, stretched, and took in a big breath of fresh air. He spread his arms out to their full length, as though reaching out into the night for something that wasn't there, then closed them around his chest in a big bear hug. He looked down at Gotch, who was still seated and was staring up at him.

"It'll be okay, Frank," he said, a slight smile on his lips. "The old Boilermaker will be ready when the time comes." With that, he turned and headed for his cabin.

After checking into his hotel room, Frank decided to take in some of the Reno nightlife, even though Burns declined, saying there was nothing to interest him in Reno at this point other than a good bed and a good night's sleep. Frank took a stroll down the wooden streets, amazed at the press of humanity. A number of men stopped in their tracks when they saw him, and asked for autographs. Just when he was about to return to the hotel, he heard his name shouted out and looked up to see a trim, elderly man walking briskly toward him. He immediately recognized him as George Barton, sporting editor of the largest newspaper in Minneapolis, the nation's foremost wrestling and boxing writer.

"Frank, how are you?" said Barton, extending a hand. "I heard you were coming out, but hadn't seen you so I wondered if it was just a rumor."

"George, it's good to see you," said Frank. "I just got in this morning. Where are you staying?"

"The street, it looks like," said Barton dejectedly. "Every damn room's taken. My secretary messed up. Got me a room in San Francisco, not Reno, for crying out loud. Said she hadn't heard the fight had been switched. By the time I discovered what she had done, there were no rooms left here."

Gotch genuinely liked Barton. Not only was he a great sports writer, he had been a top ranked flyweight boxer in his early days.

"Shoot, George, I got a huge room. The Farmer lined it up for me two weeks ago when he got here. You can stay with me, if you don't mind the floor. Maybe we can get the hotel to give us some extra bedding."

The smaller man stared up at Gotch.

"You mean that, Frank? That would be great."

"It's done, then," said Frank. "Let's go."

"Say, would you like to drop in at the Frontier Bar with me for a little snort first?" asked Barton. "I've been running all over the place in this crazy heat, and I'm bone dry."

Frank shrugged. "Sounds good to me."

Like all the bars, the Frontier was packed, and wild and noisy inside. Men were placing bets on the big fight, arguing and cursing. Several scuffles broke out, but no one seemed to care much. Gotch and Barton couldn't find an empty table, but three men at one table recognized Frank and invited them to sit with them. The three were already drunk, and couldn't believe their luck at having the heavyweight wrestling champion of the world join them. They plastered Frank with compliments and asked his opinion of the big fight over and over. Finally, one of them dropped his head on the table, out like a light, and the other two sat dazed, unable to talk any longer.

Barton had kept out of the conversation, surveying the room. For several minutes, he watched a trio of men at the bar. Finally, he nudged Frank and pointed at one of the three men.

"See that dignified old chap over there," said Barton, pointing to a slender man with a brushy mustache, leaning against the bar and talking quietly to the other two men. "He's sort of a legend out here and in California. He was a town marshal in Kansas for several years back in the eighteen eighties, and was the central figure in a real famous shootout at some place called the O.K. Corral.

"Now, he hangs around the boxing scene. He refereed the Sharkey-Fitzsimmons bout a couple of years back, you know the one with the very controversial finish. He disqualified Sharkey for some strange reason and gave the decision to Fitzsimmons, and there was talk it was because he had placed a big bet on old Fitz."

"Sure, I remember both the fight and the controversy. What's his name?" asked Frank.

"Wyatt Earp," said Barton. "Before he went west, he was raised in Iowa, I heard this afternoon. He approached me when he found out I was a writer. He's looking for someone to write a book about his exploits back in the wild cow towns when he was the peace officer."

Frank nodded, quietly regarding the old timer.

"If he's from Iowa, let's go meet him," he said finally.

They left the table and walked to where the three men were standing. Earp saw them approach, and smiled at Barton.

"Howdy," he said politely, offering his hand. "Good to see you again."

Barton returned the salutation, and then introduced Gotch.

"Mr. Earp, thought you might like to meet Frank Gotch, the heavyweight wrestling champion of the world."

The two men shook hands, Earp smiling broadly again.

"It's an honor to meet you, Frank," he said. "I've certainly read a lot about you the past couple of years or so." He introduced Gotch and Barton to the other two men, who he said were former associates from Dodge City, where he had been town marshal.

"We ran a little gambling establishment together in Dodge, but had to leave when things got too hot," chuckled Earp, winking at the two men. They nodded solemnly, regarding Gotch and Barton only half-heartedly. They turned back to the bar and continued their drinking.

"How do you regard the fight tomorrow?" asked Earp, of either of them. "Has Jeffries got a chance?"

Barton shook his head sadly.

"Well, if I was a betting man, which I'm not, I'd have my money tucked away safely and keep it there," said Frank, "even though it pains me to say so. Jeff just isn't the same fighter he was five, six years ago. I think he's in for a very bad day."

"That's the way I see it too," said Earp. "So does Bat. My old friend Bat Masterson has been following boxing very closely the past couple of years. Writes a sports column for a big New York paper. He says Johnson's way too fast and way too slick for Jeff, and that he also hits like a mule. Most folks don't realize how hard Johnson hits because he likes to be cute up there, moving and boxing. But when he wants to hit, Bat says he's murderous."

Gotch winced. Barton shook his head again.

Gotch and Earp talked briefly about their Iowa backgrounds. Earp said he was born in Monmouth, Illinois, but his family moved to Pella, Iowa, when he was only eight. He lived there for the next ten years, finally leaving home and heading to Kansas at age eighteen, to seek his fortune. Gotch enjoyed the man, though he felt he liked to talk about himself a bit too much. Earp spent at least thirty minutes telling them about his various gun fights and brawls in the Kansas towns he worked. At last, Gotch and Barton bid him so long and stepped out into the muggy night air. It was well after midnight and the streets were still packed.

"He must have thought you are a writer too, Frank, the way he kept talking to you about his past," chuckled Barton as they walked toward their hotel.

"Sounds like he's had an interesting life," said Frank. "If he hooks up with the right type of writer, a fella who can spin a yarn, he just might become famous some day."

Burns was very worried when the day of the fight dawned. He knew Jeffries was a much older, slower, and less inspired fighter than he was when champion. It hadn't been hard to figure out why he consented to the comeback - there had been the incredible pressure from white America, of course, but it had really boiled down to two things....pride and money. Jeffries wanted to prove he was still the greatest fighter in the world. And the financial considerations were tremendous. If things went as expected, he could earn nearly one hundred thousand from this one fight alone. He had been given a bonus of ten thousand for signing, and was to receive fifty thousand for the movie rights, as was Johnson. In addition, he was to receive forty percent of the purse, or around forty thousand. It was to be, far and away, the most profitable sporting event ever.

But the heat was what was worrying Burns now as the Jeffries group waited in their dressing room for the signal to begin the long walk up the boardwalk to the ring. It was blazing hot, and the heat was sure to have its effect on Jeffries if the fight went any longer than five rounds. And it was certain to do that. Burns had slipped into the Johnson camp, and was shocked by the condition and the ability of the champion. He had never seen Johnson in action before, and was amazed at the man's native talents. He moved around the ring with the grace and agility of a featherweight, bobbing and weaving and slipping punches with great skill. He was magnificently developed, as though God had intended him as the perfect model for a fighting machine. His jab was the fastest Burns had ever seen, and looked like it was delivered with as much power as a man could ever expect from that maneuver.

In addition, the mood of the Johnson camp caught Burns' fancy. There was a great deal of clowning and singing, tomfoolery and joke telling. There was a mixture of blacks and whites, and Johnson was always on center stage, flashing his brilliant smile and laughing constantly. It was the portrait of a supremely confident fighter, and the sharp contrast between Johnson's mood and Jeffries' mood caused the

Farmer great concern. That was one reason he had been working on Jeffries with the wrestling; he was trying to tell Jeffries, in a way he might understand, that the best way to go after Johnson was to brawl with him, force him into the ropes, cut the ring down, and maul him. That's why he had gotten so angry when Papke had interrupted his game plan.

The stands were completely filled an hour prior to the fight. When the promoter, Tex Rickard, spotted Frank taking a seat in the second row, he hurried over to him. Rickard introduced himself and asked if Frank would like to come up into the ring and be introduced with all the great boxing champions of the past. Frank was flattered and quickly agreed to do so.

With just twenty minutes remaining until fight time, the ring began to fill with huge men in suits. They were all sweating profusely as they climbed the four short steps and slipped between the ropes into the ring. The sight of each man elicited a smattering of applause from the crowd. A prolonged roar went up when John L. Sullivan, the last of the bare knuckle champions and now sixty-five years old, climbed into the ring. He had fought at two hundred and twenty pounds, but now weighed well over three hundred and sported a large, bushy white moustache.

Rickard motioned for Gotch to come up, and Frank took a place in the ring, standing next to Bob Fitzsimmons, the man who had taken the title from Corbett and lost it to Jeffries. Fitzsimmons slapped Frank on the shoulder and said he was glad to meet him. Sullivan, who had been Frank's hero as a young boy back in Humboldt, leaned over to shake his hand, too, as did little Tommy Burns, the man Johnson had knocked out to win the title. Also in the ring were current contenders Bill Squires and Bill Lang, and tough old Tom Sharkey, a man who fought Jeffries twice. So was Stanley Ketchel, the ferocious world middleweight champion who was known as the Michigan Assassin for his aggressive style of slugging. He stood off from the others, smoking a cigar, looking cocky. He strolled over to shake Sullivan's hand, but ignored the rest of them.

It took ten minutes for announcer Billy Jordan to introduce them all, and Gotch was pleased by the warm ovation he, the only non-boxer, received. But he was glad to return to his seat and get the show moving. He wanted it to be over for Jeff as quickly as possible.

Walking toward the ring, Jeffries was glum and silent. But then, he had been in that frame of mind for the last two days. He admitted to Gotch he felt a tremendous pressure to restore the crown to the white race, and now it appeared the pressure was weighing him down, occupying his every thought. In addition, he continued to hear disturbing reports from the Johnson camp attesting to the greatness of the black man as a fighter. Unfortunately, self-doubt had begun to show in Jeff's demeanor, and it was sapping his will to fight.

A deafening roar erupted as the two fighters made their way into the ring. The fans were going all out in their appreciation of Jeffries, who moved to his corner and stood ramrod straight, nodding his head just slightly in recognition of the thunderous ovation from the twenty thousand fight fans. He looked drawn and haggard, like a man who had been missing his sleep for many a night.

Rickard was also serving as the referee, and stood in the center of the ring sporting a straw hat and bow tie. His white shirt was soaked with perspiration as he gazed over the press row and the thousands of fans. Rex Beach, the famed outdoors writer, and novelist Jack London were at ringside, along with the many celebrities just introduced.

A loud chorus of boos and jeers broke out at the far end of the arena and Gotch looked across the way to try and catch the approach of the champion. He saw heads bobbing up and down, and once saw two black arms jam their way upwards, as in recognition of the booing. After several minutes, the figure of Jack Johnson burst into the ring. The attendants held the ropes for him, and he slipped between them as gracefully as a jungle cat, and leaped into the ring, a wide smile marking his features. His golden teeth glistened in the bright light of the summer day - temperatures were again well over the ninety-degree mark - and he spun around the ring throwing a series of beautiful, crisp combinations at an imaginary foe. He smiled brightly at Jeffries, who stared back glumly, and danced back to his corner. He moved along the ropes, peering down at the faces at press row, grinning broadly and exchanging lighthearted banner. Frank felt a knot rising up in his stomach; he knew his friend was in terrible trouble.

Jordan introduced Rickard as referee, and then the fighters. The sharp clang of the bell got the battle of the century under way at twelve o'clock sharp. And it didn't take most of those present long to realize what the outcome was going to be.

Jeffries was clumsy and ineffective from the start. He seemed confused, and moved in and out of his famous bob and weave style, trying to befuddle the champion. But Johnson began immediately to land beautifully-timed left jabs to the face, and by the third round he was connecting at will, peppering the ex-champ until Jeffries face began to swell horribly. Corbett, riding the top step at Jeffries' corner, screamed wildly at Johnson, calling him names and trying to distract him, all to no avail. Johnson merely smiled and chatted back.

"How do you like this jab, Mr. Jim," he called out as he bounced a stunning punch off Jeffries' face. He even took time from his chore to carry on a short dialogue with Sullivan at ringside, calling him "Captain John" and asking him why he had supported Jeffries when the man couldn't hit.

Johnson dominated the fight from beginning to end, and finished off the once feared Boilermaker with a devastating series of blows in the fifteenth. Jeffries, bloodied and broken, was knocked sprawling between the top and middle ropes, partly hanging off the ring apron. He rose to one knee, then stood before Rickard could count him out. Johnson chased him around the ring, the smile gone from his face. He was deadly serious now, intent upon ending the charade of a fight. He landed eight unanswered blows to Jeffries' face - any one of which would have dropped an ordinary man - and the proud ex-champ was sent sprawling once again, lying helplessly between the ropes on the opposite end of the ring.

Sickened to see his friend humiliated, Gotch gritted his teeth in frustration. He wanted to climb into the ring and take on Johnson, so deep was his pain at seeing Jeffries bested so easily. But he knew then and there he would never be able to compete with Johnson on this level; the man's skills were awesome. Never had Gotch seen a fighter move his hands so quickly, or so expertly. The only way he would take on this fellow, he knew, would be in a wrestling match, or a no-holds-barred contest. He could swarm Johnson, keep his chin protected, back him into the ropes, and then get his hands on him, and that would be all there would be to it. But he knew, watching Johnson in Reno this day, that no man in the world could hope to defeat him in a boxing match.

Fans were on their feet screaming hoarsely for Jeff to rise. But just as many were yelling at Rickard to intervene and stop the fight, calling it a technical knockout, and not a pure knockout. Many shouted obscenities at Johnson, who was standing in a far corner, sweat glistening on his marvelous body. For once, he appeared oblivious to the crowd and the press, his eyes trained on Jeffries' pathetic efforts to rise. His lips were turned back in a snarl. He was ready to move in for the kill should Jeffries somehow find the strength, and courage, to stand.

Watching Johnson closely, Gotch understood for the first time that they had something in common - the rare ability to turn on the heat when they wanted to. They both could smile and joke easily, and then turn deadly when the need arose. The fact was, they both knew how to beat a man when he needed beating. Gotch nodded faintly in silent admiration as he stared up at Johnson in the corner, waiting to finish off his foe. He recognized in Johnson his own killer instinct.

Suddenly, Rickard, at the count of seven, waved his arms wildly back and forth across his chest, signifying the fight was over. He pointed toward Jeffries' corner, where one of the assistants had placed his foot in the ring, as a gesture of capitulation. It had been done purposely, to save Jeffries from an official knockout.

The ring turned into bedlam, and Gotch, slumping in his seat, watched dejectedly as Johnson's handlers swarmed over him, and Corbett, Burns and the others hauled Jeffries back to his corner. Just before he turned to leave the stadium, Gotch caught a glimpse of Jeffries. He was sitting in his corner, staring expressionlessly ahead. His face was swollen and bleeding, one eye completely closed. He looked seventy years old, Gotch thought. I wonder if he thinks the money was worth it, he asked himself as he pushed up the aisle. He promised himself he would ask him when he saw him next.

CHAPTER 18

After Reno, Humboldt was a real breath of fresh air. It had taken Frank two days to get out of Reno, and another three days to get to Fort Dodge by train. His partner, Frank Saul, met him at the train station and brought him to Humboldt in his Mitchell, one of the finest machines on the road. After a few minutes discussing the fight, they talked business all the way, and Frank was pleased to discover all was going so well. They planned a hunting trip and talked about going fishing, but Frank's mind was occupied by other thoughts. He had made up his mind on the trip home to ask Gladys to marry him. He was lonesome, even with the companionship of Burns, Klank and others.

He had talked with Jeffries the day after the fight. When he learned Jeff had made nearly one hundred thousand from the fight, he whistled, noting it was one of the greatest paydays any man had ever made. But Jeffries, speaking through battered lips, had said the beating he took wasn't worth it.

"Nothing's more important than a man's pride and his peace of mind," he said. "And I lost both in that ring. I knew I shouldn't have come back, that my heart wasn't in it. But I got conned into it by a lot of fancy words."

Gotch had resolved then and there to retire from wrestling. In his mind, there was nothing left to accomplish. After all, he hadn't lost a match in over four years, and not even one fall in nearly the same time. He and Jeffries resumed their discussion about barnstorming around the country, with Jeff taking on all comers in five rounds of boxing, and Gotch offering one thousand dollars to any man who could avoid being pinned in fifteen minutes of wrestling. The two men would attract huge crowds willing to pay top dollar to see them in action. When Gotch left, Jeffries promised to get in touch within the next six months.

"But first I gotta go mend," said the Boilermaker. "It will take about five months of fishing and hunting just to get over this." He smiled for the first time, and the two men parted with a handshake.

Burns had accompanied Frank to Omaha, where his family was now living and where he was opening a wrestling school. Klank, figuring Gotch was thinking about leaving the ring, met them there, and rode with Frank to Fort Dodge. He then went on to Chicago, where he said he was going to work on lining up some more matches. Gotch merely nodded his approval, and Klank left with the feeling he had better work fast, and come up with a lucrative deal and an attractive foe to keep his man's interest in the game.

Gladys had written Frank once just before Reno, saying she would be home from Ames for much of the summer. In the previous letter, she mentioned several young men at the college were asking her if she knew Frank Gotch, being from Humboldt, and she had written she was very proud to have been able to say "Yes, she did know Frank Gotch - and rather well, too." The message left two impressions on Frank: he realized he was a man truly known far and wide, and that Gladys was attracting attention from other men, who could become possible suitors. It was at that moment he made up his mind not to let her get away, and his next letter to her had suggested they might consider making a strong commitment to one another about the future. But he had been dismayed that her last letter carried no response whatsoever to his proposal, of a sorts.

He spent his first two days back in Humboldt on his own farm, talking with his brother, Charlie, who was in charge when he was gone, and visiting his mother and father. His mother seemed somehow to be stronger than ever, but his father had regressed. He no longer spoke, but spent most of his days either on a rocking chair on the front porch, or in bed. Amelia was deeply interested in all her son's travels and the people he met. She was astounded to think her son had actually been to Europe and had been in a play. But what impressed her most of all was the fact he had been invited by Teddy Roosevelt to visit the White House to demonstrate his wrestling ability against a jujitsu expert from the Orient.

After two days on the farm, Frank decided it was time to

approach Gladys. He drove to her house on a beautiful Sunday afternoon. She was sitting on the front lawn with several of her friends when she looked up and saw him sitting in his Mitchell, smiling down at her. She immediately rose, excused herself, and walked over to the auto.

"Good day, Mr. Gotch," she said formally, and then, unable to hold back, she smiled. She had wanted to appear serious and detached, but she failed miserably.

Frank tipped his derby.

"Good day, Miss Oestrich," he responded, smiling. She was, he suddenly felt, the most attractive woman he had ever seen. Sure, there were those who would find a greater beauty in the flashy women out East, or in the voluptuous women he had seen in Reno. But he was, first and foremost, an Iowa boy with country tastes, and she fitted precisely his preconceived image of womanly beauty.

She stood with hands on the door of the Mitchell smiling at Frank, knowing she was being assessed, and enjoying it. Her dark hair was in the bun again, with loose strands trickling away from her face on both sides. She reached up a hand to flip back the strands.

Gotch looked past her, at the friends. They sat attentively, staring back, smiling shyly. There were five of them, and though he recognized several faces, he knew none of their names.

"Are you booked up for the whole day," he asked, "or could you take a ride with me?"

"Now?" she asked. He nodded.

She turned and walked to the group. They talked for just a minute, then Gladys returned to the auto.

"I'm free now," she said, "if you'll grant me just one wish."

"Certainly. Anything at all." He felt exhilarated to discover she would leave her friends on a moment's notice to be with him.

"They want to meet you," she said. Gotch blushed. Even though he was the center of attraction at any city in America wherever he showed up, he never expected such treatment in Humboldt. Nevertheless, he was all too pleased to oblige, especially if it meant an afternoon with Gladys.

After the introductions, they headed south of town, taking a winding ride through the countryside. Gladys was full of questions, as usual, and Frank was surprised to discover she was truly interested in the Jeffries-Johnson fight. She had read the details in the Humboldt Republican newspaper, and in papers from around the country that came to the Ames College library. The fight had captured the imagination of all levels of society. Riots had broken out all over the country, and in one place - Kaystone, West Virginia - Negroes took over the town. In tiny Mounds, Illinois, blacks shot up the town, and two blacks in Charleston, Missouri, were charged with killing a white man and were taken from their jail cells and hung. Fearful of further such outbreaks, Congress had even passed legislation prohibiting interstate passage of fight films, and the principals lost a great deal of revenue as thousand were denied the opportunity to see the fight film.

At the same time, Rickard promised he would never again promote a fight between a black man and a white man.

"And just think, you were right there, where all of this began," said Gladys.

"Wish I hadn't been, though," Frank said solemnly. "Jeff took such a beating it was sickening to watch. I hated to see a friend of mine get pasted like that."

"What happened?" she asked. "He had never lost before, the papers said."

"He's way past his peak, Gladys. A man shouldn't keep going on indefinitely. He had done all there was to do in his sport, and then retired. But folks talked him into coming back, even though he didn't want to. They used the hate angle, and started calling him 'The Great White Hope'. Why, there's some folks now who are calling me that, and want me to get in the ring with that Johnson fellow."

Gladys seemed quite concerned over the prospect, and turned to him, laying a hand on his arm.

"Oh, Frank, you're not going to box, are you? Wrestling's bad enough, but boxing....that would be just too much."

"I thought you liked wrestling," he said, with a half smile.

"I do," she said. "But that's because I know no one can hurt you there. My goodness, you're the world champion, the very best wrestler in the entire world. But, boxing would be all new and different for you, and it's such a mean sport, where the object is to knock the other man unconscious."

"You needn't worry about me boxing. I sure won't do any of that. And, as a matter of fact," he said, turning to her as he slowed the auto down to a crawl, "I'm thinking about retiring from wrestling in the next year or so."

She looked at him. Her hand was still resting on his arm.

They drove a bit farther in silence, and then Frank pulled over at a park on the outskirts of town. They left the car and walked to a set of swings and sat down. In the distance, boys were playing a game of baseball, and one of them spotted Gotch. He ran over and talked to the others in a quick huddle, and they all turned and started across the diamond, over to where Frank and Gladys were sitting on the swings. Gladys was the first to notice the approaching group of twenty boys.

"Uh, oh," she said with a chuckle, pushing back the loose strands of hair from her face once again. "I think you've been recognized."

Frank glanced up to see the boys, who had now slowed down considerably. In fact, they stopped about twenty yards away, obviously afraid to advance.

Frank stared at them in a menacing glare, and several of the boys actually began to retreat, causing Frank to break out laughing. He motioned them forward.

"Come on over, boys," he said pleasantly. Slowly, they began moving toward them again.

One of the oldest, dressed in overalls, without shirt and shoes, stepped forward. He had a big thatch of yellow, thick hair hanging down across his eyebrows. He had a ball in his right hand, and was nervously pounding it into the glove on his left hand.

"You Frank Gotch?" he asked in a high voice.

"Sure am," replied Frank, sitting with his hands on his knees. "And who might you be?"

The boy brightened considerable.

"I'm Bill Burns," he said proudly. "My pa's Tom Burns, and he says he used to know you before you became the greatest wrestler in the world."

Gotch put his hand up to his chin, rubbing it in thought.

"Hmmm, let's see. Tom Burns. Say, doesn't he have that farm just north of town?"

"Sure, that's him," said the youngster, beaming and turning to his friends, making sure they all heard that Frank Gotch knew his pa.

"Why, he's a mighty stout fellow," said Frank. "We used to roll around a bit, Tom and me. He was a pretty fair country wrestler."

The lad was beside himself with pride. Several others mentioned their names, and Gotch talked with them all, asking about their families and saying he knew their pas. Each of them, according to Gotch, was a good wrestler, ballplayer or runner. After nearly twenty minutes of talk, Frank reached down into his pocket, and pulled out a five dollar bill.

"Say, it's a mighty hot day, ain't it fellows?" They all nodded. He beckoned for Bill Burns to come closer, and the boy stepped forward, eyes wide.

"Here," said Frank, handing him the greenback. "Why don't you boys go on down to the soda shop and get yourselves some ice cream, or a soda drink to help cool off?"

"Wow, do you mean it Mr. Gotch?" asked Bill, reaching gingerly for the money. He withdrew his hand at the last second, and stood grinning.

"Go on, take it," said Frank. The boy did. He thanked him and the whole crew took off running to main street.

When they were gone from sight, Gladys laid her hand on Frank's.

"That was wonderful, one of the nicest things I ever saw a person do, Frank," she said. "They were satisfied just to be around you, to meet the champ. You gave them something extra special just by being here."

"I love kids," said Frank. "I like being around them. I remember in my youth how much I admired men like Buffalo Bill and Kit Carson, and then, later, athletes like John L. Sullivan and James J. Corbett. I'm glad I was able to make them happy."

"Do you want a lot of children when you get married?" she asked.

He stood, walked around behind her, and placed his hands lightly on her back. He pushed, and she moved forward. He stepped back as the swing came toward him, then pushed again. She lifted her legs out and leaned back in the swing, gathering momentum.

He returned to his swing, and sat swaying slightly until she had stopped. He rose and held out his hand. She grasped it, and he pulled her lightly from the swing. Still, without any words, they walked the length of the park, now deserted since the boys had taken off for their treat, and came to the bank of the Des Moines River. They walked along it for awhile, holding hands, saying nothing.

"Let's just sit for awhile, okay?" he asked.

"Don't tell me I've tired you out," she smiled.

"Well, you certainly do have some kind of an effect on me, though I'm not sure it's tiring me out."

She was serious now, searching his eyes. They sat in the lush grass.

"Tell me about it," she said softly.

He reached for a piece of thick grass, and broke it off, sticking it in his mouth. He put his right elbow in the grass, and leaned back on it, crossing his legs. She sat upright, and gazed down at him.

"Remember that night when I came over and your folks weren't at home?"

She nodded.

"That was the night I knew."

She nodded again. "Me too," she said softly.

He sat up. "You too?"

"Yes."

"That I love you...or that you....you...."

"Both," she said.

He was speechless. He had expected to tell her he was in love with her, and had been prepared to explain his feelings, and to defend them, sure she would be put off by this sudden declaration. Never in his wildest imaginings did he allow himself to suppose she might feel the same toward him.

"You mean that you....you actually....think you love me?"

"No," she said gently. "I don't think that, Frank. I know that."

He sat up, and then stood, pulling her up in front of him. Vaguely, he thought to himself, he felt the same as when Hackenschmidt said he would forfeit the match. Being in love, and knowing your feelings were shared, was as good a feeling, he would admit to himself later, as being named the heavyweight wrestling champion of the world.

He reached out for her, and she came into his strong arms. They kissed for what seemed a long time. When they parted, he held her a short distance from him, and she searched his eyes deeply. Then, they kissed again, several times.

Frank laughed quietly, and looked around. But there was no one in sight.

"Are you embarrassed?" Gladys asked, pushing back a puff of hair that had fallen down in front of her eyes. She had a slight smile on her lips.

"No," he said, truthfully. "I just wouldn't want someone to see us, then take back word to your folks that nasty old Frank Gotch was attacking Gladys Oestrich on the banks of the Des Moines River, out in plain sight, for everyone to see."

They both laughed, then stopped abruptly, staring at one another. Frank had a knot in the pit of his stomach. So, this is what love actually feels like....a knot in the stomach....he thought.

Gladys seemed so small and so insecure when he held her. He felt the need to reach out and hold her again, and he wrapped his powerful arms around her and hugged her, until she let out a slight gasp, followed by light laughter.

"Did I hurt you?" he asked, releasing the pressure immediately.

"No, it felt good," she said, snuggling into his arms even tighter and laying her head on his huge chest. For some time, neither moved, content to drink in the moment and savor it completely.

"Gladys," he said at last.

"Yes?" she answered dreamily, her hand still on his shoulder.

"Let's get married."

"Yes!" she replied, her head still on his chest.

He waited.

"Gladys?"

"Yes?"

"Are you awake? I mean, did you hear what I asked?"

She pulled away from him, raising her face to his. Her mouth was almost touching his. She put a hand on each side of his face. He could smell her sweet perfume, enveloping and captivating him.

"Of course, Frank," she said.

They kissed again, and again.

It was late at night when Frank finally left the Oestrich home. He and Gladys had approached her parents together, with Frank asking for permission from them both. They immediately consented, and Mr. Oestrich broke out a bottle of champagne he said he was holding for the most special occasion in the world. He confided to Frank, when the women weren't in earshot, he had almost broken it out the night Frank defeated Hackenschmidt, but Gladys had told him he best be holding it for an even more important occasion. He told Frank he had been harboring the feeling for some time that Frank and Gladys were headed for matrimony.

"She always had plenty of callers, but she never seemed very interested in any of them," he said with a wink. "Her conversations at the dinner table were seldom about men, but when they were, yours was the name that always came up. Why, her mother didn't act a bit surprised tonight. She even thought you might propose today when we came home and the girls told us that you had taken Gladys away earlier."

They set the date for January 11, 1911, and decided upon the Oestrich home for the site. It was to be a relatively small wedding, with just family and special friends invited. Frank was concerned with hurting the feelings of a great many fans by allowing some to come, and then drawing a line after a certain number. So they decided to keep it small from the outset.

They discussed his wrestling career, and though no one came

right out and said it, he was of the opinion all three of the Oestriches would prefer he give it up. After all, there was a lot of hard travel involved, and he certainly was no longer in need of the money. In fact, Frank had to admit he was comfortably fixed for the rest of his life, and could live very well from his land holdings alone. Then, there was the automobile dealership with Saul that was proving very lucrative, and the real estate purchases in the Minneapolis-St. Paul area had worked out very well, too. He had been world champion for over two years now, and sometimes enjoyed it immensely. He was starting to warm up to the demands of the press and the fans, but he also knew the rigors of training and travel would be much tougher after he was married.

Still, there was so much national interest in him now. A reporter from a Chicago paper, George S. Robbins of the Chicago Daily News, had sent a letter to him about the possibility of a book being written about him, and even said he had a publisher, the Joseph B. Bowles Company of Chicago, lined up. Frank responded that he was interested, and they were to meet in Humboldt some time in the next several months to discuss the project.

There were also others to consider, men who would stand to lose a great deal if he retired. Klank and Burns would suffer drastically from an economic standpoint, although Farmer had a wrestling school going in Omaha and was thinking of starting one by mail order. Klank would probably continue to wrestle on his own, but he was not a major drawing card any longer, since he had taken over the responsibilities of being Gotch's manager.

Finally, there were the people of Humboldt, who had so generously banded together to raise the money to build him a training camp. They enjoyed their moment in the sun, the prosperity that had come their way since he had become world champion. Every single day found new visitors in Humboldt, seeking the spot where Gotch trained. It certainly helped the economy of the town.

The six months leading up to the wedding were the most tranquil of Frank's entire life. He remained in Humboldt, renewing old friendships. He and Elmer Smith went hunting and fishing a dozen or more times. And Frank worked on his own farm, as well as that of his parents. He joined his brothers in the field, staying out late at night, and found he enjoyed the camaraderie he was building anew. It was like he had never really left. He enjoyed the long talks he had late in the evening with his mother. She had met the Oestrichs just once when she was in town and Mrs. Oestrich had recognized her and introduced herself, her husband and Gladys. When Frank told her who he was he was marrying, she could recall the name, but could not place it with a face. Frank brought Gladys out to the farm after they decided to get married, and Gladys stayed for dinner. She and Amelia became fast friends, and she sat back and smiled as Amelia admonished Frank, making him promise to at least consider giving up wrestling "and this notion that you have to be in twenty different states in two weeks to be happy."

By the time the wedding rolled around, it was the most talked about event in Humboldt since his victory over Hackenschmidt. Though neither Frank nor Gladys wanted it to happen, it had become the social event of the year. Despite the small attendance inside the home, hundreds gathered outside, parking their autos along the roadway, to watch the proceedings from afar. They cheered when Frank drove up, and he tipped his hat to them, breaking into a big grin. Even Burns and Klank drew cheers, and when Frank and Gladys emerged, man and wife, horns blared and rice flew wildly.

Frank had a huge house constructed in the center of town. He loved his farm, but Gladys had grown up in town and preferred city life to that of the farm. He gently bowed to her wishes, and went about hiring a contractor. The new house was among the finest in Humboldt, with a huge, enclosed front porch and a large back yard, with two apple trees and dozens of other trees. The first story was painted white, with the top half a dark green. With four bedrooms, it had all the space they could possibly ever hope for, no matter how many children came their way.

CHAPTER 19

Frank had hinted to Gladys he would retire from wrestling after they were married, but a honeymoon in Chicago showed her how difficult that would be, for several reasons. She saw first hand how the sporting public adored him - they were stopped constantly on the street for autographs and small talk, and they were introduced at their box at the theatre, and had to stand, both of them, to a long ovation. She also began to understand the need he and wrestling had for one another. She wasn't a bit concerned about his ability to protect himself, she assured him, but she didn't want him away from home for long trips. She and Amelia discussed his traveling at great length one night when Frank was in the fields with the other boys, and Amelia had confessed that Frank's absences had been very rough on both her and Frederick. The Gotch clan had always been extremely close, and the continued absences of one son had disappointed the parents. Gladys had become convinced she didn't want to endure the many nights home alone, but Frank had promised to limit the traveling and wrestle closer to Humboldt, and not so frequently, if she would consent to his continuing in the ring.

So willing - and understanding - had been Gladys to allow him to resume his career, that Frank allowed Klank to schedule matches immediately. A contest with his old foe, Fred Beell, in Des Moines on February 7, less than a month after his marriage, was his first bout in over seven months. A packed house, which included Gladys at ringside for the first time at one of his matches, watched as he toyed with the great Wisconsin grappler before flattening him in straight falls.

Both times, he used the toe hold to work Beell's shoulders to the mat, and the crowd responded to the hold, the most famous in all of wrestling, with a standing ovation. For the first time, Gladys, standing and clapping wildly, truly understood the power of the athletic spotlight.

He took on the established wrestler Gus Schoenlin, who wrestled under the name of Americus, in Kansas City and then in Boston, winning both with ease and providing Gladys her first look at the East. He whipped Peter Norgert in Hartford, Connecticut, and Paul Schmidt in Buffalo, before returning to the Midwest for another series of matches. On March 25, he won easily over an aging Tom Jenkins. The former American champ was no longer the powerhouse of eight years earlier, when they engaged in the series of brutal matches that would hasten Jenkins' decline and establish Gotch as the foremost matman in America. This match was in Denver, Colorado, and allowed Gladys her first glimpse of the Rocky Mountains. She fell in love with Denver, but was apprehensive about the match because of the terrible stories she had heard about the previous battles between Jenkins and her husband. She had expected far more from Jenkins and was surprised at how easily Frank disposed of him.

When she questioned him about it, he smiled and shook his head: "Just like old Jim Jeffries against Jack Johnson," he said. "A man should know when his day's past. Promise me, honey, that you will take me aside and tell me when I've slipped enough that I'm not the same man."

She promised, and felt a pang of sadness as she watched Frank later that night in a restaurant, signing autographs for adoring fans. He was so good with the public, and loved to be generous. Yet, she knew there would come a day when he, too, would be far less than he was now. It pained her to think of it, and she removed it from her mind.

As their first year of marriage ended, Gladys knew something was gnawing away at her husband. From time to time, she would come across a newspaper at home that had a page or more torn out, and she would ask Frank about them. She was putting together a scrapbook of his accomplishments, and became a regular reader of the sports pages. He dismissed the questions with a flip of the hand and the always-present quick smile, but she found tucked away in a shoebox in the corner of his closet a pile of stories that had been taken from the various newspapers and magazines around the country. Many, she knew, had been sent to him by loyal fans. Every one of the stories concerned Hackenschmidt, and most concerned statements from him charging that Frank had wrestled him unfairly in Chicago, and had run from him on Gotch's trip to Europe, refusing to meet him.

Matters came to a head one night in the Gotch household. Klank and Burns had been invited to dinner, and the three men had retired to the library when a heated discussion broke out. Gladys hurried in to find Frank standing by the bookshelf, staring down at his two most trusted friends. He looked angry, and his words rang with anger.

"I don't care if he is here right now," he said through gritted teeth. "I want him to first wrestle Mahmout. Let him prove himself."

"But Frank," said Klank, seated and holding out his hands as though pleading, "the promoters don't want that match. Neither does the public. We can get some incredible deals right now. You're the one everyone wants to see against Hackenschmidt." He turned to Burns for verification and support, and Burns nodded up at his protégé.

"I know that, Emil, but gosh darn it," Frank said, slamming a big fist into an open hand, "I'm sick and tired of the way Hackenschmidt is acting. I'm tired of his accusations and his excuses and his lies. I know I can defeat him without any trouble. But Mahmout is the best man I've faced in recent years, far better than Hack. Hell, I think even Roller could probably beat Hack now. He just wants the match with me for the money. He thinks he's too good to wrestle these other men. Well, I say let him prove he's better than them, then I'll meet him again."

"Folks might get to saying you're afraid of him," said Klank rather meekly. It was a last resort measure. Frank looked down at him, then slammed a fist against the table, hard. He walked across the room, and stared at Gladys before turning back to Klank.

"Nice try, Emil," he said. Seeing his wife had calmed him, but he was still angry.

Klank smiled weakly, and knew the argument was lost. Then he turned toward Gladys. Rising, he walked over to her and placed an arm around her shoulders.

"Gladys, please inform this stubborn husband of yours that he is passing up the biggest deal he's ever had. Tell him that your brother says his bank account is overdrawn and that he's in desperate need of money...."

Gladys broke out laughing, and so did Frank. She pushed Emil's arm from her, and Klank began laughing, too.

"Oh, Emil," said Gladys. "You know I never got my way with Frank. Don't come to me with your proposals."

But long after Gladys had left the men alone, retiring for the night, they devised a plan. They knew Hackenschmidt was set to meet Jess Westergard in Omaha, and a huge crowd was expected to see the former world champion.

"You take Mahmout with you," Frank said to Burns, "and let out the word that something big is going to happen. Then, walk up to the ring with Jess and Mahmout, having Mahmout disguised. They will let you into the ring, thinking you are going to make an announcement of some sort about our plans to wrestle Hackenschmidt. Old Jack Curley, Hack's manager, will go along, thinking we have finally come around. "When you get the crowd's attention, have Mahmout show himself and say he is taking Jess' place. Tell Jess we will pay him well for bowing out. Then, the crowd will demand to see the much better match, which would be Hack against Mahmout. I don't see how Hack can turn down that challenge in front of that big of a crowd. And if he does...."

"What then?" said Burns, raising his eyebrow and staring up at Gotch.

"Then," said Frank, "the sporting public will know Hack's not all he's cracked up to be. They'll know he's a lair, too."

"Will you consent to meet him then, no matter what happens?" asked Klank.

Gotch nodded.

"Then, and only then."

Two weeks later, Burns returned from Omaha with a signed contract bearing the names of Hackenschmidt and Curley. Gotch's plan had worked to perfection, with Mahmout gaining the crowd's favor and issuing the challenge, and Hack refusing to even enter the ring. After nearly thirty minutes of considerable shouting but no action, the over-flow crowd of five thousand plus demanded to see a match, and finally Mahmout and Burns left the ring, and Hack defeated Westergard. The sporting press came down hard on the Russian Lion, and said he certainly had no right to say Gotch had ducked him in Europe when he obviously wanted no part of Mahmout. That pleased Frank to no end, and now he was as eager as could be to take to the ring with Hackenschmidt for another battle.

He began training in the same manner he had for his second great match with Jenkins, with long morning runs and four or more hours of strenuous mat work each day. Burns brought in Yankee Joe, Westergard and several others to work with him, and Gladys became caught up in the training camp routine for the first time. She relished the role. She saw to it that all those training with her husband received the very best meals - cooked by her personally.

The training camp down by the river became the focus of attention for the entire community, so much so that Burns worried about Frank's ability to train. Reporters flocked in from all across the nation, and Humboldt swelled to almost twice its normal size as each day brought a new crush of fans. They sat in the bleachers, and in the grass, and stood ten-people deep through the oppressively hot afternoons of June, July and August to watch him train.

He wanted a tune up match, and tangled with Beell on May 5 in Knoxville, Tennessee. After taking a thorough beating, Beell volunteered to come to the Riverside Camp for a few days to work with Frank in his preparation. When Beell arrived in Humboldt, he brought word that Dr. Roller had signed up to work with Hackenschmidt, and Gotch frowned when he heard the news. Other than Burns, no wrestler knew as much about Gotch's wrestling style as Roller, who was a student of the game of the first rank. But the news only made Frank determined to train all the harder.

One newspaperman from Chicago reported he had come to town to write a story about Gotch's training, and was surprised to find the town deserted. The stores were closed and not a person could be found on the streets. He was about to head back to Chicago when he heard a mighty roar down by the river, and he proceeded to the Riverside Camp, where he found over two thousand people - twice the town's population - basking in the sun watching Gotch throw the huge Rogers around the training camp ring. The upcoming match was, the reporter wrote, the biggest sporting event in America since the day Johnson knocked out Jeffries in Reno.

Jeffries and Corbett had both sent telegrams of good luck, as did Theodore Roosevelt. The governor of Iowa came to watch Gotch's progress late in July, and spent thirty minutes talking with Gotch and wishing him well. He even said Frank would be a tremendous politician, should he ever tire of wrestling, because the crowds responded to him and trusted him so strongly.

But for the first time in his long career, Frank was moody and on edge. He had always gone into battle - even the first match with Hack - full of confidence. But this time he was obsessed with his training, as though he feared he might not be in good enough shape to prevail. He knew the key to winning lay in his ability to tire Hackenschmidt out, and to that purpose he trained like never before. He pushed himself so hard on his long runs that several times he actually threw up, and he pounded his training partners so fiercely on several occasions that Burns had to pull him off.

"I like a mean wrestler, particularly when he needs to be," Burns told Frank late one evening when just the two of them were together. "But, gosh darn it, Frank, you've been beating up on Jess and Fred too much. Go easy on 'em after you've whipped 'em. Save some of that anger for the Lion, will ya?"

Gotch nodded. "I know what you're saying, Farmer," said Frank. "But I'm so darned angry at Hackenschmidt that I can hardly control myself when I get in the ring. I see him standing there after our first bout acting so meek, and then I think of all the lies he's spread....and I want to make him pay. I want to make him hurt, and hurt bad."

As Burns watched Gotch walk away, he knew for certain that The Russian Lion was in big trouble this time around.

Spotting Gladys in the crowd one day at camp, Frank suddenly realized she was also part of the reason behind his obsession. He saw the pride in her face when Klank introduced him to the enthusiastic crowds, and the thunderous ovation he received as he climbed into the ring made her squirm with pride. He threw her a little wink, and she blushed quickly. This was the first time she would actually see him wrestle with his title on the line. True, she had seen him in many ring engagements so far, and he always wore his world championship belt into the ring. But this was the first time he would be up against a foe who posed a serious threat. He realized, watching her from the ring, that he could not stand to lose in front of her.

Training for the second Hackenschmidt match was a totally different experience for him. Before Gladys, he would while away the nights on his farm, either talking with Burns or Klank, or taking long walks alone. Now, he would come home from camp with several men with him and they would set down to a meal prepared by Gladys. Then, while the others would sit on the porch or in the backyard, if the mosquitoes weren't intolerable, Frank would slip away and spend some time with Gladys. She never demanded it, and would have understood if he chose to talk wrestling with the others. But he always made a point to spend at least an hour with her every night before joining Burns, Klank, Rogers and the others for strategy sessions.

The match was set for September 4, and the Gotch entourage left Humboldt on August 25, taking a train to Chicago. They were quartered in the Morrison Hotel, the forty-story building that was one of the finest lodges in the world. A huge crowd gathered at the train station in Humboldt to bid farewell, and another crowd greeted them in Chicago. Reporters also met them as they stepped down from the train and followed them all the way to the hotel.

The front pages of the sporting sections of the Chicago papers were full of stories about the upcoming bout. There were quotes from promoter Jack Curley and Hackenschmidt, who had arrived in town a week earlier, and from other prominent wrestlers. Hack was predicting victory, of course, but Gotch was surprised to read that several other matmen - foes he had defeated easily - were also on the side of the Russian Lion.

A pounding on their door the first morning after their arrival startled Frank and Gladys, and Frank rushed to let in Klank.

"Come here," he said grabbing Gladys by the wrist and motioning Frank to follow him to the window. "There," he said, pulling open the curtains, and pointing down into the street. "Look at that, if you will."

Gladys peered into the street, and stepped back, her hands over her mouth.

"What in heaven's name do they want?" she asked, looking up at Klank with a shocked expression.

"To see your husband, of course," said Klank. "Must be two thousand of them out there. And they say they aren't going away til Frank sticks that ugly mug of his out the window and says something."

Frank shook his head, a smile playing on his features. He had become accustomed to enthusiastic crowds, but this was beyond anything he had experienced. It reminded him of the scene at Reno before the Johnson-Jeffries fight. Klank pulled up the window, and Frank stuck his head and shoulders out, peering down into the street. Immediately, a man caught sight of him and pointed upwards, and several nearby began cheering and pointing, also. Within seconds, nearly every man, woman and child in the street had seen him, and was cheering wildly. Frank continued to wave out the window, feeling somewhat foolish - but very honored - and withdrew after about a minute.

He turned to Klank, and shrugged, and glanced at Gladys, who was standing back from the window, staring at her husband. There was a look of awe on her features, and she gave the appearance of one who has just suddenly discovered something new and unsettling. She had seen how the crowds in Humboldt had treated him, but she had reasoned it away by rationalizing that he was, after all, the town's only claim to fame, and he could be expected to be idolized. And he had been certainly well received in cities like Kansas City and Denver. But to draw this kind of a response in the city of Chicago was almost beyond her comprehension.

Her thoughts were interrupted by a pounding at the door.

"Go see who that is, will you, Emil?" asked Frank.

Klank opened the door, held a brief conversation, then returned.

"Some fellow from a newspaper wants an interview.....with you, Gladys."

"Me?" she exclaimed. It was getting crazier by the second, she thought. "For heaven's sakes, why me?"

Frank laughed.

"Go ahead, dear," he said. "Now, it's your turn to be done in by the press." He started to push her gently toward the door.

"But Frank," she protested.... "no, I can't do this. No. Stop pushing me." She was holding her head with her hands and half laughing as her husband directed her toward the door, where the newsman was standing, hat in hands.

"This is Mrs. Gotch," said Frank. "And I'm Frank Gotch." He held out his hand, and the newsman reached for it timidly.

"Hello, I'm Tom Hey from the Chicago American newspaper," he said. "I've been sent out to do a story on Mrs. Gotch, and what it feels like to be married to the No. 1 sports hero in America."

"Oh, goodness," said Gladys, looking first at Emil, then at Frank for support. But she was greeted only with large smiles. Both Klank and her husband were enjoying the moment.

"We'll leave you two to talk," said Frank, grabbing Klank by the elbow, "and we'll just go into the next room and figure out if we can win this thing with the great Russian Lion."

Emil nodded, looking suddenly very serious.

"Actually, I do have something we need to discuss, Frank," he said. "Better brace yourself..."

With that, the two wrestlers departed, leaving Gladys with the reporter.

"Did he really mean that....about trying to figure out if they can beat Hack?" said Hey, adjusting his glasses. He was a thin, meek man, but Gladys found him very pleasant and easy to talk with.

"On, no," she said, with a flip of her hand. "You mustn't take those two seriously. They love to tease. They know exactly what they are going to do and Frank is not at all concerned about the match."

"How about you, Mrs. Gotch. Do you worry when Frank wrestles?"

"Please, call me Gladys," she said. "Mrs. Gotch sounds so formal....and makes me sound so old." She laughed lightly.

She was beginning to feel more at ease, and led Hey into the living room, where they each found chairs. She was still in the big housecoat she had thrown on hastily when Klank's pounding had startled them, but neither she nor Hey seemed to notice.

"I'm not concerned Frank will get hurt anymore. I first saw him wrestle in Humboldt at the opera house, when I was just nine years old. I fell asleep on the lap of my father. But I didn't see him wrestle again until after we were married. When I first watched him after we were married, I was a bit nervous, but nobody knew it, for I felt that would be giving the impression Frank couldn't hold his own, and that wouldn't be fair to him."

"What was it like in Humboldt this summer, when he was training and all those other wrestlers were hanging around the house?" asked the reporter.

"I cooked for strange people - by that, I mean people I didn't know previously - all last summer. Not a morning passed that the train didn't bring in some men who knew Frank, and after watching him down at the training camp, they'd come home with him to eat. I never knew until I saw them coming who we would have for dinner, or how many besides the regular camp folks - like Emil and the Farmer, Yankee Joe Rogers, Jess Westergard, and the like - but I gave them what we had. We had some wonderful times."

"Does Frank eat a lot when he's in training?" asked Hey, leaning forward eagerly and obviously enjoying hearing about these wonderful athletes.

"Why, he can eat a whole jar of preserves at one meal," she said emphatically. "I don't know where he puts it. I guess he just works out so hard that he burns most of it up right away. But, preserves and ice cream are his weakness. He loves to go down town some evenings and find a group of young boys, and take them all over for ice cream. And believe me, Frank eats more than all of them. He often tells me that when he gives up wrestling, he'll have to give up eating, too, else he'll turn into a big butterball."

"Does Mr. Gotch want children some day soon?" asked Hey. He seemed a bit nervous about asking such a personal question, and Gladys immediately saw he was ill at ease.

"Oh, heavens, yes, and you needn't feel uncomfortable about asking such a question," she said reassuringly. "We both love children, and Frank is so good with them. He has so much patience and understanding. We hope to have several children, but don't plan to start a family until he quits wrestling, so he won't be traveling such a great deal when the children are growing up."

The two chatted for another ten minutes, after which the reporter thanked his hostess and left. Hearing the door slam shut, Frank and Klank returned from the next room. Frank wore a deep frown and Gladys saw he was upset. He stood in the center of the room, staring first at her then back at Emil.

"Emil says there's talk of a fix going around," he said slowly, measuring his words. "That Hack let me beat him the first time so we could have this rematch and make a lot of money. People are saying Hack is going to beat me handily this time, so we can have yet another match and make more money."

He dropped into a big chair and sat in a slump, his powerful frame sagging. He looked as depressed as she had ever seen him.

"Same thing that happened after the Beell match," said Klank sourly. "Just have to show 'em it ain't so, Frank."

"What about the Beell match?" asked Gladys. She knew Fred Beell well from the training camp, and knew Burns regarded him as one of the finest wrestlers he had ever seen. But he was, she recalled, a small man compared to Frank, Hackenschmidt and Mahmout.

"Oh, there are folks who think I let Fred beat me that first match we had in New Orleans back in 1906," said Frank. "Fred is a wonderful wrestler and in great shape because he was a wood chopper, working all day long cutting wood up in the Wisconsin forests. But, heck, Gladys, Fred only weighed about one hundred seventy pounds, and I was two hundred or so. He's strong and tough, but just too darned small.

"I won the first fall easily, and was sort of fooling around in the second one - you know, I didn't want to disappoint the crowd and end it too easily - when I shot in for a double leg takedown and ran into the ring post in the corner with my head. I was knocked goofy; I really didn't even know where I was. Then, Fred started doing those danged backdrops of his...."

Klank butted in, coming over by Gladys and pretending he had an opponent in his arms, wrapped up in a bear hug.

"See, it's like I'm Fred Beell, and I've got this guy like this," and Klank made a flopping motion, like throwing a sack of wheat over his shoulders backwards.

"....and he did it to me about four or five times," continued Frank, holding his head. "I was so dazed I didn't know where I was, or what was happening. Ramming my head into the corner post did it, but Fred's backdrops didn't help matters any."

"Couldn't they just stop the bout?" asked Gladys, the concern registering on her face.

Frank laughed.

"Hardly, dear. That's part of the game, and the part the fans just don't understand. I'm the champ, I have to keep going. If I get dazed in the course of the bout, well that's just too bad. A champion has to be good enough to win under all circumstances.

"Anyway, I got twenty minutes to rest up between falls, and never quite came around. Fred polished me off pretty fast in the third fall, and I lost the crown. The American crown, that is. This match took place two years before I won the world title from Hackenschmidt."

"You shoulda seen him, Gladys," chimed in Emil. He made a face, twisting his features all around, and she laughed. "He was really messed up - confused - for some time. Even more than usual..."

"But why would anyone think that was a fixed affair?" asked Gladys.

"Because Frank beat him every time they wrestled after that," said Klank. "He beat him so easily that no one would believe Fred could have beaten Frank under any circumstances, even when he was almost unconscious."

Frank sat shaking his head.

"We must of wrestled eight, nine times after that, and I never had any trouble with Fred. The truth is, I was only half conscious after hitting my head on the ring post. Accidents happen, especially in a sport as rough as wrestling. The men who know me understand I'd never throw a match, not ever. There's too much pride and reputation at stake. Money doesn't mean so much to me that I'd fake a match. But, there's plenty of others who simply don't think I could lose fair and square, and that I must have thrown the match to Beell."

"In fact," said Klank, "that's the last time you ever lost a fall, let alone a match, Frank. And what was that...five years ago?"

Frank nodded. He had wrestled the top men across the country and around the world for five years without losing so much as a fall. There had been sixty-five formal matches since Beell in New Orleans, and over a hundred exhibitions, and he hadn't even come close to being thrown once.

"Better win this one convincingly," said Klank, seriously, "or you know what everyone will be saying." Frank nodded.

"Use the toe hold," said Klank. Frank nodded again.

"If he'll let me," said Frank, quietly. "He has a great fear of it, and will do anything - anything at all - to stay away from it. He'll toss in the towel if he thinks the toe hold is coming. But, you're right, Emil. I have to beat Hack so convincingly that there will be no doubt in any-one's mind. That's the surest way to handle talk about a crooked match. If you never lose, then no one can say you're crooked, because you'll discourage people from betting against you."

"The problem there is," said Klank, "that if you ever do lose, folks will say you done it on purpose."

Frank stood, and walked to the window, staring out into the streets. Most of the crowd had gone, content with a glimpse at the world's heavyweight wrestling champ. He turned back to face Gladys and Klank.

"Then I'd better never lose again, right?"

CHAPTER 20

The first Gotch-Hackenschmidt bout was held in the Dexter Pavilion, but the rematch required a much larger venue and was set in Comiskey Park, the new home of the Chicago White Sox baseball team. It was a little south of main Chicago, and had been built just the year prior by Charles Comiskey, the club's owner. An egotistical man, Comiskey invited Frank and his entourage to the park the day before, in order to show off his posh offices in the upper level. While impressed with the facility, Frank kept his distance from Comiskey, having heard how cheaply he treated his ball players.

The match was set for 3 p.m. The day began with a drizzle, but quickly cleared. At noon, Burns told Gotch and Klank that there was already rumors floating about that Hackenschmidt had hurt his knee in a last-minute practice session and was limping slightly. Frank was furious.

"He's planning on losing," mumbled Burns, "because he's already inventing excuses for his performance."

"How many times have you competed with a bum ankle or a banged-up knee, Farmer?" asked Gotch. "Or you, Emil? Hell, what wrestler doesn't get banged up during hard practices. I've got jammed fingers and a shoulder that hurts all the time, but I wouldn't let anyone else know it. That's just a part of the sport."

"Yeah, but a part Hack obviously doesn't know how to cope with," said Klank.

The Gotch party left the Morrison at noon in two autos, and ran into a huge crowd of fans two blocks from the park.

"I can't believe this crowd," said Klank, peering out the window of the auto carrying Burns, him and Frank. "Curley estimated we would get thirty thousand people - and he may be low!"

The group moved quickly down to the clubhouse area where the ball teams changed. Gotch was in the White Sox clubhouse, while Hackenschmidt used the visitor's locker room. Frank changed slowly, taking great care to limber up precisely the way he and Burns had planned. There was lots of pushing against the wall, deep squats, and then some tussling with Klank and Rogers. After breaking a sweat, Frank sat on the edge of a long bench, away from the others, preparing his mind for the epic match that loomed ahead. He allowed himself to think about the trip to England and the crowds he had encountered, and the accusations he had been forced to endure. The anger began to swell up inside him. He stared down at his hands, clenched in tight fists. He felt ready for the match of his life, and to make George Hackenschmidt sorry he had ever come to America....Frank Gotch's America.

After receiving the call, they moved quickly down a narrow passageway, up through the players' dugout and out onto the field. Twelve men, including five Chicago policemen and his longtime friends, surrounded Frank. The size of the crowd and the roar marking their appearance was unbelievable to both Gotch and Klank, but Burns was oblivious to it all. As usual, his mind was elsewhere - already he was minutes ahead of everyone else, visualizing the opening minutes of the match. Fans shouted his name, too, and tried to reach out and pat him on the back as he passed them, but he paid little attention.

Burns bounded up the steps to the ring, and put a foot on the lower rope and pulled up the middle, allowing Frank to glide through, his long green robe flowing behind him as he entered. Westergard had an American flag with him and began tying it to the ring post, setting off a huge cheer from those in the crowd who could see what he was doing. Frank gripped the thick ropes and searched for Gladys, finally spotting her twenty rows back. He waved quickly, and she waved back, while necks strained to see who he was saluting. She was sitting in a section filled with Humboldt people, and Frank let his eyes run over them, nodding in a silent greeting. He felt a tingling down his back, and a great sense of pride in knowing his friends from Iowa would be able to see him at his finest moment.

Hackenschmidt was scheduled to appear at the same time, but was nowhere to be seen, and Gotch grew increasingly irritated as the minutes slipped away. It was a common courtesy to never keep a champion waiting, and Frank was offended. Klank was miffèd, as well.

"Where the heck is the big dumb Russian, anyway?" spit out Klank between clenched teeth.

"He's just playing his game, trying to get us riled," said Burns, calmly. He looked around for the first time, and let out a low whistle. "Never seen a crowd like this before."

"Somewhere in the neighborhood of thirty thousand," said Klank, peering up into the second deck. "At least, that's what Smith said."

Ed Smith, the sporting editor of the Chicago American who had officiated the first match, was the man in charge of refereeing this one, as well. Gotch was happy with the choice, as he felt Smith was an honest man who would show no favoritism in either direction. That was as important to him as it would be to have a referee who wouldn't favor Hackenschmidt. Frank wanted no charges of favoritism or talk of a fix to damage this match. Nothing, he vowed, would be allowed to add any claim of foul this time around. It was to be a pure shooting match, fair and simple, between the two men whom the sporting world considered the greatest wrestlers of all time.

Finally, at ten minutes after three, Hackenschmidt began his walk toward the ring. He paused several times as well-wishers stopped his progress, but he reached the ring at 3:15, fifteen minutes after Gotch's arrival. Gotch stared hard at Hackenschmidt as he entered the ring, but the Russian immediately turned his back on him, and Frank eventually turned away.

Smith called them together at ring center for photographs and instructions, and Gotch got his first good look at Hackenschmidt in nearly three years. His hair seemed thinner, and he seemed smaller and much less formidable in appearance than the first time they met, though he was still wearing his robe and Gotch couldn't see his body. They shook hands listlessly, looking at the photographers while the pictures were snapped, and stared impassively at one another while Smith read the directions. There was no mention of the toe hold, and the two men shook once more, briefly, before returning to their corners. Gotch slipped off his long robe and handed it to Klank. He wore long purple tights, with no shirt, while Hack was attired in dark green tights, and was also bare chested. Frank looked out at Gladys one last time, but he could scarcely make her out. She wore a white hat, wide at the brim, and seemed so small and frail sitting amongst so many big men from Humboldt. He winked to her spontaneously, knowing she couldn't see it, and flashed a smile of confidence. She waved back furiously.

Klank was talking a mile a minute, and Burns was pounding him on the back. He looked across the ring and saw Hack standing without expression, nodding his head slowly as his manager issued last second instructions. Sitting on the steps beneath them was Roller, a man Gotch had defeated twice, but whom he held in great respect. He knew Roller was a keen student of the game of wrestling, and he was disappointed he had tied in with the Hackenschmidt camp.

Gotch surveyed Hackenschmidt quickly. He reminded him of Tom Sharkey, the fighting sailor who had given Jeffries two of the toughest fights of his life. Sharkey was a squat, powerful athlete with short cropped hair, as was Hackenschmidt. Now that his robe was off, Frank noticed Hack was not as muscular as he was the last time, when Frank thought he was the most impressive physical specimen he had ever seen. Hack was still well developed, but the three years since their last match seemed to take the edge from the incredibly chiseled look of 1908.

The ring announcer introduced several celebrities and stated all bets were declared off by order of the Chicago Police Department. The bets were voided at the request of the officials of the Empire Athletic Club, which had made all the arrangements for the bout. Comiskey was the president, and he was firmly against gambling of all sorts. The crowd cheered at the announcement, convinced the match was on the up and up, if there was no gambling involved.

The bell rang, and the match was on. But this time, Gotch was the champion and Hackenschmidt the challenger. Frank forced a wicked smile, more of a sneer, at Hack as they approached the first tie-up.

"Well, here we are again, George," he said in a low voice. "This is your chance to prove I wrestled unfairly the first time. Here's your chance to prove how great you really are."

Hack grunted slightly, and the two men grabbed one another, collar and elbow, trying to push or pull the other out of position, and thereby gain a quick advantage. They tied up and broke apart, assessing the other man's strength. Once again, Frank found himself surprised at Hack's strength, or lack of it. He wasn't as strong this time as last, and last time he felt he was not as strong as Jenkins at his peak.

Roller shouted at Hack to move away, not to let Gotch hang on him. Hack tried to oblige, and it immediately looked to the crowd as though he was totally on the defense. Gotch smiled and moved after him, and they spent the first ten minutes of the match in similar fashion, the crowd cheering with great volume whenever the action picked up.

Gotch finally grabbed Hack's leg and raised it, pulling it into his own midsection, and then he dropped his weight on it, forcing Hack to the mat with a thud. He reached for Hack's foot and began to draw it up into position for a toe hold, but Hack, with a supreme effort, erupted, and pulled free, standing. Frank was in on him like a cat, repeating his move, and they hit the canvas once again, the champion on top. This time, Gotch tried for a half nelson and crotch hold, but Hackenschmidt spun away and came to his feet. Gotch reached for him and Hack dipped beneath the extended arm and swept behind Gotch with more speed than Frank thought he possessed. The speed of the movement convinced Gotch there was nothing wrong with Hackenschmidt's leg or knee. Securing a waist lock, he lifted Gotch and slammed him to the mat, hoping to work his way up into a control hold.

But hundreds of hours working with Burns had made the Iowan a master at escaping, and he pushed his weight back into Hack, at the same time grasping the Russian Lion's hands, and forcing them apart. He pushed harder into Hack, and the two of them came off the mat, with Gotch controlling Hack's hands. Suddenly, he pivoted, facing Hack. Gotch smiled, and Hack took a step backward. He seemed perplexed, and depressed, by the ease with which Gotch pulled loose. Hackenschmidt was used to overpowering foes with his awesome strength once he was behind them, and yet he had seen no opportunity to try anything with Gotch from behind.

In a matter of moments, Gotch took Hack down to the mat and began working on his legs. The fans cheered wildly, thinking the toe hold was imminent. Hack was horror stricken, and turned to watch Gotch's activities. He strained desperately to keep his leg straight, and not allow Gotch to bend it upward. Suddenly, Gotch pivoted on his stomach, and spun to the front of Hack, catching him on his side. Hack was half on his back, with Gotch on top of him, and a furious struggle ensued, Hack trying to fight off his back and Gotch straining to drive him further onto it, in a pinning maneuver.

For several moments they were like an oil painting - poised in effort, unmoving, each straining mightily against the other. But slowly, Gotch's position prevailed over Hackenschmidt's strength, and he forced the Russian's shoulders closer and closer to the mat. For several long seconds there was no movement on the part of the Russian, and Smith tapped Gotch on the back, signifying the fall....the first pure pin in Hackenschmidt's entire wrestling career.

It had taken just twenty-seven minutes. Gotch stood and walked away from Hackenschmidt, not even glancing back to watch as the Russian rolled slowly to his stomach and came to his hands and knees, and then his feet. His head hung in despair as he trudged to his corner amid the deafening roar of the crowd.

"He was easier than last time," shouted Klank as he wiped the perspiration from Gotch's back with a thick towel, glaring across the ring at Hackenschmidt's corner, where his trainers were trying desperately to revitalize him. "He's lost it."

Burns shook his head.

"Hardly lost it. Just up against a man, and a style, he can't cope with. Frank's the fastest heavyweight of all time....no one even close. Hack just can't keep the pace. He's a great wrestler, but he's in over his head."

Frank listened to the words, but said nothing. He looked for Gladys, and saw her half hidden behind rows of standing cheering fans. He wanted to rush out and hold her, to say it was all over....that he was ready to retire after just one more fall with Hackenschmidt, which he knew now would be nothing more than a mere formality. He had wrestled far too many matches not to know when an opponent had resigned himself to defeat. It was over for Hack, he knew. In fact, he wouldn't have been surprised if Hack forfeited the next fall.

During the rest period, both men sat in their corners while several boxers were introduced to the crowd and Mahmout climbed into the ring to challenge the winner of this match. When the ten minutes had expired, Smith called for Hack to show. A second call followed, whereupon he broke from a small group about ten feet from his corner and headed for the ring. Curley and Roller were at his side, and both looked dejected.

Hack started out the second fall strong, his teeth clenched, desperate to make a go of it. But Gotch was far too fast and evaded his every move, finally tripping him to the mat after five minutes of wrestling. Immediately, he went for the toe hold, and was surprised to hear Hackenschmidt yell out.

"What?" asked Gotch, who had his back turned toward Hack while working hard to bend the leg back so he could grip the foot in preparation for his favorite submission move.

"Don't break my leg," said Hack in a strange tone. Gotch looked up at Smith, who was bending low, and heard the Russian Lion.

"There'll have to be a fall," said Smith firmly, aware Hackenschmidt was asking for mercy and, therefore, ready to submit.

Worried the crowd would be disappointed if there wasn't a dramatic conclusion to the bout and mindful of Hack's charges that the first match was won unfairly, Frank started to pull up the leg all the harder, intent upon securing the toe hold. He knew Hack was finished, but he wanted to at least secure the toe hold so there could be no doubt the Russian had submitted. But before he could lock in the torturous hold, Hackenschmidt turned so that his shoulders were forced onto the mat, and Smith called the fall at the six-minute mark.

It was all over. The Russian Lion, once the pride of the entire athletic world, had suffered his second loss in over four hundred matches, both at the hands of the same man.

Frank rose slowly, disappointed at the ending. He wanted to make Hackenschmidt cry out in pain and submit. The crowd was cheering, but not as boisterously as at the end of the first fall. It was pleased, no doubt, that the title would remain in America, but it had hoped for a gamer show from the famed Russian Lion. Frank sensed a feeling of disappointment not only in his own heart, but in the crowd, as well. He, and they, had hoped for a fierce battle to the very limits of human endurance.

Frank looked down at Hack, and then turned and walked to his corner. Hackenschmidt had not looked up at him; both knew something immeasurable had passed. Hackenschmidt had lost forever the air of invincibility he had fashioned in over ten years of wrestling, and Frank had lost the greatest opponent, at least in terms of reputation, he would ever face. Never again would Americans rally to the site of a wrestling match like they had that afternoon in Comiskey Park. Even in total victory, Frank sensed he had lost a part of himself.

The photographers were in the ring, snapping pictures frantically as Frank tried to leave. Once again, he searched for Gladys, and saw her standing atop her chair, waving joyously, but only for a moment, before being swallowed up by a sea of faces and bodies. As he was climbing from the ring, he glanced back in the opposite direction one last time, but the Russian Lion was already gone from view.

The Marquis of Queensberry, the man who had written the rules for modern boxing, traveled from London to cover the fight for several newspapers. The day before the big match he had asked in his column for the Chicago Daily American "what on earth sporting Chicago was going to do with itself" after the big match was over. But while life continued just as before in the big city by Lake Michigan, it was far different for Gotch and Hackenschmidt. For them, and wrestling itself, life was dramatically altered. Hackenschmidt left town in a hurry but Frank and Gladys stayed a week in Chicago to relax and do some shopping. They were greeted by enthusiastic crowds wherever they appeared. They were celebrities of the first rank, the toast of Chicago, the Midwest and the entire nation.

Roller wrote an article for one Chicago paper stating that Hackenschmidt had indeed suffered a minor leg injury prior to the match, but that it shouldn't have played any type of determining factor in the outcome. The truth was, said Roller, that Hackenschmidt simply lost his nerve. "I don't know why," Roller wrote, "unless he was just overcome by fear at the prospect of facing Gotch again."

The match met all expectations from an attendance standpoint. Over thirty three thousand fans had paid a total of eighty seven thousand nine hundred and fifty three dollars - both records for a match. The Empire Athletic Club, which sponsored the match, collected eighteen thousand dollars, with the promoter's office picking up thirty four thousand. Coming from Europe and incurring far heavier traveling and training expenses, Hackenschmidt collected forty three thousand. Gotch had been guaranteed twenty one thousand dollars as a fee and picked up another ten thousand from his share of the gate and film rights.

But aside from the financial rewards, the match had established Frank's supremacy once and for all. Without a loss in six years, he had removed all competition from the horizon. There was talk of a match with the legendary Great Gama of India, a man of gargantuan strength who had reportedly never tasted defeat, and threw most opponents in less than a minute. Gama had apparently agreed verbally to a match with Gotch, but first decided to wrestle Zbyszko in London. They wrestled for three hours and forty-seven minutes without a fall, and the match was declared a draw. Perhaps disheartened by the knowledge Gotch had pinned the Polish giant twice within thirty minutes, the Hindu champion promptly returned to India, the talk of a match with Gotch forgotten.

Frank and Gladys returned to a tremendous welcome in Humboldt, and began to settle into married life. He wrestled nine more matches in 1911, winning all with ease. Nine matches the next year also ended without him losing a single fall, much less a match. By the end of 1912, he was riding a string of eighty-five consecutive victories, and had eliminated any and all worthy competition.

But the year had brought some stunning surprises, as well. Like the rest of the nation, he was shocked by the sinking of the ocean liner Titanic on April 15, during its maiden voyage from England to New

York City. When he first heard the reports, he was reminded of his own narrow escape from a watery death in Alaska some twelve years earlier, on the ill-fated Skagway. Contemplating the death of an estimated fifteen hundred people under such terrifying conditions in the frigid North Atlantic sent a shiver down his back.

And then there was the setback suffered by his White House friend, Teddy Roosevelt. When his second term ended in 1909, Roosevelt said he would never run for the nation's highest office again. But apparently three years of travel and big-game hunting had left him with the urge to get back into the political fray. When his followers formed the Bull Moose party, they nominated him for their candidate and he accepted. The name cropped up when a newspaper reporter asked Roosevelt how he felt after a long hunting trip and he, in typical Roosevelt fashion, responded he felt "strong as a bull moose."

But Roosevelt's decision to run for president split the Republican Party, ruining not only his chances but those of President William Howard Taft, as well. Taft had served as Secretary of War under President Roosevelt and the two had once been very close. Taft was elected president after Roosevelt left office, but they became enemies in the ensuing years and their rift split the party and allowed Woodrow Wilson to claim the presidency in 1912.

Frank could only shake his head in disbelief at all that was transpiring in the world as 1912 drew to a close. Henry Ford's automated assembly plant had made automobiles such a common sight now that it seemed everyone had one. The popularity of little movie theaters was exploding all across the nation, as well. The unsinkable ship had sunk, and the unbeatable Teddy Roosevelt had been beaten. Times were changing so quickly that it was hard to keep pace. Maybe it was an omen that he should consider stepping down as heavyweight wrestling champion of the world before the unthinkable happened to him, as well!

CHAPTER 21

After walking across the well-manicured yard in front of the huge white house, Frank climbed the steps and passed through the front porch. Entering the fashionably decorated living room, he marveled once again at how Gladys could make a home look so comfortable and lived in, without making it look messy. She had exquisite taste, in his mind, and he left all decorating decisions to her. Just as the wrestling ring had been his domain, so the house was hers..... and she had spent nearly five thousand dollars on furnishings in Chicago the week following the Hackenschmidt match.

He called out her name, but heard no response. He stopped for a moment to inspect the mail sitting on top of the white wicker table in the hallway, then climbed the stairway to the second floor, slipping from bedroom to bedroom looking for her. He stopped in the long hallway at the back window and peered out, and saw her sitting in the back yard. He grinned, and turned away, heading down the stairs and hustling out the back door. When she looked up at him, she broke out laughing.

"If you don't look a sight," she said, as he hurried toward her. He was attired in heavy black boots, and bulging, thick pants, along with a thick sweatshirt and a beat-up hat, with a long bill in front. And, he was caked with mud halfway up the front. He had a shotgun in his right hand, and three pheasants in his left, so big that they were trailing along the ground behind him.

"Yeah, I may not look so sharp, but look at these babies," he said with a grin, holding up the dead birds. "Plenty of work for you right here." He knew she would cook anything he brought into the house, and she would gladly set the table for as many friends as he wanted to drag home, and on as short a notice as he wanted. But one thing she would never do - not even for him - was clean birds, or fish.

She smiled up at him, reclining in her chair, and kept right on knitting. He waited for a response, but didn't receive one, so just shrugged.

"Sure, make me do all the work around here," he said.

He was gone for about thirty minutes, then came out of the small building at the back of the yard, his hands bloody from the work inside. She saw his hands, pointed at the pump in the backyard, and he mumbled something about forgetting and walked quickly to the pump, cleaning his hands. He came back and pulled up a chair.

"Where's the little guy?" he asked. Robert Frederick Gotch had been born on February 24, 1914, and was the apple of his eye. Frank couldn't wait until his son was big enough to go hunting and fishing with him, and to even begin to roll around on the living room floor. He wasn't determined to make his son a wrestler, but he sure wanted him to take an interest in at least some sport. Right now, he thought base-ball looked pretty good, although Frank wasn't convinced the sport would ever pay well enough that a fellow could earn a handsome living from it.

"Upstairs, sleeping," she replied, "unless you woke him when you barged through the house."

"Don't think so," said Frank. "Didn't hear him, anyway."

They sat talking quietly, Frank rattling on about the day's catch. He and five others had been out since before dawn, on his eight hundred acres south of town, and had an exceptionally good day of it. Since his retirement from the ring, he had gotten caught up in a series of business ventures, including real estate and the raising of stock. He had dabbled in the banking business, become the president of a street railway company and an electric light company in Humboldt. He had played a large role in the building of a new train depot in Humboldt, and other civic projects. But he had not lost his love of the outdoor life, and had turned to hunting to take up the emptiness he felt when he decided he would no longer wrestle.

He had made the decision to give up top-flight wrestling after a win over George Lurich, another powerful Russian, in Kansas City on April 1, 1913. In truth, he began to lose interest in wrestling as a pro-fession after the Hackenschmidt battle. The fever pitch which gripped the nation's sporting fans seemed to evaporate after the Chicago bout, as the public felt there were no other opponents on the horizon who could be expected to challenge him.

Besides, Jeffries had been pushing him to tour with him as a member of the Sells-Floto Circus, taking on all comers, and the idea appealed to Frank. The management was offering one hundred dollars to any man who could last three rounds with Jeffries or fifteen minutes with Gotch and in the summer of 1913, Frank hit the road with the circus.

In over two hundred bouts, the circus was never forced to pay off once on Gotch, and the two champions earned huge paychecks. The money was easy because he didn't need to be in the same fighting shape as he did for a bout against a top professional like Beell or Jenkins. But he disliked the premise almost from the start and knew it was beneath the dignity of his title. After five months with Sells-Floto, he and Jeffries decided they had seen enough. Frank returned home to Humboldt and Jeffries took a train to California, deciding to settle there and set up a boxing school, similar to what Burns was doing for wrestling in Omaha.

The next two years seemed slow and monotonous for Frank. He engaged in a few pickup bouts, mostly exhibitions where people paid not to see him take on a top professional, but simply paid to see the great Gotch in action. He found himself growing restless and began to stay out late with fans who wanted to be in his presence. He was being invited constantly to make appearances in Des Moines, and in other Midwestern cities, alongside politicians and others who wanted to share the spotlight with him. His late nights led to several long discussions with Gladys.

"You said you always wanted to be a Humboldt farmer, and yet you want to leave Humboldt all the time," she stressed during an emotional debate in the spring of 1915. "Frank, I just don't understand. Please don't go on the road any more."

"It's not that easy saying no, Gladys," he said. "I've got offers from everywhere. Big promoters in the East are after me all the time. I could make a ton of money out there. I've been traveling since 1899, going up to Alaska at age twenty. It's just not easy to quit the road."

"But we don't need any money," she pleaded. "What we need is time together to build our family life. And besides, you've even admitted those Eastern promoters want you to agree to lose matches..."

Frank snorted in disgust.

"They know better!" he growled. "There ain't enough money in the entire world to get me to go into the tank. They say if I'd agree to lose a match to someone, then the return bout would break every record for attendance, even the second match with Hackenschmidt. I told them fast enough where they could take that proposition.

"One of the promoters even had the nerve to suggest I threw the first Beell match in order to sell an entire series with Beell. I grabbed him by his shirt collar. I think he believed me then when I told him I have never, ever wrestled in any fixed bout, including Beell."

Despite the serious objections from Gladys, he accepted an offer to tour with the Buffalo Bill Circus. In late summer of 1915, he was taking on all comers again across the nation. But Jeffries was gone, replaced by the young Kansas boxer, Jess Willard.

A giant at six foot six and two hundred and fifty-five pounds, Willard upset Jack Johnson and won the heavyweight boxing title with a knockout in Havana, Cuba, on April 5, 1915. Some insiders said that Johnson took a dive in the twenty-sixth round because he had been chased out of the United States by hatred, and wanted to come back. Johnson was telling his friends he had to give up the title to a white man in order to be accepted back in the States, and Frank wondered if he had really thrown the fight. Almost from the start, Frank disliked Willard, who he found to be sullen and arrogant, and he didn't believe for a minute that the awkward, slow-moving Kansan could whip Johnson under any conditions.

Frank also missed the comradery he had known with Jeffries. After just three months with Buffalo Bill and his wild cowboys and indians crew, Gotch headed home. He had certainly seen enough of circus life, he told himself as he gazed out the window of the railroad cabin on the way back to Humboldt.

There were several reasons to bring his traveling days to an end. On the long road trips, he began drinking heavily for the first time in his life. Even worse, Frank had allowed himself to be seen in the company of women on several occasions, when the circus owners had demanded he and Willard go out with them and their financial backers in the evenings after the shows. Rumors of long and wild parties lasting into the wee hours of the morning reached all the way to Humboldt. When the circus hit Atlanta in late summer, Frank had partied hard into the morning hours and wound up nearly arrested when police came to a nightclub and a large riot broke out. Upon his return home, Gladys had immediately confronted him about the stories she had heard. Once again, they sat up long into the night discussing his future, and he agreed to give up the road life and its many pitfalls.

After quitting the circus for good, Frank was content to spend his time in Humboldt, concentrating on his various business ventures, as well as hunting, fishing and playing with his son, whom just about everyone was calling Frank, Jr. instead of his given name. He joined the Masons and even spent time with local political leaders.

But just when it seemed he had put wrestling behind him once and for all, the wrestling bug struck again. It started with a trip to Omaha in late 1916 to visit with the Farmer, who had pushed him to take an interest in his wrestling school and booming mail order business.

On the way to Omaha, Frank stopped in tiny Walnut, Iowa, to watch a match which featured a young amateur star named Earl Caddock. He had heard that Caddock was possessed of tremendous natural ability, and Frank was impressed by what he saw. A three-time national Amateur Athletic Union champion, Caddock was lean and powerful, quick as lightning, and showed great skill in the ring.

"It was like seeing myself in Fort Dodge almost twenty years ago," Frank told Burns in Omaha. "I think this kid can go all the way to the top. I think he can beat Stecher."

The name Joe Stecher had become a sore point with Frank ever since his retirement. After it was apparent to the top promoters that Frank had left the ring for good, a tournament was held in early 1915 to crown his successor. Charley Cutler, who had once fought Jack Johnson for the world heavyweight boxing title, losing by a knockout, defeated Henry Ordeman to claim the championship. Cutler then took his title on the road, taking on all comers. But just three months after winning the championship, he traveled to Omaha to face a young farmer named Joe Stecher, and was dealt a severe beating.

Stecher was similar to Frank in several ways. He had come off a farm near Dodge, Nebraska, to capture the imagination of his state. His victory over Cutler made him a state hero, and Nebraskans began to clamor that their boy could have even whipped the great Gotch. Sports writers called Frank constantly to ask him if he was thinking of coming out of retirement to face Stecher, and promoters all over the nation beat a path to his door. Even Jack Curley, who had served as Hackenschmidt's manager and promoter, tried to get in the picture and line up a match between the two.

In January of 1916, Klank drove to Humboldt to inquire about his plans, and even Gladys had said she would not stand in his way if he wanted to make a comeback on that level, despite her objections to his circus wrestling. On the long drive to Omaha, Frank had gone over in his mind a thousand times what he was going to say to the Farmer. He had not wrestled a real match for three years at this point.... not quite the same amount of time Jeffries had taken off before coming back to meet Johnson.

"Say, how good do you think this Caddock fellow really is?" asked Frank when he and the Farmer finally had an opportunity to sit and talk.

"Darn good. Heck, might be about as good as you were at the same stage," said Burns. "He's fast, very fast. Too fast for most heavyweights, just like you were. But he ain't as strong as you were, Frank."

"Why, most folks never thought I was that strong," said Gotch.

Burns looked at him.

"But we knew different, didn't we?"

"Yeah, I guess we did."

"Caddock can be the champion," said Burns. "I'm trying to match him up against Stecher."

"I was shocked at how easily Stecher beat Charlie Cutler for the title," said Frank.

"He's a great natural athlete," said Burns. "He even had a tryout with the Philadelphia major league baseball club and Ty Cobb talked to him about signing with his team in Detroit, I heard. They say Stecher could have played in the majors if he had been inclined that way. But he realized he could make more money wrestling. Like you and me, he's a product of the Midwestern farm lifestyle.

"You know, Frank, there's something about the farm life - the clean air, hard work, discipline....the individual nature of work. Like wrestling. Farm life produces good wrestlers. The only problem with Stecher is he's from the wrong state."

Frank chuckled. "Nebraska's close enough to Iowa. We can adopt him."

After a pause, Frank asked the question that had been on his mind for several weeks.

"Farmer, I'm thinking about making a comeback. There's talk of me and Stecher hooking up. Two undefeated champions. They say it could be as big as the Hackenschmidt match in Chicago. An Omaha promoter has been calling me every day. Even Jack Curley's gotten in the picture. What do you think?"

Burns shot him a hard look.

"Hell no, you can't come back," he spit out, swearing for the first time since they had met back in 1899. "Don't you remember Reno? Are you forgetting how pathetic old Jeff looked up there against a younger, faster man? I know what life was like for you in the circus,

Frank. All that travel. Women and booze and late nights. Don't tell me those things didn't happen, because I can see for myself that you ain't the same."

There was a long pause as the two old friends regarded each other seriously. Gotch knew there was a great deal of truth in what the Farmer was telling him, and he suddenly felt ashamed. It was true that he had neglected his physical self, and it was also true that he hadn't been as faithful to Gladys as he wanted to be. But it was tough - really tough - to just walk away from the bright glare of the spotlight. He had been one of the nation's best known athletic figures for well over a decade, and he was having trouble adjusting to life as an ordinary person. But he couldn't tell the Farmer all of that; the Farmer would simply shake his head in disapproval. Any kind of a weakness, physical or spiritual or emotional, was something the Farmer disdained.

"The fact is, you ain't the same athlete now as you were in 1911," said Burns finally.

There was another long pause.

"I know what's eating at you," said Burns. "They say Stecher's good enough to have tested you real hard. You want to know if you were better. Well, I seen a lot of both of you. I've been to Stecher's camp up in Dodge and seen him wrestle three or four matches so far. He's good, darn good. But he's no match for what you were in your prime. You woulda handled him easy. But now, at age thirty-seven? Facing a young and hungry twenty-two year old warhorse after being off for three years, or more? I doubt it."

Frank pondered the Farmer's words over and over all the way back to Humboldt, and over the next two weeks. But he still couldn't let go of the idea of making a comeback. A month after visiting Burns, he decided to travel to Waukesha, Wisconsin, and train with an old friend, Bob Managoff, who was making some money with a new gimmick. Managoff was wrestling under the name "The Terrible Turk" and was drawing good crowds all across the Badger state. There had been "Terrible Turks" traveling the wrestling circuit for decades, and the first few had indeed been from overseas. There was a fascination with the Turks because Turkey was a country that loved wrestling like no other country, and the Turkish wrestlers who came to America in the 1890-1900 period were big, rough and talented athletes. So, some enterprising American matmen began to adopt a new personality and a new background in order to attract certain ethnic fans. Frank didn't like the show business angle that had begun to creep into the profession since his retirement, but he understood the promoters' determination to pump more excitement into the sport.

"When you were the champ, the title was indisputable, beyond question," said an East Coast promoter who had come to Humboldt to talk to Frank about sanctioning a world championship match in New York. "Everyone knew Frank Gotch was the king, and we knew out in the East we weren't going to get you very often, because you would stick to the Midwest for your big matches. But when you retired, all the promoters decided they wanted their own 'world' champion. The world title means newspaper coverage, big crowds and big bucks.

"Sure, the best wrestlers are in the Midwest, everyone knows that. You, Burns and Beell, Stecher and Caddock, and this new kid, Ed Lewis. Shooters and hookers. But we can't wait for a Midwestern champ to come East once every two years. We need the world champion out here on a regular basis to draw the big crowds. So, we just waited for you to retire, and we crowned our own world champion."

The sudden popularity of Stecher had thrown a wrench in their plans. He had become the darling of the Midwestern newspaper gang, almost as popular as Gotch had been, and the East Coast promoters were still without a champion they could count on to make regular appearances.

Frank spent a week in Waukesha, a small town just west of Milwaukee, training with Managoff. He felt slow and sluggish at first, but after a week of hard workouts his timing and reflexes began to improve. Just when he was beginning to believe he could successfully return to the ring, he suffered a crushing setback. Lifting Managoff from the mat and preparing to slam him to the canvas, Frank's ankle buckled. It snapped as he fell heavily to the canvas, writhing in pain. It was the worst injury he had ever suffered in a career that dated back almost twenty years. He went back home two days after the accident, thoughts of a comeback all but eliminated.

"Maybe it's an omen," Klank told him when he came to Humboldt for a visit, and found Frank sitting on his front porch, his ankle in a cast and resting on a footstool. "I've been talking to the Farmer, and I agree with him now. You've got everything you need right here, Frank. You've got a wonderful wife, a handsome young son, and an entire state that loves you. You're the most popular man in all Iowa. Forget about a comeback, and learn how to enjoy your retirement, and your blessings."

The ankle was slow to mend, so Frank took some solace in helping groom Caddock. He invited the young wrestler to Humboldt and worked out with him when his ankle was well enough that he could do some limited work on the mat. He counseled him and trained him, always with his eye on the goal of beating Stecher.

Frank was ecstatic when Burns sent word that Stecher had agreed to give Caddock a shot at the title. The match was set for April 9, 1917, in Omaha, and was billed as a match for supremacy of the Iowa-Nebraska border, as well as for the world title. It was a dream battle, almost on the scale of the first Gotch-Hackenschmidt bout. Stecher was riding a winning streak of sixty-two straight wins and reportedly had never lost an official match. Caddock had compiled a record of fifty wins and no losses as an amateur and was now unbeaten in twenty-five bouts as a professional.

The match produced a quick sellout of the Omaha Auditorium. Over ten thousand fans - most of them from either Iowa or Nebraska - cheered themselves hoarse as the two great athletes struggled valiantly. Stecher finally scored a pin in eighty-two minutes of hard wrestling to win the first fall, but Caddock roared back to take the second fall in an even one hundred minutes. With the world title waiting to be decided, Stecher conceded from his dressing room after the ten-minute break. After three hours of wrestling, he was simply too exhausted to continue.

Prior to the start of the match, Frank had been called into the ring to pose between Caddock and Stecher, and he drew the largest ovation of the night. During the match, he sat nearby Caddock's corner, shouting encouragement to the native Iowan. He was delighted at the outcome and spent the next day at Burns' wrestling school, discussing the match from start to finish with the Farmer and assorted friends and wrestling fans.

Before leaving, he made a startling confession to his old mentor.

"You know, Farmer, in a way I'm glad that the ankle gave out when it did. After watching these young fellas go at it, I'm not sure I would want to get in there and tangle like that any more. I wrestled nearly five hundred matches the last eighteen or so years - from the gold fields of Alaska to New York, and all stops in between. Chicago, Kansas City, Des Moines, Buffalo, Seattle, Montreal, even in front of the President of the United States. I guess I've wrestled enough for one lifetime."

He paused: "Besides, I ain't been feeling too well lately. The ankle healed up fine, but the stomach's been giving me lots of problems." He tapped his abdominal area gently, glancing down. "Things just don't feel so good down here. Guess I'd better get over to see the doctor one of these days and get a real good checkup."

The Farmer nodded.

"You do that, Frank. I've been worried about the stories I heard about you on the road with those darn circus people. That life's not the right one for men like you and me. Good clean living, early to bed and early to rise. That's the Iowa farm way, Frank. And the wrestling way. Take care of that body, Frank, as it's the only one the Good Lord is gonna give ya."

CHAPTER 22

Despite Caddock's big victory, the first half of 1917 was turning sour for Frank, and just about everyone else in America. He simply couldn't shake his health problems and was experiencing severe pain throughout his back and abdominal area, along with occasional migraine headaches. He had been to see several doctors, and had even traveled to Glenwood Springs, Colorado, and Little Rock, Arkansas, to take special hot sulphur water treatments. Nothing had helped much.

Meanwhile, America was trying hard to keep out of the world war that had developed in Europe in 1914. President Wilson was walking a tight rope, and Roosevelt was making things tough on him. Roosevelt was demanding that America be prepared to engage Germany, calling it "a strong, ruthless, ambitious, militaristic" nation. Finally, on April 6, 1917 - just three days before the Caddock-Stecher showdown - the United States declared war on Germany. Slightly over two months later, on June 24, the first American fighting men landed in France.

The news of the great world conflict hit hard everywhere, including Iowa. Camp Dodge, situated in a beautiful area just north of Des Moines, was quickly transformed into an elite training center. Caddock made national news again in July when he signed up with the army, and demanded he be given no special treatment even if he was the heavyweight champion of the world. He said he wanted to enlist as a private and declined an officer's commission. Joe Stecher enlisted in the navy; the world war was delaying the much-anticipated rematch between the two wrestling stars.

Frank was sitting in his backyard chair reading the paper about the events in France when he heard Gladys' voice. He looked up at her as she approached.

"That Caddock is quite the fellow," he said. "He's got a ton of grit, that guy. Signing up to fight and then demanding to be sent overseas as a private. He'll probably wind up in a foxhole in some backyard in France, fighting for his life like all the other doughboys." He shook his head slowly in admiration of the young man from Walnut.

"Yes sir, he's a real fighter, that's for sure. And a patriot, too. Iowa can be real proud of Earl Caddock." He paused, then added, "Sure wish I wasn't so old, and felt so bad. I'd like to go overseas too and help win this war."

He looked back down at his paper, ignoring his wife, who had reached his side and was staring down at him.

"Frank, did you call on Doctor Arent, like I asked you to?" There was a sudden seriousness to Gladys's voice. She had been after him to see about the headaches and the sudden loss of appetite. If there was anything in the world that was uncharacteristic of him, it was the fact he had begun to eat less and less of late, and had shown little interest in meals. He had always, from the days of his youth, been a hearty eater, and he greatly appreciated the lengths she went to in creating large and delicious meals.

"Aw, Gladys," he said, shaking his head slowly. "No, I didn't. But honey, I'm fine. Just need to lose a little weight, that's all. Heck, I wrestled best at two hundred pounds, and I was all the way up to two thirty there for awhile. I'm just too short to carry that kind of weight. That may be all right for old Jim Jeffries, but he doesn't have to see the Farmer as often as I do and catch a verbal licking for it."

Gladys always brightened when Frank spoke of Burns or Klank. They hadn't been to Humboldt much since Frank's decision to give up his comeback plans. Klank was busy scouting for a new wrestling sensation, having missed out on signing up Caddock or Stecher, and Burns was preoccupied with his wrestling school in Omaha. Gladys missed them both, and knew Frank did, too.

"What have you heard from the Farmer lately?" she asked. "Didn't I see a letter from him on the table?"

Frank fiddled with his knife, cleaning his fingernails. He always liked to keep well groomed.

"Guess his school's going pretty well, and he's kind of tired of traveling, too. He wants me to come down and take a look at some of his students, maybe spend a little time with them. You know, teach a thing or two."

"That would be nice, Frank. Are you thinking about going?"

"Yeah, maybe I will," he said softly, laying the paper down in his lap. "Just for a week, or so. Farmer kind of wants me to. What do you think?"

He looked over at his wife of six years. She was only twenty-six, but it seemed to him that he had known her for at least that many years. She was so strong, he thought, for her size. What she had, he reasoned, was a big, good heart. He had recognized it that day years ago when she had approached him to buy a church raffle, a lass of just twelve years. Suddenly, he stood up and hugged her. She gasped, and he quickly released her.

"Why, Frank, I'm not Joe Stecher," she said teasingly. She loved it when he grabbed her like that, and she wasn't as fragile as she liked to let on.

"Almost forgot for a minute there," he said. "Then, it's settled. I'll go visit Farmer. You could come, too, if it wasn't for Frank, Jr."

She glanced up at the second floor of the house, and nodded. Frank Jr. was too young to be doing the kind of traveling they were talking about. Besides, she felt it would do Frank a world of good to visit the Farmer by himself. He hadn't been away from the family for several months in a row, and for a man who had done the kind of traveling he had, there needed to be a break from time to time.

"Just one thing," she said, as he rose to leave, grabbing his hand. "See Doctor Arent before you go."

He shrugged, smiled quickly, and started to move away.

"Promise?" she asked, pulling on his hand.

He looked down at her.

"Yes," he said, "I promise."

He wasn't a man to show his emotions easily, but Farmer Burns couldn't hide the fact he was delighted to see his old protégé again. When Frank walked into the school of wrestling in downtown Omaha, there were nearly fifty men in the practice room, going through moves and slapping holds on one another. Word of his arrival spread fast, and in less than two minutes all activity came to a halt, with all eyes trained on Gotch. He still cut a magnificent figure at thirty-nine years of age. He wore a three-piece suit, and a black derby, and carried a cane, a habit he had picked up from Gentleman Jim Corbett. He still had a full head of dark brown hair and deep set eyes, and was as handsome as any man could hope to be.

Burns, clad in gray sweats, walked across the gym and stuck out a hand.

"Couldn't believe my eyes when I read your letter saying you was coming," said the Farmer. He called all the men around, and began introducing them to Gotch one by one.

"They never would have forgiven me if I hadn't introduced them to the great Frank Gotch when he came calling," said Burns later. Frank was flattered as he watched Burns holler out instructions and, from time to time, turn and ask him for advice. After all, Burns had been his mentor for almost twenty years, and Frank still envisioned him as the greatest wrestling authority in the world, especially in the art of hooking. Maybe he was nearing sixty, but Burns was as tough and as rugged as the day they first met, and more than a match for just about any young up-and-comer who wanted to try him out. Now, here he was acting like Frank was his equal. Sure, Frank admitted he had accomplished more than Burns - after all, he was the only American ever to win the world heavyweight title, and had held it for seven long years.

The two left the school together and retreated to Burns's home for dinner. The Burns' three children had grown up and left home, and only Martin and his wife, Mary, were left these days. Gotch asked about the two boys and his daughter, and was pleased to discover all were doing well, according to the Farmer.

"But, what about you, Frank?" asked Burns, as the two sat on his front porch after the supper hour had ended. "How are things going with you?"

"Very well," replied Gotch, settling back on the porch, his back resting up against the house. He put his hands behind his head, and locked his fingers, using them as a cushion for his head against the wood of the house.

"Business has never been better - the automobile business, I mean. The Model T Ford craze seems to have finally slowed, and we're selling lots of Mitchells. And I'm enjoying being on the bank board, and the real estate dabbling."

"Humph," said Burns. "I hardly call it dabbling when a fella owns most of Humboldt and half of St. Paul, and a little bit of South Dakota."

"All farfetched exaggerations," said Frank, but he knew he couldn't fool Burns. He looked over at the old warrior, and smiled, throwing a hand on his shoulder.

"How's retirement been?" asked Burns, arching an eyebrow. He hoped to hear that Frank had given up all thoughts of any kind of a comeback.

"Not bad," said Gotch, withdrawing his hand. "I can live with it. With the big war going on in Europe, sports is taking a real back seat anyway. Caddock and Stecher are both serving their country, and no one's talking much about wrestling matches. Besides, I've got other considerations right now. You know, the Republican Party's even talked some about running me for governor. Can you believe that?"

"Sure, I can," said Burns. "You'd be a natural. Most respected name in the entire Midwest. Known for your honesty and your integrity, always a straight shooter."

Frank shrugged.

"There's still some talk about fake matches years ago. I hate that, Farmer. There's even rumors about Roller or some hooker ruining Hack's leg before the second match. Can you believe that? What fair-minded person would think that I'd need any sort of advantage, or want one? Heck, I could've beaten Hack with two bad legs myself. The heart was the difference, not the legs."

"Let 'em talk," said the Farmer. "Who cares? Some people just can't accept the truth. Why, there's even some folks who think Jesus Christ didn't rise from the dead."

Frank looked at his old friend - and they both chuckled loudly.

They sat in silence, relishing one another's company and the quiet of a beautiful autumn evening.

"How's the health?" asked the Farmer suddenly.

Frank looked over at him. Burns' features were half hidden by the fading light of day, but Gotch could see the eyes straining to look into his own. His lips were set tight beneath the dark, thin mustache that he had worn most of his life. His hard, craggy features bore an expression of concern.

"Been talking to Gladys, have you?"

"She sent me a letter."

"Figured that," said Frank.

The silence lasted for nearly a minute, before Burns repeated the question.

Frank stood up and walked a few paces, then turned back to him.

"I can't understand it, Farmer," he said quietly. "Heck, I was never sick a day in my life. Nothing at all. You know that. And now, suddenly...." His voice trailed off.

Burns stood and walked to where his friend stood.

"What is it?"

"Don't really know for sure," said Frank. "Ever heard of Bright's disease?"

Burns shuddered involuntarily, and hoped Frank hadn't seen him. He hadn't; he was staring off at the moon, hardly visible but taking shape as day gave way to night.

"Yeah, I've heard of it."

"Well, it could be that....or something very similar to it. Doctor isn't sure. But whatever it is, I'll whip it. Just like Hack and Mahmout and Jenkins. Nobody thought I'd win those matches, either."

"Don't forget Stanislaus," said Burns, and they both laughed, recalling Gotch's memorable victory over the Polish giant, Zbyszko.

They walked to the fence that enclosed the Farmer's yard.

"You got a nice place, here, Farmer."

"It'll do, but it ain't like it was when the kids were here."

"Nope, I suppose not," said Frank.

"But, you wouldn't know about that, would you?" said Burns lightly, shaking off the earlier mood. "Your child-raising days are just beginning."

"If I ever get to them," said Frank. The words cut through Burns like a knife. He grabbed Gotch by the arm.

"What the hell does that mean?"

The two men stared at one another until Frank spoke up.

"My doctor in Humboldt says it don't look good, Farmer," he said. "He won't say I've got Bright's, but my kidneys ain't working right, and the urine is not like it should be. Guess there's enough of it, but it doesn't contain the right ingredients....at least that's the way I understand. It's what he called a toxic condition, and it don't look good."

Burns was eyeing his longtime friend in disbelief. He had spent his whole life advocating healthy living and hard training. He couldn't allow himself to understand how any disease could take hold of a man like Frank Gotch. After all, he lived a healthy life for the most part....didn't use tobacco, or drink hardly a drop in the early days. He lived in the clean air, ran regularly for years, and just plain took care of his body. He had never known a tougher man, physically or mentally.

The two talked for another hour, and then retired. Burns watched as Gotch walked toward the guest room - where the boys had slept before they left home - and disappeared behind the dark door. He set for awhile at the kitchen table, his chin resting in his palms, his elbows on the hard wood table. Then, he rose and slipped into bed.

His wife, Mary, felt the bed lower, and turned toward him.

"How sick is he, Martin?" she asked softly. Burns looked over at her, waiting for her features to come into focus as his eyes adjusted to the darkness of the room. Finally, he saw her faintly.

"He's darn sick, but then he's also Frank Gotch," he said. "He ain't never lost one in the past ten years, Mary, and he's not losing this one, either."

The cop leaned back against the seat of the auto and picked up an apple, taking a big bite. He chewed slowly, and glanced at his pocket watch for the fourth time in the last hour. It was just half past eleven. He shook his head. Another long, boring night, he thought. He sighed and took another bite of the apple. He glanced to the right down the long, dark street, and then to the left. He continued looking down the street, then sat the apple down.

"What the heck...." He mumbled. He leaned forward, gripping the steering wheel. He squinted hard, trying to make out the figure walking slowly along the street. The man was having trouble negotiating the sidewalk, and he bounced once off the building which ran next to the sidewalk. It appeared as though he was inebriated, but officer Kelly knew better....that in reality the man was much worse off than if merely drunk.

Kelly shook his head sadly and stepped out of the auto. He adjusted his belt, cleared his throat, and began walking toward the man.

"Good evening, Mr. Gotch," he said slowly, standing in front of the husky man who was wearing a long black coat and a black derby. "Are you out for a late stroll tonight, sir?"

Frank looked up at patrolman, but said nothing. There was a far-away look in his eyes.

"I've got to get to the arena," he said in a soft voice. "The Russian Lion is there."

Kelly nodded, and placed a hand gently on the large shoulder. He had known Frank for much of the last ten years and was among his legion of devoted fans. Kelly had even driven up to Humboldt to watch Gotch train for the second match with Hackenschmidt, joining the other spectators in the Riverside Camp. He had met Gotch when he came to Fort Dodge to give a speech several years ago. Now, here he was, for the third time in the last half year, about to try and talk his hero into going home.

"Mr. Gotch, the match is over," he said gently. "You won. The Russian Lion quit on you again. You're the champion." He paused while Frank looked into his eyes, and began to nod slowly. "Listen, can I buy you a cup of coffee? I'd like to have the honor of drinking some coffee with you, Frank, and then see about getting you home."

Frank nodded. Together they walked down the street to a small café. Kelly opened the door for Frank and they went in. The place was empty, except for the counter man. He saw immediately who Kelly had with him.

"Oh my gosh, Kelly. It's Frank again," said the counter man, a thin fellow in his late fifties. "What should we do?"

Kelly led Frank to a table and they both sat down.

"Bring us a couple of coffees, will you Joe" he asked.

Joe brought the two coffees and Frank picked up a cup with both hands, sipping slowly. He sat the cup down and looked directly at the cop.

"Hack quit again," he said with a half smile. "Just doesn't have the heart, does he officer?"

"No sir," said Kelly, with a shake of the head. "But Frank, who can blame him? He's so darned scared of that toe hold of yours. Who ain't?"

Frank sat back in his chair and chuckled, slapping his large hands on his thighs. Then he leaned forward, his eyes locked on Kelly's.

"You know what, officer? The toe hold ain't so dangerous. Sure, it hurts like hell if I get it on you. But it ain't easy to get on a smart wrestler. It's easy to defend against. The real power of the toe hold is that it makes a fellow so scared. I mean....really scared, deep down inside. Then, that's when you got 'em whipped, and you can pin 'em with the crotch and half nelson."

Frank laughed several times, then turned quiet, staring down at his coffee. Kelly watched him for a moment, then stood up.

"Wait here for me, Frank, will ya please? I gotta make a call."

Kelly walked over to where Joe was standing behind the counter, and reached for the telephone on the wall. Joe watched Frank as Kelly reached into his pocket and pulled out a thin black book, thumbing through the pages. He found the page he wanted and dialed a number from it.

It took a dozen rings before a voice came from the other end.

"It's officer Kelly, down in Fort Dodge," said Kelly. "We....have

Frank again." He paused. "No, he's okay. Just a little....confused again. I'll bring him home." He paused, nodding. "Yes, Mrs. Gotch. No, honestly, it's an honor to be able to help out."

He hung up the telephone, and glanced over at Frank, who was sitting at the table still holding his cup.

"What a shame," said Joe softly. "The greatest wrestler who ever lived. A national celebrity, the man everyone admires and who every kid in Iowa wants to be like. And now, just a sick man who can't remember nuthing."

Kelly glanced at Joe, and shook his head.

"He can remember some things," he said. "It's just he gets so confused, they say. He don't really know where he's at some of the time. It's this disease he's got. They say it affects the kidneys first, and then the mind. It's kind of like the mind gets poisoned and you begin to forget all kinds of things."

He walked over to Frank, who looked up at him.

"Frank, can I take you home now? I just talked to your wife, and she wants me to bring you home. She'll send someone for your car tomorrow."

Frank nodded and stood up. They walked out the door together and back down the street to Kelly's auto.

Gladys liked to drive, and had ever since her early days with Frank. He used to take her for rides when they were courting, she remembered, and she always looked forward to a ride in the newest, nicest automobile in town. He had teased her at great length when she first began handling the auto, but he had admired her pluckiness, and the ease with which she caught on. Not many women were driving in Humboldt in 1917, but Gladys had always been one to forge ahead rather than lag behind, and Frank had always encouraged her to do just that. It was one of the many reasons she loved him so dearly.

She parked the auto and stepped down to the boardwalk. It was a quiet day in Humboldt. There was a chill in the air, but it was not near as cold as one would think for the first week of December. Still, she wrapped the scarf tightly around her neck. She adjusted the wide-brimmed hat, set her chin high, and started for the small office located at the end of the string of shops and buildings.

She hoped she wouldn't encounter anyone, and she was in luck. Not many ventured out at this time of year, except for the necessities. And it was early in the morning. She had planned it this way, and

Doctor Arent had agreed. Neither wanted her subjected to the kind of questions that would have to be asked if she should meet any friends.

She opened the office door, stepping into the little waiting room. Beverly Reiter, Dr. Arent's secretary, looked up, smiled and motioned her through.

"The doctor is waiting for you, Mrs. Gotch," she said.

Gladys thanked her and stepped into the next room. Dr. Arent, working at his desk, turned and glanced over his shoulder, rising the second he saw who it was.

"Good morning, Gladys," he said, taking her arm at the elbow and guiding her to a chair. "Sit down, please."

He returned to his chair, and faced her, in silence. He smiled, and so did she.

"Lovely morning," he said, in jest.

"Yes," she replied. She liked Dr. Arent. He had been her physician for years. Frank, however, had grown up without seeing a doctor. He was never sick, it seemed, and always went to the Farmer with the series of nagging injuries and bruises accumulated in his profession. He had always laughed lightly when she had mentioned doctors and check-ups, and said they were fine for folks who needed them, for folks who had neglected their bodies and their health, and who were unfortunate enough to need a professional's help and advice. But, that had been a long time ago, she thought to herself. Now, Frank needed help, desperately.

"How has it been?" he asked, the smile gone. He had a sympathetic demeanor, and eyes that seemed to understand suffering. He had seen far more than his share of that, ranging from farm accidents which left men crippled to horrible diseases that snatched young children from their parents in the dead of night. Often, he could help; just as often, he was powerless to do more than administer support and treatments designed to alleviate suffering.

"Not good," she said bravely. "He's so tired all the time. He has headaches, and mood swings, just like you said he probably would. He acts.....so irrational sometimes. And he just won't eat. I know he's lost at least thirty pounds in the last three months. And his eyes....they get so puffy. He gets confused. At times he doesn't seem to know where he is. Three or four times he's driven to Fort Dodge by himself, and then forgets where he is, and where he left the auto. Each time, a police officer brought him back home, and I've sent someone down to pick up his auto."

Her voice trailed off. She sat leaning forward in her chair, a tiny slip of a person, her hands clenched tightly in her lap. "Now, he can't drive any more at all, of course...."

Arent nodded, and adjusted his glasses.

"Yes, that's the way it works. I told you when you came back from Arkansas that these moments would arrive."

"But the treatments, the hot baths in Arkansas," she stammered. "I thought they'd help. I thought they would...."

"Make him well? No, Gladys, not that. I wish I could say there was a treatment for uremic poisoning. But there just isn't, that's all. We just don't understand it. We know the symptoms are very similar to Bright's disease, and there are doctors who feel they are really one and the same.

"When Frank first came to me with the headaches and frequent nose bleeds, I thought it was the result of his heavy schedule and his many years of wrestling. But the first time you told me of the slight confusion he experienced, and the tendency to drowse much of the day, I became fearful. His checkups showed his kidneys are diseased, and not acting properly. They are retaining some materials that should be excreted from the body. Consequently, these poisons are retained in the system. The kidneys are a weak organ in that they are not able to force the toxins which corrode the minute tubes and choke the system."

There was a pause; he had said all he felt he should, and yet she seemed to have not heard.

"The diet....I've kept him off the meats altogether, as you've said. He is drinking lots of milk, but it seems hard on him. And he drinks water like he's dying of thirst....he vomits a lot...."

Her voice trailed off, and she brought her hands up to her face. Her eyes grew wide, and she gasped once, loudly. Arent stood and stepped to her side. She lurched forward, as though she were choking, and he caught her, fearful she would topple on the floor. She was rigid, hard as a board, and he lifted her petite body easily to her feet.

He shook her, and she gasped again. She looked into his face, her eyes still wide, with a growing realization and terror. She tried to push away from him, but he held on to her arms tightly. He wanted to shock her back into reality with the pain of his hands tightening on her arms. And he succeeded.

"Oh!" she exclaimed, looking down where he held her arms. He loosened immediately. Suddenly, she seemed like she would wilt and collapse on the floor, and he eased her back into the chair.

"Are you all right, Gladys?" he asked, a note of grave concern in his voice.

She nodded.

He drew up his chair, and sat in front of her, holding her hands. Slowly, she regained her senses. Her face, which had lost all of its color, was a slight pink now. He stared hard into her dark brown eyes, and thought to himself how very pretty she was, and how exciting her life had been in the past few years. She was married to the best known man in all of Iowa, and maybe all of the Midwest, if not America. He was lionized the length and breadth of the country as the greatest wrestler in American history. He was a successful banker, automobile dealer, land developer and speculator. He was admired and liked by nearly every man, woman and child in Humboldt, and loved by most. He was a friend of national figures and dignitaries, invited to the White House and mentioned prominently as a potential candidate for governor.

He was handsome, she was attractive. They had a young son, friends and relatives galore. They had traveled widely and had never had to worry about such matters as finances and family illnesses, until now. Soon, her life would be far, far different.

He had been so busy reflecting that he failed to notice she had fully recovered and was staring at him, expectantly. He cleared his throat. The time had come.

"Frank will die," he told her. He knew of no way to soften the blow. She could not be fooled, nor did he want to deceive her. She was strong....on her own, and from living with such a man of strength. She would endure it, he knew.

She sat before him, unmoving.

"How long?" she asked. Her voice seemed strangely husky, almost masculine.

"Gladys, he can't last more than a month. And it will probably be less than that."

"Then, I had best be getting home, hadn't I?" she said with an air of reserve. She stood quickly, smoothed her long dress and pulled the long coat tightly about her. She had not bothered to take if off, for she had felt secure with it wrapped about her. Frank had given it to her the night before they left for Chicago for the second Hackenschmidt bout. It had always been her favorite.

She started for the door, and Arent came up behind.

"Did you drive?"

She nodded, her hand on the door know.

"Let me take you home, and visit Frank," he said.

She nodded again, her back to him. He placed her hands on her shoulders, as they shook heavily.

They drove up to the big white house on Sixth Street. It was one of the largest homes in Humboldt, yet it was not near what it could have been for a person of Frank Gotch's wealth and celebrity. He had always chosen to live relatively modestly.

They walked up the front steps onto the porch, now shut tight for the winter. On summer days, Gladys had the porch screens up and chairs all around, with a table or two, as well. She liked to sit and slice apples for pie or sauce on nice summer evenings, and entertain the many wrestlers who passed through in the warmer months. Her pie and applesauce were well known in wrestling circles.

They moved into the main house, into the long hallway. Immediately, Gladys glanced up the open stairway, with the top half of the first bedroom door visible. She stood for a moment, as if expecting to hear something, then moved into the living room, motioning for Dr. Arent to follow. An elderly woman came around the corner from the dining room. She was very old, but sturdy appearing, with her silver dark hair tied in a tight bun at the back of her head. She had strong, craggy features, and looked to have been a strong, if not beautiful, woman in her youth.

"Dr. Arent, this is Mother Gotch, Amelia," Gladys said.

"Oh, yes, Mrs. Gotch. It's been a long time," he said quietly.

She stopped short and looked first at the doctor, and then at Gladys. Her expression was one of bewilderment.

"Is Frank resting?" asked Gladys.

Amelia nodded.

"Millie is with him," she said in a voice that sounded tired and old. It still had traces of a Germanic accent even after all the years she had lived in Iowa, far from her native country. In fact, she was proud of the fact she had not lost all traces of her ancestry.

"Millie is Frank's sister," said Gladys.

"Of course," said the doctor. "I remember her well."

"And Frank, Jr., is asleep," said Amelia. Gladys smiled, and touched her on the shoulder.

"We're going up now, Mother," said Gladys. "We want to see Frank."

They had taken two steps when they heard the frail voice behind them.

"He is going to die."

They halted, and turned. Amelia stood facing them, as solid as a rock. Her lips were set tight. There was no trace of weakness in her, even in the eyes.

"Yes, mama," said Gladys. The two women stared at one another, and then Amelia turned and walked slowly back into the dining room, and disappeared into the kitchen.

"You needn't worry about her," said Gladys. "She is very, very strong. That's where Frank got it, you know. His father was always such a gentle man. He gave that to Frank. But Amelia....she gave him the strength, the will, the drive."

"I remember her when Frederick died," said the doctor. "When was that, 1910?"

"No," said Gladys, climbing the stairs. "It was October 21, 1911. Just a month after the second match with Hackenschmidt," She stopped on the stairs and looked down at the doctor, three steps behind her. "He lived just long enough to see Frank through his greatest moment."

They continued up the stairway and turned left at the top, passing two doors and stopping at the last one on the left. It was slightly ajar. Gladys took a deep breath, and then pushed it gently open.

Millie had left and Frank was sleeping. They walked softly to the side of the bed. He didn't stir.

Arent had not seen him for nearly two weeks, and was surprised once again at the loss of weight evident in the face. He had always thought Frank was an extremely handsome man, though he had the tendency to gain weight easily and develop pudgy cheeks in the years since he gave up wrestling. His long, dark hair was parted in the middle, as had always been his style, but seemed thinner than usual. His eyes were puffy. He was thirty-nine. Arent would have guessed his age, at this moment, closer to mid fifties.

Frank stirred, and opened his eyes. The twinkle that was always there was gone, replaced by a dull, flat look. Gladys was preparing to speak, but he shut his eyes too quickly. She stood with hands folded in front of her, staring down at her husband. For several minutes they waited for Frank to reopen his eyes, but when he didn't they slipped quietly from the room.

In silence they walked down the hallway and back down the stairs. Arent walked to the door, then turned to face her.

"I must start making the arrangements," she said in a voice barely audible.

The doctor nodded.

Burns and Klank fought the cold, bundling up and lowering a shoulder and walking straight into it. Their pace quickened and they fairly leaped into the automobile, which Westergard had left running. They had been the very last to leave, and they drove slowly through the cemetery.

Burns wiped at his eyes; the cold had bitten into his face, and a tear had run from each eye, down the red cheeks. His hard face was drawn with many lines, and the scars of battle, nearly six thousand in all, if anyone had ever bothered to count.

There were still folks out on the road that led south to Humboldt. They were walking in groups, bundled tightly, and sitting in slow moving automobiles. Nearly three thousand had shown up this day, braving the icy winds to visit Union Cemetery and to say goodbye to Frank Gotch. In the distance, a church bell tolled.

The automobile clanked along toward town, and Burns found himself remembering the day he had first seen Frank Gotch. It was December 18, 1899, in Fort Dodge, he recalled, and a smile worked its way across his thin lips. When the big, brawny lad had emerged from the stands with that sly smile, Burns had known he was different. He had realized just how different after only five minutes of wrestling.

He recalled the conversation afterwards, when he told Frank he could be the best. Not just the best in Iowa, or the Midwest, or even America, but the best in the entire world. Burns had known it as sure as he had known anything in his lifetime. There was the blinding speed, the tremendous strength, the desire to win. And there was that heart....so big, so strong. Could it really have stopped?

The auto broke from the crowd, and sped on by itself. Westergard kept his eyes on the road, while Klank, in the back, stared out across the wide-open plains, now bare in the grip of winter, Iowa style.

There was the trip to Alaska, and the big money. But it hadn't changed him. Then, those grueling matches with Jenkins, who Gotch had always admired first and foremost among American wrestlers, after Burns, of course. And the culmination of it all. He had beaten Hackenschmidt, the feared Russian Lion. Not once, but twice. He had made him quit the first time - the most convincing victory of all - and then had merely pinned him in the second encounter. There were over thirty thousand people, cheering wildly. How they loved that man, Burns thought.

Burns wasn't cold now, but he was startled by a strange sensation. There was no longer a wind in his face, but there was a wetness in his eyes. He dabbed at them, quickly, then looked at Westergard, to see if he had noticed. But Westergard drove on, looking straight ahead.

"What now, Farmer?" came a voice from the back.

"Guess I'll just go back to the wrestling school in Omaha," Burns sighed. "Maybe we can get another Caddock-Stecher match lined up. Maybe we can find us another world champion, huh Emil?"

Westergard looked over at Burns, and chuckled. He hunched forward, and chuckled again.

Klank joined him from the back, chuckling softly, and then Burns, too; and then they drew silent.

"Don't matter what happens now, right boys?" said Burns finally. "We saw the best. We were with him for nearly twenty years. We won't see his like ever again."

The auto rambled on, its passengers silent, lost in the memories of days gone by.

POSTSCRIPT

W hen he died from kidney failure at his home in the afternoon of December 16, 1917 at the age of thirty nine years and eight months, Frank Gotch was so weak he could barely lift his head off a pillow. Yet the power of his name and his fame has endured for nearly a century - both in the sport of wrestling and in the State of Iowa.

In the book 100 Greatest Sports Heroes, author Mac Davis paints a marvelous word portrait of Gotch and his impact on the nation's sporting scene:

"As the idol of millions in the United States, Canada and Mexico, Gotch made wrestling a big-time sport in his day. By the time Frank was ready to return to his farm, he had earned about a half a million dollars - a great fortune in those days. Added to that were the honors Gotch had won over the years. Babies had been named in his honor, as had buildings, toys, farm implements and a hundred other things. The word 'Gotch' was a synonym for quality and strength."

"He was a mighty box office draw," wrote famed boxing and wrestling historian Nat Fleischer in his book, From Milo to Londos. "There was a glamour about him that made huge crowds willing to pay top prices to watch him perform....Gotch did for modern wrestling what John L. Sullivan accomplished for boxing in the old days. It was Gotch's victories over the hitherto invincible Hackenschmidt that made him the most popular mat star in America and started a move-ment among college men to take up wrestling."

George Barton, perhaps the most respected wrestling writer ever, reported on all the top wrestling stars from 1903 until retiring in 1957, and ranked Gotch as "the greatest professional wrestler of all time." He was, wrote Barton, "a remarkable physical specimen. He was tremendously strong, amazingly fast, and catlike in movements. Frank was master of all holds on offense and blocks for these holds on defense. He also mastered leverage to the nth degree and was the last word in courage.

"Topping off his wrestling skills, Gotch was a handsome, intelligent fellow, gifted with the personality and friendliness which made Jack Dempsey the most popular sports figure of all time."

"No breath of suspicion (of fake matches) ever attached itself to Frank Gotch," wrote Graeme Kent in his book, A Pictorial History of Wrestling. "By 1913, Gotch had run out of opponents and retired. When he left the ring, the golden age of wrestling came to an end."

Gotch's popularity was such that he remained in the public spotlight for decades after his untimely death. A 1928 poster entitled Celebrities in the World of Sports included Gotch among its eighty-eight athletes. His photo is alongside photos of such legends as Babe Ruth, John L. Sullivan, Red Grange, Knute Rockne, Jack Dempsey and Johnny Weissmuller - even though Gotch had been gone for eleven years! It was a remarkable tribute to his legacy.

The Gotch name also endured across the state of Iowa. In 1924, the state's largest newspaper, The Des Moines Register, conducted a poll to find out what Iowan was most admired by the residents of the state. Gotch won by a large margin, seven years after his passing.

His fame was used to help sell products for decades. A 1934 advertisement in a national magazine boasted "Frank Gotch had the power that wins and so does the 1934 Harley-Davidson," promoting the motorcycle. As late as the 1970s, a bank in his hometown of Humboldt was still using his picture in ads.

His name came into prominence again in 1977 in the best-selling Book of Lists, where he is ranked as the greatest wrestler of all time. George Hackenschmidt was ranked second.

Gotch was a member of the initial class of the Des Moines Register Sports Hall of Fame in 1951, and was inducted into the Madison Square Garden Hall of Fame shortly after. He was the very first person inducted into Professional Wrestling Writers Association Hall of Fame in 1972, and the first wrestler to go into the George Tragos/Lou Thesz Professional Wrestling Hall of Fame in Newton, Iowa, in 1999.

Today, the Humboldt school district sponsors a Frank Gotch Wrestling Tournament for young amateur wrestlers each winter. The local kids wrestling club is named in his honor.

And a ten-acre park just south of Humboldt bears his name. The acreage is near where he grew up on his father's old farmstead. On the large stone marker in the park is an etching of a smiling Frank Gotch, and the following words:

"The sports world has never known his equal."

About the author

Mike Chapman is one of the nation's top wrestling historians. He has been named National Wrestling Writer of the Year four times and created the popular amateur national wrestling publication, W.I.N. (Wrestling International Magazine). He is the founder and executive director of the International Wrestling Institute and Museum in Newton, Iowa, and has been a newspaper editor for over twenty-five years. He has been studying the life and career of Frank Gotch for three decades. This is his twelfth book. He and his wife, Bev, live on a small acreage near Kellogg, Iowa.